FUNDAMENTALS
OF
SCALING
AND
PSYCHOPHYSICS

WILEY SERIES IN BEHAVIOR

KENNETH MacCORQUODALE, Editor

University of Minnesota

FUNDAMENTALS OF SCALING AND PSYCHOPHYSICS

JOHN C. BAIRD

Dartmouth College
Hanover, New Hampshire

ELLIOT NOMA

University of Michigan
Ann Arbor, Michigan

A WILEY-INTERSCIENCE PUBLICATION

JOHN WILEY & SONS, New York • Chichester • Brisbane • Toronto

This material was prepared with the support of National Science Foundation Grants No. GJ-28456 and EPP71-01952. However, any opinions, findings, conclusions, or recommendations expressed herein are those of the authors and do not necessarily reflect the views of NSF.

Published by John Wiley & Sons, Inc.

Copyright © 1978 by John C. Baird and Elliot Noma

Library of Congress Cataloging in Publication Data:

Baird, John C
    Fundamentals of scaling and psychophysics.

    (Wiley series in behavior)
    "A Wiley-Interscience publication."
    Includes index.
    1. Psychometrics.   I.   Noma, Elliot, 1950–
joint author.   II.   Title.

BF39.B32   150'.1'82   78-6011
ISBN 0-471-04169-6

Printed in the United States of America

10 9 8 7 6 5 4 3 2

FOR FRIENDS

SERIES PREFACE

Psychology is one of the lively sciences. Its foci of research and theoretical concentration are diverse among us, and always on the move, sometimes into unexploited areas of scholarship, sometimes back for second thoughts about familiar problems, often into other disciplines for problems and for problem-solving techniques. We are always trying to apply what we have learned, and we have had some great successes at it. The Wiley Series in Behavior reflects this liveliness.

The series can accomodate monographic publication of purely theoretical advances, purely empirical ones, or any mixture in between. It welcomes books that span the interfaces within the behavioral sciences and between the behavioral sciences and their neighboring disciplines. The series is, then, a forum for the discussion of those advanced, technical, and innovative developments in the behavior sciences that keep its frontiers flexible and expanding.

KENNETH MacCORQUODALE

Minneapolis, Minnesota
December 1974

PREFACE

Research in scaling and psychophysics has facilitated the emergence of psychology as a behavioral *science*. In fact, many consider the birth of psychophysics in 1860 to be the origin of scientific psychology. Since then, the field has provided useful techniques for the study of perception, decision making, psychobiology, and environmental psychology—to mention only a few examples. Therefore, a sound background in scaling and psychophysics is an excellent jumping-off point for work in related disciplines.

There are many facets to psychophysics, but the topic can be meaningfully divided into two major branches, methodology and theory. The first concerns the practical matter of experimental procedures and data analyses. Many texts deal with only these topics. Although important in its own right, excessive attention to methodology at the introductory level can sometimes lead to superficial understanding of underlying assumptions and boredom among persons with more abstract inclinations. The second branch emphasizes the theories behind the techniques and how they illuminate psychological principles. Most mathematical treatments relate this side of the story. Unfortunately, this information often doesn't generalize to specific issues or generate an intuitive feeling about the scope of applications.

In this work we have chosen to present both branches of psychophysics but to devote more attention to theory than to applications. We feel that the person who follows the arguments in the text and gains some laboratory experience with the techniques will have an excellent grasp of the fundamentals of scaling and psychophysics. Our hope here is to convey a sense of understanding and excitement about theoretical matters while still providing the necessary tools for applications.

The major arguments can be organized into two sections. Chapters 1 through 6 and Chapter 8 deal with the more traditional areas of psychophysics—the measurement and scaling of sensations and responses popularized by Fechner and Stevens. In later chapters (7, 9, and 10), generalizations of the classical methods are treated as scaling models in the larger arena of decision behavior. The models of cluster analysis and information theory are presented in Chapters 11 and 12 as supplements to the scaling models described earlier.

It was impossible in a text of this sort to give full attention to the recent attempts to combine all psychophysical results into a unitary structure. This exciting prospect may be realized in the near future (and there is probably more than one solution!). However, we see the present text as a necessary primer for this level of theoretical analysis.

Much of this book was written in 1974–1975 with the partial support of a grant from the National Science Foundation administered by Project CoMPUTe at Dartmouth College in Hanover, New Hampshire. We would like to thank Arthur Luehrmann, Director, and A. Kent Morton, Assistant Director, for the technical and financial support provided by the project staff. We have a special word of thanks to Jean Maier for her expert typing of the manuscript (with the help of the Dartmouth Time-Sharing System), and to Mary Cartwright-Smith and Margaret Olsen for editorial assistance. In addition, many friends and colleagues offered valuable suggestions for improving the text. We especially benefited from R. Duncan Luce's insightful and scholarly comments on earlier versions of the material. We also wish to express our gratitude to Bruce Carlson, Clyde Coombs, Trygg Engen, Janice Johnson, Jill Nagy, and Robert Z. Norman for their aid in upgrading the readability and technical accuracy of the manuscript.

JOHN C. BAIRD
ELLIOT NOMA

Hanover, New Hampshire
Ann Arbor, Michigan
June 1978

CONTENTS

FUNDAMENTALS
OF
SCALING
AND
PSYCHOPHYSICS

CHAPTER

$$\boxed{1}$$

INTRODUCTION

Psychophysics is commonly defined as the quantitative branch of the study of perception, examining the relations between observed stimuli and responses and the reasons for those relations. This is, however, a very narrow view of the influence it has had on much of psychology. Since its inception, psychophysics has been based on the assumption that the human perceptual system is a measuring instrument yielding results (experiences, judgments, responses) that may be systematically analyzed. Because of its long history (over 100 years), its experimental methods, data analyses, and models of underlying perceptual and cognitive processes have reached a high level of refinement. For this reason, many techniques originally developed in psychophysics have been used to unravel problems in learning, memory, attitude measurement, and social psychology. In addition, scaling and measurement theory have adapted these methods and models to analyze decision making in contexts entirely divorced from perception. In this book we concentrate on the traditional link between scaling and psychophysics, but with a mind toward elucidating the broader role of scaling in psychology.

There are many possible ways to study the human organism as a measuring instrument. Some of these merely measure sensitivity to change in the environment, whereas others attempt to sketch a person's internal organization of the world. It is our intent to describe each within its own philosophi-

1

cal and historical framework to further an appreciation of its full beauty and complexity. Several major themes are recurrent throughout all these methods. We will explore these themes and show how they lead to a shared set of beliefs (*paradigm* in the sense of Kuhn, 1962) that transcends individual approaches.

The theme of this paradigm is that human beings perform as measuring instruments interpreting the myriad of physical stimuli impinging upon sensory systems from the surrounding environment. These stimuli come in many forms, but all can be analyzed as values along component dimensions, such as light intensity, sound pressure, and size; and each of these dimensions is open to physical measurement, at least in theory. The key question is "How does the human being use sensory and cognitive mechanisms to perceive the type and amount of stimulus energy?" In brief, psychophysics investigates the correspondence between the magnitude of stimulus properties as assessed by the instruments of physics and as assessed by the perceptual systems of people.

PSYCHOPHYSICAL THEORY

Many psychologists unfamiliar with the subtleties of psychophysics are apt to treat it more as technology than as science. This is because their exposure to the field is often limited to the blind application of specific methods without consideration for the historical and theoretical rationale behind their development. The scientist working in psychophysics sees matters in quite a different light. To this person, psychophysical theory shapes the interpretation of results as well as the experimental procedures. Whatever the subject population, the theorist searches for invariant relations among stimuli and responses and the constraints these relations place on models of the underlying mechanisms of information processing. The technical machinery required to reach this goal is important and interesting in its own right, but for most scientists this aspect is clearly subservient to substantive issues in psychology.

In brief, a psychophysical theory is a set of statements (assumptions) that describe how an organism processes stimulus information under carefully specified conditions. The assumptions usually concern hypothetical processes that are difficult or impossible to observe directly. Once these assumptions are made explicit, however, formal models can be devised. The validity of the theory can be tested by comparing observations against the predictions of the model. In other words, a theory represents a set of "reasonable" guesses about exactly *how* a person behaves as a measuring instrument when asked to judge properties of stimuli.

Detailed predictions of what a person will actually *do* in an experiment are based on models especially designed to test one or more theories. Although in recent years the terms "model" and "theory" have often been used interchangeably, a model is thought to be a concrete synthesis of the assumptions of a theory. This synthesis specifies the interrelationships among the postulated primitives of the theory. Often these statements are in the form of mathematical formulas, computer programs, or logical truisms. In this way they are both more specific and yet more general than the theory giving rise to them—more specific in that the theory, through its models, is now amenable to laboratory test, and more general in that an abstract model may be used to quantify theories in many areas of study.

In some cases, a model combines only a few explicit assumptions and therefore can be readily accepted or rejected by an examination of relevant data. This is particularly true when mathematical functions are fit to results in hopes of producing a more economical representation. For example, the mathematical function $y = ax + b$ might be employed as a model, where y is the magnitude of a subject's estimate, x is the stimulus intensity giving rise to that estimate, and a and b are determined by examining pairs of x and y values. By appropriate statistics we can quickly decide whether or not the model is adequate to describe the data. This is not to say that *no* assumptions are involved in its use. Critical assumptions may simply be well hidden or left unstated; for instance, it may be assumed that the relation between stimulus (intensity) and response (magnitude) may be modeled by a smooth curve without jumps or discontinuities.

One important example of such a descriptive model is the *power function*, which has played a dominant role in modern psychophysics, mainly because it handles an impressive array of experimental results. For example, a person's perception of the intensity of electric shock can be studied by comparing numerical estimates (verbally stated) with actual physical intensities. One can often approximate the relationship between stimulus intensity (S) and mean response magnitude (R) by the equation

$$R = \lambda S^n \tag{1.1}$$

where λ and n are constants. The λ is merely a scaling constant that depends on the particular experimental conditions. By contrast, the attribute under study is characterized by a unique value of the exponent n. For electric shock, n is approximately 3. This general relation, often called Stevens's law, holds for many stimulus continua, including visual line length, sound intensity, luminance, and force of handgrip (Chapter 5). The interesting invariant here is the power function, because it transcends the particular nature of the stimulus and suggests an underlying order in the perceptual transformation of the environment.

Some investigators argue that this is all we can ever expect from a psychophysical function and that consequently there is no need to delve further into its underlying assumptions. On the other hand, one can argue that a theory is still required to explain why the power function works so well, and this theory will come equipped with assumptions and rules about why it holds under some conditions and not under others. We offer such a theoretical structure in Chapters 4 and 5.

SCALING MODELS

The level of understanding in various scientific disciplines is closely linked with the extent to which quantitative methods are employed. This is true in psychology, where the concept of a dimension or a scale extends beyond the field of perception and psychophysics. A scaling model is employed in a variety of situations to represent empirical relations among a set of observations by the mathematical relations among a set of numbers (Krantz et al., 1971). Hence, we can "scale" not only the perceived intensity of electric shock but also such attributes as the excellence of handwriting or the desirability of automobiles. Therefore, the use of scaling models in psychophysics is a subset of their total use in psychology. While emphasizing psychophysical applications throughout this work, we also hope to provide some insights into some of the broader issues raised by the use of scaling theory.

MEASUREMENT AND SCALE TYPES

One of the key ideas throughout psychophysics and scaling is the concept of measurement invariance. That is, across a variety of conditions, the data from experiments should be consistent in predictable ways. The theory need not say that the response to a given stimulus will be *absolutely* invariant over many replications, but only that the pattern of response magnitudes will stay the same. Measurement theory is the study of these patterns; numbers are assigned to objects or attributes so that the relations among the attributes are represented by the relations among the numbers. Such a pattern is called a *scale type*. Although a fair variety can be formulated (Coombs, Raiffa, and Thrall, 1954; Krantz et al., 1971), we will concentrate on the four most commonly distinguished: *ratio, interval, ordinal,* and *nominal* (Stevens, 1946, 1951). The thing to note here is that the type of scale employed in any instance depends on theoretical expectations and restricts the kinds of statements one can make about empirical data represented by points along the scale. Less information about the empirical world is conveyed by a nominal scale (essentially a set of labels) than by a ratio scale (a ruler, for example).

The rules of numerical assignment are logical or mathematical, and the objects or attributes are phenomena whose existence is agreed to on either empirical or theoretical grounds. In psychophysics the stimulus attributes are light intensity, sound level, electrical current, and weight; the measuring instruments include the photometer, sound level meter, voltmeter, and balance; and the rules of interpretation of the system are taken from mathematics (for example, $1+1=2$, $3>2$, $5=5$, and $4\neq 7$). An unusual side of this enterprise is that numerals (emitted by subjects) are treated as numbers satisfying the rules of mathematics. In this way, the subject is treated both as the originator of an attribute (numerals) and as the measuring instrument for that attribute.

Only in a few special cases is the assignment of numbers absolute. One example is the counting of distinct objects. In most situations, however, numbers are assigned relative to some standard. For example, the values assigned to lengths depend on the unit of measure (the length of an object could be given the value 100 if the units were centimeters and the value 1 if the units were meters). This does not mean that the values assigned to lengths can be *anything*. In this case the numerical assignments are constrained by what will later be more formally described as a ratio scale. For instance, a pair of lengths assigned 12 and 24 cm could not be assigned the numbers 1 and 50 in another unit of measure. This would not satisfy the rules of a ratio scale, since $24/12\neq 50/1$. (The values 20 and 40 would satisfy the requirement, since $24/12=40/20$.) Often the requirements of a ratio scale are too stringent, for reasons either theoretical or experimental (the data do not satisfy the conditions). But luckily we can substitute other criteria for the equal ratio requirement and still "do science." Different sets of criteria determine different types of scales, each implying a particular uniqueness for the relations among the data represented. As the uniqueness requirements of the ratio scale are relaxed, we obtain the interval, ordinal, and nominal scales.

It should be emphasized that there is nothing sacred about these four scale types. This classification scheme is due primarily to the relative simplicity of specifying and testing their requirements. In addition, it helps us to decide which mathematical models are appropriate for analyzing the data. A related point of view is that these four types specify the degree of invariance expected when scaling data. This means that certain relations among scale values will remain true when another scale is constructed from a second data set obtained under the same, or similar, conditions.

Table 1.1 Hypothetical results from light measurement

Black box 1, Ratio scale

Trials	Lights					Scale transformations
	A	B	C	D	E	
1	2	5	8	10	15	x
2	6	15	24	30	45	$x' = 3x$
3	1	2.5	4	5	7.5	$x'' = 0.5x$

Black box 2, Interval scale

Trials	Lights					Scale transformations
	A	B	C	D	E	
1	2	5	8	10	12	x
2	5	8	11	13	15	$x' = x + 3$
3	0	1.5	3	4	5	$x'' = 0.5x - 1$

Black box 3, Ordinal scale

Trials	Lights					Scale transformations
	A	B	C	D	E	
1	2	5	8	10	12	x
2	2	6	6.5	9	200	$x' = \mathrm{mon} f(x)$
3	1	75	90	92	99	$x'' = \mathrm{mon} f(x)$

Black box 4, Nominal scale

Trials	Lights					Scale transformations
	A	B	C	D	E	
1	2	5	8	10	90	x
2	3	1	6	2	0	$x' = f(x)$
3	8.5	60	1.5	90	10	$x'' = f(x)$

$f(x)$ is a relabeling of each light such that all the new labels are different from one another.

To illustrate the connection between theoretically expected invariances and data, consider a hypothetical experiment. Let us say we have a generator that produces lights of five different intensities. (We will denote the lights as A, B, C, D, and E.) To avoid some philosophical problems, let us assume that light A is always of a constant intensity and that the same is true for the other four lights. Suppose also that we have four "black boxes" (could be people, photometers, or Martians), each producing scale values consistent with one of the four scale types (a ratio-scale black box, an interval-scale black box, etc.) Let us suppose, further, that through some misfortune we have mixed up the labels and now wish to accurately relabel the boxes. To do this, we run an experiment and collect responses from all four boxes. This is done on three occasions (replications) for each of the five lights. The hypothetical results are summarized in Table 1.1.

Ratio Scale

Black box 1 produces responses that maintain their relative sizes across trials. For instance, the ratio of responses for lights A and C is always $1/4 = 6/24 = 2/8$. This could be interpreted as meaning that once a value for the standard, A, is established, the value for C is fixed. Alternatively, this means that values obtained from one trial can be transformed into those from another by a single multiplier. That is, each repetition (trial) produces a scale, and to go from a measure x from one scale to a measure x' on another, multiply by a positive constant a:

$$x \rightarrow x', \qquad x' = ax, \qquad a > 0 \qquad (1.2)$$

Other qualities make this pattern of numbers unique among the four scale types to be mentioned later. The ratio scale is the only one in which the concepts of "twice" or "ten times as bright" have any meaning. One of the distinctive characteristics of a ratio scale is the existence of a unique zero, so a stimulus attribute maintains the same zero point on all trials regardless of the multiplicative constant a. In addition, a ratio scale satisfies all the criteria for the other three scale types. So, even though black box 1 could be labeled as any one of the four types, it is probably best to say it produces numbers on a ratio scale, because this gives us the most information about the invariance of the scale values. The empirical data (measures) are best modeled by the numerical rules of a ratio scale.

Interval Scale

Next, let us consider the data collected from black box 2 in Table 1.1. Here the *ratios* among the measures of the four lights can vary over trials (for example, comparing measures of A and B on trials 1 and 2, $2/5 \neq 5/8$), but the *relative size* of the intervals is retained, as well as their intensity order. To illustrate this, consider the interval AB and the interval CD on trial 1.

$$|A - B| = |2 - 5| = 3$$
$$|C - D| = |8 - 10| = 2$$

Rather than look at the ratios of the scale values, as we did for ratio scales, we look at the ratio of the two intervals

$$\frac{|C - D|}{|A - B|} = \frac{2}{3}$$

This ratio is the same for each of the other trials. For instance, on trial 3,

$$\frac{|C - D|}{|A - B|} = \frac{|4 - 3|}{|1.5 - 0|} = \frac{1}{1.5} = \frac{2}{3}$$

Hence, transformation from a measure x on one trial to x' on another is given by the linear equation known in mathematics as an *affine* transformation:

$$x \to x', \qquad x' = ax + b \qquad a > 0 \qquad (1.3)$$

If each pair of trials produces a set of measures that constitute a scale, corresponding measures may be related by a wider range of transformations than that permitted for ratio scales. That is, adding a constant is now a permissible transformation. This also eliminates the significance of zero (zero always being mapped to zero in a ratio scale) since it can now be transformed into numbers other than itself [i.e., $(x = 0) + b = b$]. Measures satisfying the conditions for an interval scale also satisfy all conditions for ordinal and nominal scales, but we shall label black box 2 as producing interval scale results. As in the case of box 1, this gives us the most information about the invariance of the scale values.

Ordinal Scale

Among the measures from black box 3, only the order of scale values is constant over trials. Light A is always less intense than light B, and so on, but the ratios and the ratios of intervals among scale values may change from trial to trial. The integrity of the ordinal scale is maintained by any monotonic transformation:

$$x \rightarrow x', \qquad x' = \operatorname{mon} f(x) \qquad (1.4)$$

where x' is a monotonic function of x. Therefore, if $y > v$, then $y' > v'$, since $f(x)$ is a transformation that maintains the *order* of y and v.

Nominal Scale

The measures from black box 4 seem to have very little consistency. All we can say is that the measures within a single trial distinguish the lights from one another. In addition to a loss of ratio and interval information, stimulus order may change from trial to trial. The simple substitution of unique labels within each trial is indicated by the expression $x' = f(x)$. The only information available is whether two stimulus attributes are the same or different. Labeling can be said to produce a scale of sorts, but since numbers need not be involved (we could use letters, or dogs' names), it is debatable whether this scale should be included in the list (Torgerson, 1958). In any event, the nominal scale adds a final note to the hierarchy of types most often discussed in the literature.

CONCLUDING COMMENT

We began the previous section by claiming that numbers could be attached to stimuli according to different rules. In the measurement example, the meaning of numerical reports depends upon theoretical considerations and the invariant properties of the measures over trials. Therefore, the critical question is: What scale properties are left invariant? The answer determines the scale type and hence the particular significance given to the measures. In order for scaling to be a scientifically useful tool, one must know the invariances and permitted scale transformations in the data produced. This allows measurement in, and sometimes generalizations to, situations beyond those in which the scale was originally established. It also restricts the various analyses that may be performed on the data.

The major point, then, is this. If a person is viewed as a measuring instrument in the psychophysical paradigm, the pattern of responses will contain certain invariances over different experimental conditions. Theories capitalize on these invariances by organizing responses into a scale type, which restricts the kinds of meaningful statements we can make about the data being modeled. Only four scales have been discussed here since they are the ones most relevant to modern psychological research.

Occasionally in psychophysics, often on the physics side, it is helpful to deal with other types of scales (see Krantz et al., 1971). For example, scale values may be invariant up to a power transformation.

$$x \rightarrow x', \qquad x' = cx^{\gamma}, \qquad c > 0, \qquad \gamma > 0 \tag{1.5}$$

Assuming x and x' are positive, this formula may be rewritten as follows:

$$\log x' = \gamma \log x + \log c \tag{1.6}$$

We see that with suitable transformations of the initial scale values, the formula is identical to that prescribed by an interval scale (Eq. 1.3). In both cases two values are needed to specify the scale: the multiplicative constant a or γ and the additive constant b or $\log c$. For this reason, scales that are invariant up to a power transformation are called *log-interval* scales.

In actuality, the early history of psychophysics contains little in the way of references to scale types, whose importance only became apparent during the course of applying classical methods to new problem areas. However, the psychophysical paradigm of the human-as-a-measuring-instrument was laid down from the start in the writings of Gustav Fechner who also provided the field with its first theory and accompanying mathematical model (the logarithmic function). This historical development is the subject of Chapter 2.

REFERENCES

Coombs, C. H., Raiffa, H., and Thrall, R. M. "Some views on mathematical models and measurement theory." *Psychological Review*, 1954, *61*, 132–144.

Krantz, D. H., Luce, R. D., Suppes, P., and Tversky, A. *Foundations of Measurement. I. Additive and Polynomial Representations*. New York: Academic, 1971.

Kuhn, T. S. *The Structure of Scientific Revolutions*. Chicago: University of Chicago Press, 1962.

Stevens, S. S. "On the theory of scales of measurement." *Science*, 1946, *103*, 677–680.

Stevens, S. S. (Ed.) "Mathematics, measurement, and psychophysics." *Handbook of Experimental Psychology*. New York: Wiley, 1951, 1–49.

Torgerson, W. S. *Theory and Methods of Scaling*. New York: Wiley, 1958.

CHAPTER

| 2 |

CLASSICAL PSYCHOPHYSICS: FECHNER'S LAW

Our study of psychophysics begins most naturally with its founder, Gustav Fechner, a German philosopher and physicist who combined his philosophical inclinations and scientific talents into the production of the now classic *Elemente der Psychophysik*, published originally in 1860. This work contains a strange mixture of philosophy, mathematics, and experimental method, making it difficult to treat individual aspects of his approach in isolation. In this and the succeeding chapter, we will outline the kinds of problems Fechner posed, his suggested solutions, and the relative success of these efforts compared with more recent formulations.

Fechner's major concern was with philosophical matters. His guiding mission throughout a productive intellectual life was to undercut materialism as a dominant style of thought. In place of this view, he championed a more mystical approach to philosophy and science, giving full attention to the conscious experience he believed accompanied all physical processes. Most remarkably, in anticipation of later thinkers, Fechner attributed consciousness to organisms at all levels of the animal hierarchy, as well as to other living matter (such as plants; Fechner, 1848; Goude, 1962). To him the physical environment was a womb containing the life spirit, which could find complete unity with the universe only after death of the corporeal form. A true theoretician, he clearly states in one of his books (1905) that, after death, the human spirit is able to comprehend all patterns, relationships, and meanings of the universe *simultaneously*. To Fechner, this was tantamount to comprehension of God, whom he equated with the spirit of the universe.

PHILOSOPHY OF PSYCHOPHYSICS

Elemente der Psychophysik is limited to one manifestation of this philosophical position: the conscious experience (sensation) accompanying activity of the brain induced by external stimuli—in short, the mind-body problem. For Fechner, this area of inquiry served only as an example, which hopefully would generalize later to broader epistemological issues.

When it came to psychophysics, Fechner dealt primarily with three concepts and their interrelations: (1) the external physical environment, (2) the brain (called bodily) activity accompanying environmental stimulation, and (3) the conscious perception (sensation) accompanying these external and internal physical processes. Of the three possible pairings, the mapping between brain activity and conscious sensation was the most critical. Fechner termed the theoretical study of this relationship "inner psychophysics." Unfortunately, as so often happens in science, this most crucial relationship proved to be inaccessible to direct observation. Therefore, one could only speculate about the exact properties of inner psychophysics, and this created a seemingly insurmountable barrier. To avoid this barrier, Fechner hypothesized that measured brain activity and subjective perception were simply alternative ways of viewing the same phenomena. One realm of the universe did not *depend* on the other in a cause-and-effect fashion; rather, they accompanied each other and were complementary in the information conveyed about the universe (Fechner, 1907, 1966; Arguelles, 1972).

In this regard, his world view was similar to that introduced some years later by the physicist Neils Bohr (1961) to explain the apparently contradictory behavior ascribed to light when defined in alternative ways (waves or particles). That is, a single phenomenon may be modeled in several ways with each model revealing only part of the overall picture. The complementarity principle in psychophysics involved a distinction between what Fechner called the "night view" (materialism, body physiology) and the "day view" (mysticism, mind).

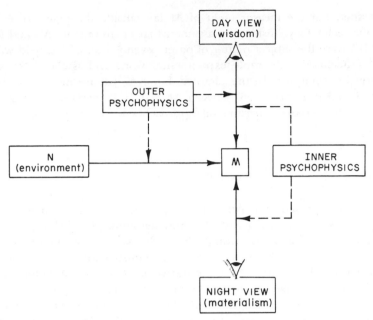

Figure 2.1. Schematic diagram of Fechnerian psychophysics.

This conception is illustrated in Fig. 2.1, where the environment N is shown impinging on the person and producing an internal event. When viewed from below the page, one sees the M of "materialism," but from above one sees a W, which might stand for conscious "wisdom." The geometric pattern on the page is identical in either case, but its interpretation varies depending upon one's location vis-a-vis the page. Acceptance of this dual but functionally interdependent view of the same phenomena represents Fechner's basic epistemology. The scientific problem then becomes one of finding the correct transformation between these two standpoints and expressing this transformation mathematically.

Now consider the following transformations. The change from perception of M to W in Fig. 2.1 is accomplished by rotating the page 180°. The transformation required to change from the night (material) to the day (psychological) view of perceptual events is not so obvious. Before focusing on that primary issue, it is helpful to state the possible relationships among N, W, and M and Fechner's ground rules concerning them (Fig. 2.1). The hypothetical relation between bodily activity (M) and conscious sensation (W) is inner psychophysics. The relation between M and N involves principles of physics, chemistry, and physiology. This relation was of interest to Fechner, but the measurement of M lay outside the power of existing scientific technology. Instead he assumed that environment (N) and sensation (W) were the subject matter of outer psychophysics. This field was the basis of Fechner's admirable experimental work and is the precursor of modern psychophysics. In this chapter, however, we are most interested in the proposed transformation between M and W (inner psychophysics). In the next chapter the experimental approaches to outer psychophysics are discussed.

INNER PSYCHOPHYSICS

Fechner was primarily looking for a quantitative means to express the relation between brain activity (M) and sensation (W) following the presentation of environmental stimuli. Since he assumed a one-to-one correspondence between elements in N (environment) and M, he indirectly measured the latter using a quantitative scale of the N intensity. (He actually spoke of the amount of internal kinetic energy.) That is, environmental stimuli (say, line lengths, or lights presented to the eye) have their M analogs in the central nervous system. Theoretically, the length of each line or the intensity of each light could be measured and ordered by the magnitude of this internal physiological effect.

Second, in his search for a mathematical relationship between M and W, Fechner assumed that sensation could be measured (theoretically) and properly located along an internal scale. The function relating values of physical and psychic magnitude then represents the psychophysical transformation. The general form of this transformation was thought to be the same for all physical attributes (lights, sounds, lengths, smells). In effect, the idea was that conscious experience is *unitary*, can be ordered along an intensity scale, and bears a constant relation (except for changes in stimulus parameters) to both internal brain processes and external conditions giving rise to those processes. Hence, a pluralistic, materialistic environment is mapped into a unitary scale of conscious sensation. Although some mechanism must also be provided in this scheme for recognizing qualitative differences among attributes, this difficulty did not receive much attention from Fechner and consequently played no role in his further development of a quantitative mapping between M and W.

We see that Fechner had little hope of measuring M and W directly, and therefore the mapping between them was similarly out of scientific reach. How, then, did he decide upon a particular mapping? We can, of course, never know the actual conditions leading to the proposed mapping. We do know, however, that he was familiar with the work of the mathematicians

Bernoulli, Laplace, and Poisson, who proposed that the subjective utility of an increase in personal wealth was a function of the amount one already had. Different increments in monetary wealth are required to produce equally noticeable subjective changes for the rich and poor. Not a highly debatable hypothesis! For example, in order to obtain the same significant increment in subjective utility, both the rich and the poor might have to double their existing wealth (see, for example, Bernoulli, translated by Sommer, 1954). In expressing this rule quantitatively, the subjective utility of money is logarithmically related to its monetary value. This in turn was the rule Fechner used to describe the relation between M and W. He tells us that the solution came in a flash of intuition, a hunch, as he lay in bed on the morning of October 22, 1850 (Boring, 1950; Fechner, in translation, 1966). This date, "Fechner Day" is still celebrated in scattered laboratories and homes throughout the world. Since we can be sure a man of his caliber was familiar with numerous functional relations, it would be a mistake to think he simply extended the earlier mathematical formulations on utility of money to apply to psychophysics. The hunch was undoubtedly the outcome of many hours of sifting through alternatives, casting about for new formulations, and checking ideas against reality (as he knew it from the experimental literature). On the other hand, the early mathematical work probably influenced the quantitative expression of this important hunch.

Whatever the actual antecedents, the field of psychophysics was founded on the following premise: *A geometric increase in brain activity (M) is accompanied by an arithmetic increase in conscious sensation (W).* In other words, a constant increment in W is paralleled not by a constant increment in M, but by an increment in M that is proportional to the existing amount. This relation is shown in Fig. 2.2, where equal arithmetic steps in W are accompanied by geometrically increasing steps in M. That is, the units on the W axis are stepped off in equal intervals of size c. On the other hand, these equal steps of W are accompanied by geometric changes (equal ratios) in M of the form

$$M_1 = kM_0$$

$$M_2 = k \cdot kM_0$$

$$\vdots$$

$$M_{i-1} = k^{i-1}M_0$$

$$M_i = k^i M_0$$

(2.1)

where M_0 is a threshold or initial value. Here, i is the number of steps along

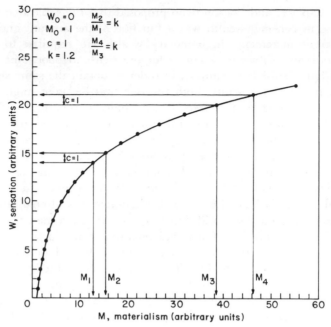

Figure 2.2. Fechner's conception of inner psychophysics. Equal steps on the sensation scale (W) are related to equal ratios on the materialist scale (M).

the W axis and k is a constant ratio obtained in the following way:

$$\frac{M_i}{M_{i-1}} = \frac{k^i M_0}{k^{i-1} M_0} = k \qquad (2.2)$$

It is convenient to graph the relation so that a constant interval on the W axis accompanies a constant interval (instead of ratio) along the M axis. This can be approached by taking logarithms[1] of both sides of Eq. 2.2:

$$\ln M_i - \ln M_{i-1} = \ln k \qquad (2.3)$$

---

[1]Logarithms are the inverse of the exponential function, so if the following equality is true for constants c and b

$$c = e^b$$

then the following equality is also true: $\ln c = b$. This is read: "log of c to the base e is equal to b." In this chapter, all logarithms are to base e (a constant approximately equal to 2.71828), which is written "ln" (natural log) instead of the more verbose "$\log_e$."

Since k is a constant, $\ln k$ is a constant, so if we assume that W is a linear function of the logarithm of M, each constant interval c corresponds to a constant interval $\ln k$. Typically, a linear function is written $y = ax$, where x and y are the two variables and a is a constant slope. In our case, x corresponds to $\ln M$, y corresponds to W, and a is the ratio $c/\ln k$. Therefore, the equation may be rewritten as follows:

$$W = \frac{c}{\ln k} \ln M \qquad (2.4)$$

Although the general form of Eq. 2.4 is considered to be invariant, the constants c and k may depend on the stimulus attribute and the experimental conditions. Fechner himself did not give much attention to these variables, but modern psychophysics does, as we will see in later chapters. With some modifications (outlined later), this logarithmic relation is the one proposed by Fechner to describe the transformation between the materialistic and mentalistic views as reflected in the smaller, but most crucial, arena of inner psychophysics.

OUTER PSYCHOPHYSICS

As noted earlier, the original idea for the psychophysical transformation was based on a hunch, and Fechner was surely not satisfied to let it rest at that. Consequently, he proceeded to develop a theoretical rationale for the logarithmic function that depended more on logic than on personal whims and historical precedent. Since he knew what to look for—that is, the final outcome had to agree with his intuitions—the task was much easier, although success was not inevitable. His eventual solution was truly creative and still stands as one of the most interesting theoretical arguments in the history of psychology. We will now trace a line of thought that probably captures at least some of the factors considered in arriving at a rational argument for the logarithmic function.

Although the relation between the internal events M and W was the object of attention, it was clear that this relation could not be verified by direct measurement. Therefore, an alternative approach was necessary. It was possible, of course, to obtain a direct measure of N, the environmental stimulus. This, then, was a starting point, although there was no hope of measuring the brain processes triggered by N. That left W. If some measure of W were possible, however indirect, the relation between N and W could probably be determined. Fechner called the experimental quest for this relation "outer psychophysics." With the assumption of a one-to-one connection between N and M, one could infer the all-important mind-body function within the realm of inner psychophysics. This situation may be clarified by reexamining Fig. 2.1.

The problem, then, is to find a relation between N and W, where the former can be measured directly and the latter cannot. The initial conditions for this problem are diagrammed in Fig. 2.3. Suppose the N-meter in Fig. 2.3 is an instrument recording the magnitude of an external stimulus impinging on a person along some dimension of interest (such as light, sound, or length). Treat the W-meter as purely hypothetical for the moment. It would be nice if the W-meter could measure internal sensation so changes in it could be correlated with changes in the N-meter. Fechner thought that reading the W-meter was impossible or, at best, would produce unreliable results. In other words, a person would be incapable of reporting the absolute magnitude of his or her sensations by saying something like: "This light is 17 units on my sensation scale," or "This sensation is three times as intense as the previous one." Presumably a person could report whether one sensation were less than, equal to, or greater than the intensity of another. The cornerstone of all Fechner's measurement procedures was this assumption that an internal scale of sensation does exist. Differences between sensations can be detected but their absolute magnitudes cannot.

Two types of changes in scale value are relevant here. The first is the change from zero sensation to unit 1; that is, the *threshold* or starting point of the W-meter is triggered by the stimulus intensity (magnitude) necessary for any sensation at all to be experienced. This is called the *absolute threshold* (or *absolute lower threshold* to distinguish it from the upper threshold encountered at the other extreme of the intensity scale). The second type of change proceeding from one unit to the next on the W scale is the smallest

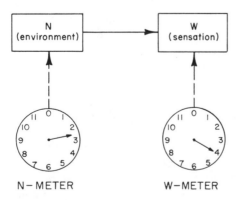

Figure 2.3. A schematic view of outer psychophysics. The external environment (N) is observable, the internal sensation (W) is not.

difference in intensity required for one stimulus to be perceived as different from a second. This is called the *just-noticeable-difference* (*jnd*) in sensation. Corresponding stimulus changes are known as *difference thresholds, difference limens* (DL's), or *stimulus jnd's*. In what follows we will try to maintain the distinction between these two sorts of jnd's (subjective and physical).

At this juncture we arrive at a critical postulate: All jnd's measured hypothetically along the scale of sensation are assumed to be of identical size. Another way of saying this is to state that the *W*-meter operates only in whole number steps of a size equal to one jnd. A jnd in sensation is a constant in this scheme. Given this postulate, we can proceed to construct a quantitative transformation between stimulus intensity measured in absolute (physical) units, and subjective magnitude measured in jnd (sensation) units.

Here is how this would work in an ideal experiment. Initially, both the *N*-meter and the *W*-meter are set at zero. This is probably impossible in practice (we might approach it temporarily by extreme measures, such as suspending a person, blindfolded, in a tub of water kept at body temperature, etc.), but for our purposes it is not really *that* important. In any case, we slowly crank up the intensity along some physical dimension, say, sound, and continuously monitor the absolute output with the *N*-meter. For a while, the person hears nothing, but eventually a sensation is aroused, the subject reports this fact, and simultaneously the *W*-meter jumps to unit 1 on the sensation scale. The current reading on the *N*-meter is then said to represent the absolute stimulus threshold for that particular dimension under those particular conditions.

The stimulus intensity is then increased from the current energy level registered on the *N*-meter, and once again we wait until the person says the subjective magnitude has increased (changed one unit). The *W*-meter now reads "two" jnd units, and the corresponding stimulus value can be recorded from the *N*-meter. The increment on the *N*-meter over the previous value is called the *stimulus jnd*. The experimenter maps the relation between successive units of *W* and corresponding intensities of *N* until the upper threshold is reached.

This hypothetical procedure is shown schematically in Fig. 2.4. Each jnd on the *W*-meter can be linked to a corresponding intensity from the *N*-meter, which gives some hypothetical results from our experiment. If the *W* values are plotted against the *N* values, the transformation between the two scales is apparent. This procedure is done in Fig. 2.2, where *M* may be replaced by *N*. The function is, of course, logarithmic and illustrates the results Fechner both expected and required to verify his hunch about the transformation between *N* and *W* and consequently between *M* and *W*. Appropriately enough this function has since been known as *Fechner's law*.

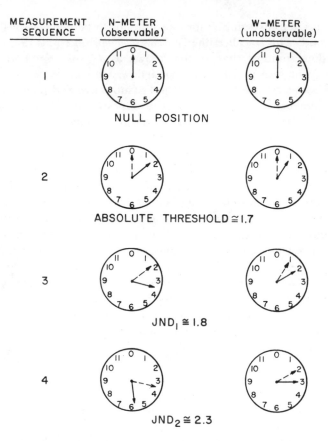

Figure 2.4. Hypothetical results of a method to obtain absolute threshold and stimulus jnd's. The successive thresholds on the sensation scale (subjective jnd's) measured by the W-meter are of equal size (1 unit). The corresponding stimulus values measured by the N-meter vary as indicated (1.7, 1.8, 2.3).

The magnitude of a sensation is defined as the sum of the jnd's beginning at a threshold value. The corresponding stimulus intensity can be taken directly from the N-meter and equals the sum of the stimulus jnd's. Presumably, a person experiencing an intensity would be unaware of this breakdown into a series of jnd's on either a subjective or physical level. In other words, it is important to understand that the summation discussed is a theoretical transformation between environmental and sensation values. We need not believe that people are actually aware of some little adding process involving jnd units. One must also realize that a logarithmic function is not the only possible transformation that can arise from such an adding procedure. The nature of the final relation depends on the assumed size of all units on the W scale as well as on the experimentally determined sizes of the stimulus jnd's. More will be said about this in Chapter 4.

Let us summarize our progress so far. Fechner's major interests lay in philosophy, where he attacked a purely materialistic view of the universe by claiming equal status for conscious awareness. He pared down this general concern to the study of the transformation between brain states and sensations. This discipline was formally called inner psychophysics, but since it was not amenable to direct study, outer psychophysics was invented. This enterprise was designed to explore the quantitative relation between external intensities and internal sensations. Because the former could be measured directly, but the latter could not, a theoretical trick was introduced. The key idea was that a series of experimentally determined stimulus jnd's was linked theoretically with a series of sensation jnd's. Each increment in sensation was triggered by one stimulus jnd. The latter is a measurable quantity, such as 1 cm or 3 foot-lamberts (a measure of luminance). The total sensation magnitude is the sum of sensation units associated with the appropriate stimulus level. The outcome of this procedure could subsequently be compared with Fechner's hunch that the true relation between M and W is logarithmic. Having satisfied himself that such an approach was theoretically sound, Fechner then set out to formalize the equations needed to describe the results of this hypothetical procedure.

MATHEMATICAL DERIVATION OF FECHNER'S LAW

The major derivation is illustrated by the following line of argument. Suppose we keep the assumption that steps are equal along the W scale. Therefore, for each step, $\Delta W = c$. Suppose also that the stimulus jnd (ΔN) is a function of N; that is, $\Delta N = f(N)$. Now we can combine the two equalities and set up the following equation[2]:

$$\frac{\Delta W}{\Delta N} = \frac{c}{f(N)} \tag{2.5}$$

At this point a decision is necessary with respect to $f(N)$. Fechner was confident that ΔN was proportional to N:

$$\Delta N = f(N) = kN \tag{2.6}$$

[2]The symbol delta (Δ) may be loosely interpreted as "change in," so ΔW is "the change along the W scale," and ΔN is "the change along the N scale."

This confidence came from two sources. First, there was evidence that the experiment just described with the N and W meters would yield Eq. 2.6. These data were obtained by Weber (1846) and will be discussed more fully in the next chapter. Second, Eq. 2.6 was consistent with Fechner's hunch that the psychophysical function was logarithmic. In other words, arithmetic increases in W were accompanied by geometric increases in N.

Let us see why Eq. 2.6 was consistent with Fechner's views. We noted previously in the discussion of Fig. 2.2 that a geometric progression is equivalent to a constant ratio (k') between adjacent N values.

$$\frac{N+\Delta N}{N} = k'$$

$$1 + \frac{\Delta N}{N} = k' \tag{2.7}$$

$$\Delta N = (k' - 1)N$$

Substituting k for $k' - 1$, we have

$$\Delta N = kN$$

and equating N with M in Fig. 2.2 completes the connection.

Now returning to Eq. 2.5, we can substitute for $f(N)$ to obtain

$$\frac{\Delta W}{\Delta N} = \frac{c}{kN} \tag{2.8}$$

Rearranging,

$$\Delta W = \frac{c\,\Delta N}{kN} \tag{2.9}$$

The terms ΔW and ΔN are small values, but they are still large enough to be measured and counted. But let us assume that what is true for values as small as jnd's is also true for even smaller values. This would imply that the relation (Eq. 2.9) is also true when ΔW and ΔN become infinitesimal. In other words, by substituting dw and dn for ΔW and ΔN, respectively, Eq. 2.9 may be rewritten as a differential equation,

$$dw = C\frac{dn}{n} \tag{2.10}$$

where C is equal to c/k times a constant. This is used to make a smoother transition from discrete to infinitesimal values. Fechner justified this transition by recourse to his "mathematical auxiliary principle" (more on this in Chapter 4).

Suppose further that the zero point on the W scale ($W_0 = 0$) corresponds to a threshold, N_0. Then, integrating[3] both sides of Eq. 2.10

$$\int_{W_0}^{W} dw = C \int_{N_0}^{N} \frac{dn}{n} \tag{2.11}$$

From calculus we know that the integral of dw is W and the integral of dn/n is $\ln N$. Therefore, the result between N_0 and N is

$$W = C \ln N - C \ln N_0 \tag{2.12}$$

$$W = C \ln (N/N_0)$$

A linear function exists between W and $\ln(N/N_0)$ with slope C.

Perhaps the most important advantage of Fechner's approach is that only a single stimulus attribute must be measured. Most modern methods of sensory scaling require a person to match the intensity of one attribute to that of another (Marks, 1974). In order to make sense of the results, one should understand the psychophysical mapping of two attributes independently, but this is usually very difficult to do solely on the basis of the matching data. Consequently, one ends up grappling with Fechner's old problem of making realistic assumptions about internal jnd's except now one is stuck with two attributes instead of one. We will have more to say about this problem in later chapters.

Thus far, we have described a hunch supported by a theoretical explanation. Fechner's next step was to search for empirical data to help bolster the viability of this "law" between sensation and stimulation (outer psychophysics). Luckily, someone (E. H. Weber) at his own university had collected data to suggest that the relation between ΔN and N was indeed linear (Eq. 2.6). The details of this story are the subject of the next chapter.

REFERENCES

Arguelles, J. A. *Charles Henry and the Formation of a Psychophysical Aesthetic.* Chicago: University of Chicago Press, 1972.

Bernoulli, J. "Exposition of a new theory on the measurement of risk." Translated by L. Sommer. *Econometrica*, 1954, *22*, 23–36.

Bohr, N. *Atomic Physics and Human Knowledge.* New York: Science Editions Inc., 1961.

Boring, E. G. *A History of Experimental Psychology.* New York: Appleton-Century-Crofts, 1950.

[3]Integration is equivalent to finding the area under a curve. In the case of Eq. 2.11, we could also derive a value by drawing the curve $y = 1/n$ and finding the area contained under the curve for n, taking all values between N_0 and N.

Fechner, G. T. *Elements of Psychophysics*, Vol. 1, Translated by H. E. Adler. New York: Holt, Rinehart and Winston, 1966.

Fechner, G. T. *Elemente der Psychophysik*, Vol. 2. Leipzig: Breitkopf and Hartel, 1907.

Fechner, G. T. *The Little Book of Life After Death*. Translated by M. C. Wadsworth. Boston: Little, Brown, 1905.

Fechner, G. T. *Nanna oder über das Seelenleben der Pflanzen*. Hamburg: Verlag von Leopold Voss, 1848.

Goude, G. *On Fundamental Measurement in Psychology*. Stockholm: Almqvist and Wiksell, 1962.

Marks, L. *Sensory Processes: The New Psychophysics*. New York: Academic, 1974.

Weber, E. H. "Der Tastsinn und das Gemeinfühl." In R. Wagner (Ed.), *Handwörterbuch der Physiologie*, Vol. 3. Vieweg, Braunschweig, 1846, pp. 481–588.

CHAPTER

$$\boxed{3}$$

CLASSICAL PSYCHOPHYSICS: WEBER'S LAW

The theoretical study of psychophysics was initiated by Gustav Fechner, but relevant empirical work began at least a hundred years earlier (Bouguer, 1760). The data reported by Fechner's contemporary, E. H. Weber (1846), however, have been the most influential in terms of both stimulating early developments and maintaining interests up to the present day. Weber's chief contribution was to show that sensitivity to changes in stimulus intensity is measurable and predictable. Since the measurement of sensitivity in terms of a just-noticeable-difference (jnd) is carried out with specific stimuli such as lights, sounds, odorants, and pressures, S and ΔS are used in place of the symbols N and ΔN that stand for general environmental inputs. In addition, we often will refer to stimulus *continua* or *dimensions* to emphasize the notion of a quantitative scale in place of the more general term *attribute*.

Weber measured the stimulus jnd by experimental means similar to the procedure outlined in Chapter 2. The intensity of the stimulus was changed along some dimension until the subject noted a difference, and the physical increment required to accomplish this was the jnd. Its size (ΔS) was not constant but increased as a function of S. In fact, the ΔS needed to obtain a unit step in subjective magnitude (ΔW) was a linear function of the initial intensity S. The generality of this function led to its designation as *Weber's law*:

$$\Delta S = kS \tag{3.1}$$

There are several reasons why this law has had a lasting impact on psychophysics.

The first was Fechner's persuasive influence on the scene. To reiterate, he thought that mental activity was logarithmically related to bodily activity (inner psychophysics), but this relation could not be directly observed. Because of this difficulty, he was willing to settle for an objective determination of the function mapping external stimuli into sensation (outer psychophysics). One side of this function could *not* be approached experimentally: internal sensation (W). Therefore, he simply assumed that all steps along the W scale were equal. Fortunately, the stimulus side of outer psychophysics could be measured experimentally and was described by Weber's law. This was ideal for Fechner, since he could then propose on theoretical grounds that

$$\frac{\Delta W}{\Delta S} = \frac{a}{kS} \tag{3.2}$$

which could be rewritten as a differential equation and rearranged in a form called the *fundamental formula*:

$$dw = C\frac{ds}{s} \tag{3.3}$$

Integrating both sides of Eq. 3.3 yields the logarithmic law:

$$W = C\ln(S/S_0) \tag{3.4}$$

where S_0 is the lower or so-called absolute threshold. It is important to realize that not just any relation between ΔS and S leads to the logarithmic function. It is rather special in this regard. Fechner definitely required the empirical evidence of Weber's law to support his philosophical views about the mind-body connection, and so he naturally took every opportunity to inform the scientific public of its generality and importance.

The second reason for the prominence of Weber's law was less tied to the personal status of those involved in its promulgation. Namely, the very existence of such a law made it clear that human perception could be studied reliably with scientific methods. A person could be considered a sort of measuring instrument, coding external stimuli in terms of an internal scale. The techniques used by Weber and expanded upon by Fechner were available to answer a number of interesting experimental questions about this coding. (1) Over what range is the stimulus effectively coded? (2) What is the resolving power of the coding for different intensities? (3) Does resolving power depend upon the stimulus continuum (for example, sound, light)? (4) How stable is the coding under changes in stimulus conditions (contextual variables)? We will consider questions 1, 2, and 3 in this chapter, reserving discussion of 4 for Chapter 6.

Yet a third reason is given most often for the influence of Weber's law: It may provide a valid index of the relative sensitivity of different sensory channels. The classical approach to psychophysics postulates a fixed sensation scale onto which all external stimuli are mapped. Therefore, the argument goes, differences in sensitivity to different continua are due to differences in the underlying sensory mechanisms mediating the transformation onto the sensation scale. This situation is described by the scheme in Fig. 3.1. Each of the three stimulus continua is transformed by its own sensory system (magic box), but the output from all three converges on the same internal W scale. It is at this level that conscious perception arises and leads to a subjective report.

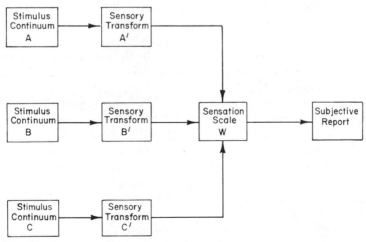

Figure 3.1. Schematic diagram of information flow from the environment to a subjective report.

GENERAL THRESHOLD THEORY

Having brought Weber's law to the fore, we can now discuss the methods used to measure the jnd (ΔS). Before proceeding, however, we ask the reader to put aside Fechner's philosophical inclinations and consider the methodology for observing the relation between ΔS and S. It should be recalled, for example, that S and ΔS are physical quantities. For instance, in a study of perceptual sensitivity to line lengths, S might be 10 cm and ΔS 1 cm. The Weber constant (k in Eq. 3.1) would then be .1.

Basic to the ensuing argument is a theory in which the subject samples the stimulus at a particular moment and compares its magnitude with that of a threshold on the sensation scale. If the stimulus value is greater than the threshold, the subject reports an increment of the stimulus intensity (a jnd). Otherwise, no increment is reported. We will refer to this as the "classical theory." To see how this theory might be converted into a working model, first consider a situation where the stimulus sampling is infallible. The subject knows the exact subjective intensity of each stimulus. If it is also assumed that the internal threshold level is fixed, the subject would be infinitely sensitive to stimulus differences.

From the standpoint of this theory let us first consider the detection of the presence or absence of a stimulus (the absolute threshold). In this case, a direct pipeline is assumed to link stimuli and sensations. What one reads on the stimulus scale is what one has on the sensation scale. Suppose now there is a fixed sensation threshold below which a stimulus is never detected (sensed) and above which it is always detected. Then, if a series of stimuli are presented in the general vicinity of the threshold, there will be a sharp separation between those that are noticed and those that are not. Therefore, a step function is the proper model to describe the probability of detection as a function of stimulus intensity, with the rise occurring at the absolute threshold (as shown in Fig. 3.2, top).

Next, suppose a standard stimulus is selected that is well above threshold. A subject is given the task of reporting whether a comparison stimulus is greater than or less than the standard. On the sensation scale there are three locations of interest: the standard, the threshold separating the standard from less intense stimuli, and the threshold separating the standard from more intense stimuli. Call the stimuli producing these locations S_1, S_2, and S_3. Then, as depicted in Fig. 3.2 (bottom), the probability of reporting that the comparison is greater than the standard can be plotted against the intensity of the comparison. Below S_1 the probability is 0. From S_1 to S_3 assume the subject guesses randomly over many trials. So the probability is .5. Beyond S_3 the probability jumps to 1 because comparison intensities are always reported to be greater than S_2. The appropriate model to describe

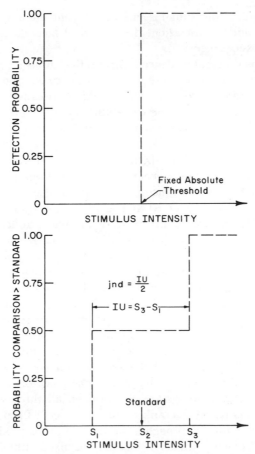

Figure 3.2 (top) Theoretical step function predicted when the absolute threshold is fixed and the subject is infinitely sensitive to stimulus presence and absence. (bottom) Theoretical step function for determination of a jnd with fixed thresholds symmetrically located above and below the standard.

this behavior consists of two steps, with the tread width of the lower one representing the distance (stimulus) between thresholds S_1 and S_3. The jnd (ΔS) can now be defined as either the distance from S_1 to S_2 or the distance from S_2 to S_3. If the thresholds are roughly symmetrical around the standard, it does not matter which measure is chosen, so an average is computed as $\Delta S = (S_3 - S_1)/2$.

The foregoing theoretical argument and the resulting means for obtaining a jnd are implicitly in effect throughout Chapter 2. In the hypothetical experiment mentioned there, stimulus and sensation meters were read to determine the size of the stimulus jnd at different intensities. Although a useful starting point for discussion, the empirical facts do not support this version of the classical theory.

Rather, the experimental evidence indicates that subjects are not infinitely sensitive and are not even consistent in their evaluations of the same stimulus and the same threshold. This could be because of the inherent noisiness of sensory systems and the variability introduced through imperfect stimulus production and measurement. Therefore, it is probably best to accept the variability as inevitable and work with statistical measures for determining ΔS. That is, we accept the occurrence of uncontrolled factors such as quirks in the stimulus generator, residue from prior stimulation, noisy neurons, and so on, and incorporate their effects into the theory. In such a situation, it is often assumed that a bell-shaped (normal) distribution gives a reasonable picture of the sum of all uncontrolled factors. This mathematical model is a useful representation frequently encountered in the theoretical arguments of both classical and modern psychophysics.

Returning then to the general theory, there are two primary ways to describe the location of an internal threshold in respect to an external stimulus, as demonstrated in Fig. 3.3. In each we have a stimulus generator, a subject receiving the stimulus, and the possibility for sensation awareness on the part of the subject. The appropriate intensity at each level is measured by the three scales (S, I, and W), where the I scale is at the interface between the person and the environment. Suppose, for our first example, that the stimulus generator A and the receptors are infallible, in that constant intensity readings are obtained on all three scales (Fig. 3.3, left) whenever generator A is cranked up to deliver a fixed intensity. The internal threshold, however, is jiggling around and thus produces a normal distribution of thresholds on the W scale. The fixed stimulus intensity is compared with a single value randomly picked from this internal distribution. Over a large number of trials the threshold will fall above and below the stimulus in accord with the probabilities given by the normal distribution. Therefore, we can visualize the stimulus as a probe dividing the distribution into two parts. On those occasions when the sensation threshold is below the stimulus, the latter *will be* noticed; and on those occasions when the sensation threshold exceeds the stimulus it will *not be* noticed. This is one possible notion of what happens when a stimulus is presented to a subject.

Alternatively (Fig. 3.3, right), the stimulus generator B is fallible, and hence does not always produce the true intensity indicated by the S scale. This variability can theoretically be recorded by the I and W scales and describes a normal distribution. If the sensation threshold is considered fixed, however, it slices the distribution into two areas, leading once again to the

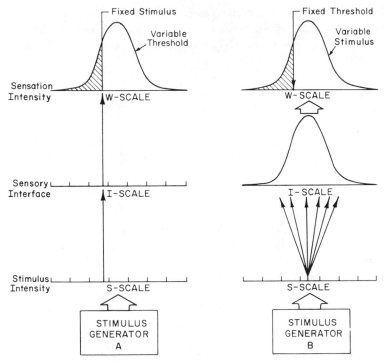

Figure 3.3. Schematic diagram of two classical threshold models. (left) A variable internal threshold is probed by a fixed stimulus intensity. (right) A variable stimulus is imposed on a fixed threshold. The scale types (S, I, and W) are described in the text.

situation depicted on the left at the level of the W scale. Since both conceptions of the problem lead to the same reliance upon the normal curve, the classical theory does not differentiate between the two. One realizes that in both cases the W scale does not yield to direct measurement, since it is a purely hypothetical construct. Only the S scale is observable; hence, it is assumed that both threshold and stimulus variability can be revealed by proper observation of the S scale. So we must proceed from there.

Suppose now we have a series of stimulus intensities and the percent of occasions that each was judged more intense than the standard. This is still not equivalent to computing ΔS for a given S. Some decision must be made as to a cutoff percentage for the stimulus at one jnd above the standard (that is, what is ΔS?). The customary approach is to assume that a standard stimulus leads to variable effects described by the normal curve. Empirical percentages, corresponding to stimulus intensities, are plotted as points on the distribution (or a curve derived from the distribution). The dispersion of this empirically determined curve is then used as a measure of ΔS. To gain an understanding of how this all works, one must know a little more about the normal curve.

THE NORMAL CURVE AS A MODEL

Given the central value (μ) and the dispersion (σ), the probability distribution for the normal curve may be defined by the equation:

$$f(x) = \frac{1}{\sigma\sqrt{2\pi}} e^{-(1/2)[(x-\mu)/\sigma]^2} \tag{3.5}$$

A particular value x, be it line length, brightness, or a value along some other continuum, is plugged into the equation, resulting in a value $f(x)$, which is the probability density that x will occur. In other words, we may compute the probability that a stimulus of value x will occur if we assume a normal distribution and provide the central value (mean $= \mu$) and dispersion (standard deviation $= \sigma$). Since Eq. 3.5 is a probability density function, the total area under the curve is 1. Area and probability are therefore synonymous in what follows. By integrating Eq. 3.5, the area under any section of the curve, from x_a to x_b, is determined.[1] In the methodology to be described shortly, x_a will usually be $-\infty$ and x_b will represent a stimulus cutoff on the x axis. That is,

$$P[x_a < x < x_b] = \frac{1}{\sigma\sqrt{2\pi}} \int_{x_a}^{x_b} e^{-(1/2)[(x-\mu)/\sigma]^2} \, dx \tag{3.6}$$

Another convenient way to compute cumulative probability (area) is to dispense with the units of measure for x in favor of a standard z score. Note that the exponent in Eq. 3.6 can be rewritten as

$$-\frac{1}{2}\left[\frac{x-\mu}{\sigma}\right]^2 = -\frac{1}{2}[z]^2 \tag{3.7}$$

The bracketed expression is the standard score used throughout statistics. It is a measure of the distance separating a raw score from the mean in units of standard deviation. One of the features of this measure is that the area under the normal curve between two particular z values is always a constant

[1]There is no analytic solution to the integral of the normal distribution, but approximations are available in most statistics books.

independent of the original units of measure on x. You can obtain z values and their associated areas from tables in many of your favorite statistics books. By converting to z scores in Eq. 3.6, we obtain a standardized normal curve with a mean of 0 and a standard deviation of 1. All other raw scores can be represented as positive or negative z scores depending on whether they lie above or below the mean, respectively. These tabled scores are commonly used as indices of location along the x axis of a normal curve; more extensive treatment of the normal curve can be found in most statistics books (see, for example, McGee, 1971).

To recap, the classical theory assumes that a stimulus intensity is compared to an internal threshold. There is noise somewhere in the system that may be represented as points with a normal distribution on one of the scales in Fig. 3.3. As a cutoff is moved along the S scale, the area to its left is the integral of the normal curve, as shown in Fig. 3.4. This cumulative probability (area) function is called the *normal ogive*. Since the mean and standard deviation uniquely specify the normal curve, they also specify the normal ogive, which is just another way of describing matters. Increasing the mean

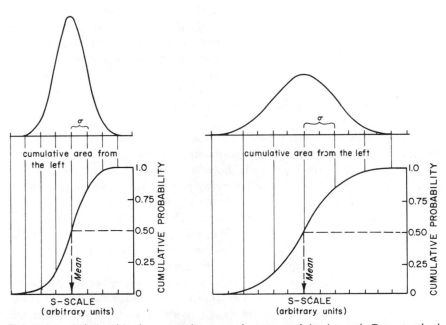

Figure 3.4. Relationship between the normal curve and its integral. Two standard deviations are illustrated as well as a graphical procedure to obtain the mean from the cumulative probability function (after McGee, 1971).

simply shifts the function along the S scale; increasing the standard deviation decreases the steepness, as shown in Fig. 3.4.

When applied to psychophysics, the normal ogive serves as a model of the relation between psychophysical judgments and stimulus intensity. For example, the probability of judging a comparison as more intense than a standard can be plotted against stimulus intensity after the manner of Figs. 3.2 and 3.4 (bottom). When certain mathematical constraints are met (Luce and Galanter, 1963), as they usually are for average data, this relation is called a *psychometric function*. Its relevance is this: If we can collect data on such a function, the mean and standard deviation (or some related measures) can be computed on the S values and used to describe the underlying distribution. In the case of the absolute threshold, the mean of the distribution is critical. On the other hand, the standard deviation is important in studies of the difference threshold. Standard deviations (σ) are illustrated in Fig. 3.4, as well as a graphical procedure to obtain the mean from the cumulative probability function (after McGee, 1971).

To briefly summarize, the foregoing version of the classical theory assumes either that the stimulus is variable and the threshold fixed or, conversely, that the threshold is variable and the stimulus fixed. From either perspective it is concluded that the normal curve is a satisfactory model of the composite distribution. The psychophysical methods to be discussed next use the cumulative area (integral) of the normal curve to fit data points. The pattern of such points is often referred to as a psychometric function.

PSYCHOPHYSICAL METHODS

To many people the classical psychophysical methods are important because of their extensive range of application in experimental psychology. Learning the ins and outs of these methods, however, can also be the most boring exercise in psychology because of the many possible variations in application and analysis. However, several excellent treatments are available for those wishing to pursue this matter in more depth (for example, see Engen, 1972; Gescheider, 1976; Guilford, 1954). We will gratefully leave most of the variations for laboratory study and concentrate upon the three chief methods: adjustment, limits, and constant stimuli.

All three methods depend on some technique whereby the presumed threshold is bracketed by comparison stimuli. The relevant statistic is either the mean of a group of measures or an index of variability such as the standard deviation. For the following examples, the model of a variable threshold and a fixed stimulus will be emphasized. The absolute and difference thresholds may be determined using any of the three methods.

Method of Adjustment

In this method the subject controls the intensity of the stimulus and attempts to match the threshold. To determine the *absolute threshold*, the stimulus intensity is preset to random points above and below threshold (the general region is found by preliminary research), and the subject adjusts intensity from this point until he or she either just detects the stimulus (ascending trials) or just ceases to detect it (descending trials). The adjusted intensity is then measured by the experimenter, and the mean value over a number of trials is the absolute threshold.

The *difference threshold* (or limen) (ΔS) is obtained in a similar way. In this case, a standard stimulus is presented, and the subject matches its perceived magnitude by adjusting a comparison stimulus. Over a series of trials the mean adjustment is usually quite close to the value of the standard and is called the *point of subjective equality* (PSE). The PSE, however, tells us nothing whatsoever about the subject's sensitivity to stimulus change. Rather, this is indicated by the size of the difference limen, which is often defined as half the range (interval) of uncertainty around the PSE. There is no objective way to decide how this range should be determined. A common criterion is plus or minus one standard deviation, which encloses an area (probability) under the normal curve representing approximately 68% of the cases; one standard deviation (σ) equals ΔS. Tradition dictates that this is the region of indifference, where comparison targets are "indistinguishable" from the standard. We could choose some other cutoff for our boundary, for example, 2 or .5 standard deviations, and these choices would not alter theoretical conclusions surrounding the cumulation of jnd's, Weber's law, and the like.

Method of Limits

In practice this method is essentially the same as the method of adjustment, except that the experimenter adjusts the stimulus intensity in a systematic way and the subject merely renders a yes-no (binary) judgment at each step as to whether the comparison is equal to or different from the standard. The calculation of the threshold value is also somewhat different.

To measure the absolute threshold, the stimulus is randomly set to a value above or below the threshold (whose approximate location is found by preliminary exploration). The subject indicates the relative location of the stimulus by saying something like "I don't see the light" or "yes, I see it." The experimenter then increases or decreases intensity in equal steps, noting the subject's judgment each time. At some level the response will switch from "no, I don't see it" to "yes, I do see it" or vice versa. Generally, the procedure is continued a few more steps to ensure that the change in response is not a fluke. The mean of the values where the response category changes is calculated separately for ascending and descending trials, and the average of these two values is the absolute threshold.

The difference limen is found in a similar fashion. The subject makes a judgment with respect to a fixed standard, as the comparison intensity is stepped in either an ascending or descending direction. The standard is bracketed, delimiting the region on the stimulus scale where the response category switches from "less than" to "not less than" on ascending trials or "greater than" to "not greater than" on descending trials. The width of this region is defined as the *interval of uncertainty* (IU). It is analogous to the region from -1σ to $+1\sigma$, as derived from the method of adjustment. Since the IU is assumed to be roughly centered on the mean, one-half the IU is appropriate as a measure of the difference limen in either a positive or negative direction from the standard intensity. As before, all measures are based on average data collected over many trials.

Alternatively, the difference limen is measured by analyzing the distribution of category switches on ascending and descending trials as if they were method-of-adjustment data. First, compute the standard deviation of the stopping points on the ascending trials only. Then compute the same measure on the stopping points of the descending trials only and average the two values. In this way we measure the jnd using the method-of-adjustment model while removing the effects of response anticipation or habituation that are often reflected in the difference in means of the ascending and descending trials.

The method of limits is quite time consuming. A common variation is the *staircase* or *up-and-down* method (Cornsweet, 1962; Engen, 1972, p. 20). Here, multiple measures of the threshold are secured on the same trial, since a trial consists of a sequence of judgments concerning the relative locations of the standard and the adjustable comparison. When the response category changes, the direction of the stimulus is reversed until the response switches back, and so on. That is, on an ascending trial the comparison will initially be judged less intense than the standard. But after a number of step increments the comparison will eventually be judged as more intense. At this point the experimenter initiates a descending series, etc. A plateau is usually quickly reached and the stimulus hovers around the threshold until a predetermined number of reversals occurs. In this sense, staircase can be viewed as an experimenter-controlled method of adjustment. Considerable information is obtained in a short time period, bringing relief to experimenter and subject alike.

The method of limits appears to provide a more intuitive measure of ΔS than the method of adjustment because it is more directly tied to changes in the response category. It is also interesting to note the similarity between this method and Weber's original procedure, where the subject indicated when the comparison was *different* from the standard as they were separated in a series of steps away from initial equality. This procedure is the origin of the term "just-noticeable-difference." In contrast, the comparison stimulus for the method of limits is initially set well above or below the standard and the subject must indicate when it is "just-noticeably-*not*-different" from the standard. This modification of Weber's method was introduced by Fechner. Since the abbreviation jnnd is longer and more confusing than jnd, the latter has been retained despite the misinformation conveyed about the experimental operations involved. As mentioned previously, the best way to think about the jnd (ΔS) is as a physical measure, which in turn reflects the dispersion of a hypothetical normal distribution. This stimulus jnd should not be confused with the internal jnd (ΔW), which the classical approach assumes to be of constant size, subjective, etc.

Method of Constant Stimuli

Once the inherent variability of perceptual processing is granted, applications of the methods of adjustment and limits follow rather directly. One has the feeling that any intelligent person faced with similar requirements could have invented these methods. It always looks easy after the fact! The method of constant stimuli, on the other hand, provides a more imaginative approach to the measurement of thresholds.

Suppose there is a variable absolute threshold, and a comparison stimulus is introduced at different locations within the range of the thresholds. On any given trial the subject samples a single threshold from his or her distribution (which is assumed to be normal) and compares it against the stimulus. Over a number of trials we calculate the relative frequency with which the comparison stimulus is detected (that is, stated to be greater than the threshold). We can then plot the relative frequencies for various comparison stimuli to obtain the psychometric function (see bottom half of Fig. 3.4).

The mean of the distribution is the stimulus value corresponding to $p = .5$ on the y axis. Even though this exact stimulus may not have been included in the experiment, it can be found quite easily by the graphical procedure illustrated in Fig. 3.4. The stimulus value so determined is the absolute threshold.

The difference threshold is similarly obtained; a standard is fixed, and a series of comparisons symmetrically located around the standard are compared with it. In this case, the relative frequency of calling the comparison greater than the standard is plotted on the y axis against the comparison values plotted on the x axis.

Sample data from an experiment using the method of constant stimuli are given in Fig. 3.5, based on a study by Weissmann, Hollingsworth, and Baird (1975). This experiment was conducted at a cathode ray terminal linked to a computer time-sharing system. The stimulus continuum was the number scale, so the particular stimuli were numbers presented on the scope of the terminal. Random samples were drawn from a "standard" distribution and a "comparison" distribution and presented in two separate rows. The subject judged whether the numbers in the parent distribution of the comparison set were larger or smaller than the numbers in the parent distribution of the standard set. The mean of the standard was fixed at 150 with a standard deviation of 5. The standard deviation of the comparison distribution was also 5, but the mean varied in 15 steps between 129 and 171 according to the usual procedure with the method of constant stimuli. The sample numbers were randomly chosen from these distributions, which were speci-fied beforehand by the experimenter. Numbers are not commonly used for this type of investigation, but they have the advantage of allowing us to exactly simulate the stimulus conditions presumed by the classical theory.

The data analysis proceeds in the standard way. The PSE (mean) can be found graphically as previously illustrated for the absolute threshold. It is approximately 152. For the difference threshold a decision must be made concerning the appropriate statistic. One candidate is the standard deviation of the normal distribution assumed to underlie the psychometric function.

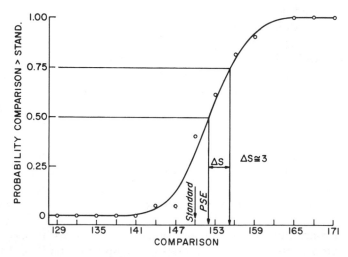

Figure 3.5. A psychometric function fit to data obtained by the method of constant stimuli. The PSE and ΔS (jnd) are obtained as illustrated (after Weissmann, Hollingsworth and Baird, 1975).

But the measure commonly used with the method of constant stimuli is the distance along the stimulus axis corresponding to the difference between $p = .5$ and $p = .75$.

The graphical determination of ΔS ($\cong 3$) obtained with this index is shown in Fig. 3.5. By referring back to Fig. 3.4 it can be seen that large ΔS values imply large variability of the underlying distribution of stimulus or threshold values. If this method is considered too crude, more accurate curve-fitting procedures can be used (Bock and Jones, 1968; Guilford, 1954).

Similarly, ΔS below the mean corresponds to the difference between $p = .5$ and $p = .25$. Either index is acceptable, as long as we are consistent in our choice of statistic. The need for consistency arises when we make assumptions about the equality of the corresponding internal jnd's and sum them to obtain scale values.

A more formal description of this requirement is expressed by the psychophysicist's litany, "Equally often noticed differences are equal, unless always or never noticed." To illustrate how this places some constraints on the definition of ΔS, first define $p(y,x)$ as the percentage of time that stimulus y is judged greater than stimulus x. So if $p(y,x) = .75$ and $p(v,x) = .75$, then $y = v$ in terms of being equally discriminable from x. But if y is *always* discriminated as larger than x: $p(y,x) = 1$, so any v with $v > y$ also has $p(v,x) = 1$. However, we would not want to conclude that they were equally discriminable from x. A subject may clearly distinguish y and v from x but just as clearly distinguish y from v. Similarly, if x, y, and v are stimuli such that $p(x,v) = 0$ and $p(y,v) = 0$, we again should not consider x and y as equally discriminable from v.

Theoretically, then, we can use any probability cutoff above the absolute threshold to define ΔS as long as $0 < p < 1$. The criterion of $\Delta S = \pm 1\sigma$ (when $\Delta S = -1\sigma$, $p(v,x) \cong .16$; and when $\Delta S = +1\sigma$, $p(v,x) \cong .84$) is an attractive choice because it is used throughout statistics and psychology as a measure of dispersion. On the other hand, the alternative criterion divides the normal distribution into four equal areas (one-half the interquartile interval). When $p = .5$, the normal curve is split in half, so it seems natural to divide each half once again to define the upper and lower boundaries of the "equal" category. This latter measure has held sway and will probably continue to do so until someone can give a sound theoretical reason for preferring some alternative.

Comparison of Methods

Clearly, the magnitude of ΔS will depend upon the psychophysical method and the accompanying analysis. Nonetheless, we would hope to find invariant relations among jnd's secured by these alternative procedures.

Surprisingly little research has been published on this problem. Early work by Fechner, together with experiments by Crozier and his associates (1940) indicate that jnd's obtained by different methods can be related by a multiplicative constant (that is, that jnd's are measured on a ratio scale). Specifically, if ΔS_a is the jnd from the method of adjustment and ΔS_c is the comparable value obtained by the method of constant stimuli, then

$$\Delta S_a = \phi \Delta S_c \tag{3.8}$$

In a recent study by Wier, Jesteadt, and Green (1976), these two methods were compared as a means for determining the jnd in sound frequency with a fixed 1000-Hz standard. Their results agreed with earlier research showing that the jnd obtained by the method of adjustment is approximately one-half the size of the jnd obtained by the method of constant stimuli. If this proportion were the same for all frequencies, the value of ϕ in Eq. 3.8 would be set at $\frac{1}{2}$.

The validity of Eq. 3.8 has two important consequences. First, the relationships between the jnd and other stimulus measures (for example, the stimulus intensity at which it is assessed) varies by a multiplicative constant as one changes psychophysical methods. And second, the relative sizes of Weber fractions among stimulus continua stay the same. That is, sensitivity to visual length of line would always be greater than sensitivity to sound intensity, etc., independent of the method (as long as the same one was used for both continua). This invariance is important for establishing sensitivity indices.

It is obvious that different methods would yield different size jnd's since each has its own arbitrary criterion for determining a probabilistic jnd cutoff point. Two other considerations could also affect the relative sizes of the jnd's measured using different methods. First, psychophysical methods may differentially alter the variance of the underlying normal distribution. Hence, the size of the jnd would change accordingly, even if the same statistical criterion were employed in defining the jnd (for example, standard deviation or one-half the interquartile interval). A second possibility is that the variance of the distribution is constant, but the methods induce the subject to use different judgment criteria. The modern theory of signal detectability allows one to distinguish between these two possibilities, but full consideration of this topic is deferred until Chapter 8. One thing is clear. When we wish to compare jnd's for different stimulus conditions, it is best to rely on the same psychophysical method. This is particularly crucial when the goal is to develop functions describing the reliance of ΔS on stimulus intensity and attribute. In both of these cases, discussion eventually centers on the most famous empirical relation in psychophysics: Weber's law.

WEBER'S LAW

If ΔS is measured at a number of intensities S, the relation between the two is expressed by Weber's law, as given by Eq. 3.1. Since ΔS is a linear function of S, the steepness of the psychometric function (Fig. 3.4) must decrease as S increases. In other words, the variance of the underlying normal curve increases with intensity, as is illustrated in Fig. 3.4.

The rate at which ΔS increases is k, the Weber fraction. This fraction is a dimensionless number indicating the sensitivity of a subject to a particular continuum.

$$\frac{\Delta S}{S} = k \qquad (3.9)$$

One often sees $\Delta S/S$ plotted directly against S, in which case the function is a straight line horizontal to the stimulus axis and with a y intercept equal to k. The smaller k is, the greater is the perceptual sensitivity. Figure 3.6 gives examples of these two graphs for three hypothetical continua (A, B, and C).

Two empirical examples of the relation between ΔS and S are shown in Fig. 3.7 for the intensity of a 1000-Hz tone. The open circles on the graph represent data collected by Riesz (1928), who employed the method of limits in a somewhat unusual way. Two tones of similar frequency (1000 and 1003 Hz) were presented simultaneously. When the intensity of one was altered by the experimenter, the subject experienced a fluctuation in loudness (beats) of an apparently single tone. The difference threshold (ΔS) was defined in terms of the intensity change needed to produce beats.[2] Riesz reported his results in energy units with respect to absolute threshold, and as such, the intensity range was considerable (1 to 10^8). Since sound can also be expressed in pressure units, and since pressure is proportional to the square root of energy, the stimulus range in those units is compressed to 10^4, which is still too large for our purposes. (We will want to talk about some details in the region of 1 to 10.) Consequently, we show data only over the range of 1 to 100, where the points are based on some corrections of Riesz's calculations suggested recently by Burbeck (in press).[3]

The filled circles on the graph were determined 49 years later by Jesteadt, Wier, and Green (1977). They employed a variation of the staircase method

[2]For further discussion of this method see Green, 1976 or Gulick, 1971.

[3]Our analysis to secure measures in pressure units proceeded as follows. From Burbeck's table of intensity I_1 in logarithmic units (decibels, dB) we first computed I_1 in energy units as $10^{dB/10}$ for each level. Next, to convert to pressure we let $S = \sqrt{I_1}$. Values for ΔS then were obtained by determining ΔI in energy units and then transforming into pressure: $\Delta S = \sqrt{I_1 + \Delta I} - S$, where ΔS and S are in pressure units proportional to some standard intensity (e.g., .0002 dyne/cm^2). This derivation was based on equations given by Green (1976, p. 255), who also advised us on their application in the present context.

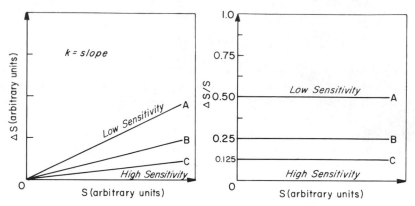

Figure 3.6. Two renditions of Weber's law for three hypothetical continua (A, B, and C). (left) The jnd (ΔS) as a function of stimulus intensity (S). (right) The Weber fraction ($\Delta S/S$) as a function of S.

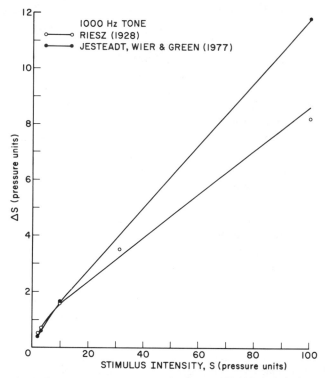

Figure 3.7. The jnd size ΔS as a function of S for a 1000-Hz tone that varied in sound intensity. The open circles are transformed values from Reisz (1928). The filled circles are transformed values from Jesteadt et al. (1977). Representation of intensity is in pressure units (proportional to a reference value; e.g., .0002 dyne/cm^2). The solid lines were drawn by visual inspection. For more details, see the text.

noted earlier in the chapter. A 1000-Hz tone was fixed in intensity while the comparison intensity was stepped toward or away from the standard depending upon the subject's response. On a given trial the two tones were presented successively and the subject had to indicate which was louder. An error in identification led to an increase in separation between the two intensities until the subject correctly identified the tones, at which point the separation was decreased, and so on. The eventual measure of ΔS was the average separation of standard and comparison for approximately the last 20 turnaround points.

Returning now to Fig. 3.7, we see that both sets of data can be fit reasonably well by straight lines, indicating that Weber's law holds over most of the range. The solid lines on the graph have been drawn in freehand to capture the major trends. The slope of the linear portions are $k \cong .08$ for Riesz and .11 for Jesteadt et al. Hence, greater sensitivity was evident in Riesz's experiment. At higher stimulus intensities (not shown), the Weber fraction slowly decreased to approximately .05 in both experiments (.10 in energy units).

Apart from the general trends, important deviations from Weber's law occur near the lower absolute threshold. In the first place, linear extension of each function to the y axis does not intersect the origin. Therefore, a better description would involve the addition of a small constant on the right-hand side of Eq. 3.1. The second deviation is the slight curvature near threshold, suggesting that a linear function, with or without the additive constant, does not offer a completely satisfactory account of the results. Both of these deviations from Weber's law will be treated more thoroughly in Chapter 4.

Empirically, k ranges from 0.02 for finger span to 0.24 for some chemicals used in studies of odor discrimination (Baird, 1970; Teghtsoonian, 1971). A representative list of Weber fractions for different stimulus continua is given in Table 3.1.

One of the advantages of the Weber fraction as an indicator of sensitivity is its independence from physical units of measure on a ratio scale. For example, although distance may be measured in centimeters or meters, both ΔS and S are measured along the same physical scale, so k is simply a dimensionless ratio. Because of this property, one can compare sensitivities for different continua. If we further assume that the internal scale (W) is fixed for all continua, the relative sensitivity of different sensory systems can be inferred from k (or more accurately, from $1/k$). Since the jnd probably depends on the method used to obtain it, comparison of Weber fractions should ideally be made for data collected in the same way. If Eq. 3.8 is correct, the relative size of Weber fractions for different continua will be the same regardless of the method (as long as it is the same for each continuum).

Table 3.1 Representative Weber fractions for common continua

Continuum	Weber fraction $\Delta S/S$
Finger span	.02
Saturation (red)	.02
Electrical (skin)	.03
Position of point (visual)	.03
Length of lines (visual)	.04
Area (visual)	.06
Heaviness	.07
Brightness (naive observers)	.08
Loudness (1000 Hz, energy units)	.10
Loudness (white noise, energy units)	.10
Taste (salt)	.14
Taste (sweet)	.17
Skin vibration (100–1100 Hz)	.20
Smell (several substances)	.24

This is because the jnd size, and hence the Weber fraction, will increase proportionately (ϕ) for all continua. As will become apparent in Chapter 4, all is not well with Weber's law as originally formulated. Although approximately correct for many continua, failures do occur, especially for very weak or strong stimuli.

The Upper Threshold

It is difficult to use the classical methods to determine the upper threshold for a stimulus continuum. Experimental results for very intense stimuli are scarce, since there is always the risk of physiological tissue damage. No complete table of dynamic ranges (differences between lower and upper thresholds) of continua has been published, although it appears from some studies (Valter, 1970) that there are substantial differences in this regard. It has been suggested by Teghtsoonian (1971) that dynamic range is directly related to the Weber fraction (a logical conclusion from the classical notion of a fixed internal scale of constant range). So far the relevant data analyses do not lend much weight to this hypothesis (Valter, 1970). For instance, the smell continuum has large jnd's but a very short dynamic stimulus range over which the sensory system reacts. This is clearly contrary to the hypothesis, although it still may apply to other continua; more analyses are required to find out for sure.

Fechnerian Integration

If Weber's law is correct and we grant Fechner his assumption about the equality of internal jnd's (ΔW), the logarithmic function (Eq. 3.4) follows. So Fechner was right! Well, maybe. In the next chapter we will see that Fechner was correct only to a first order of approximation and only when his special assumptions about internal jnd's are granted. In fact, Fechner was aware of some of these problems, but time constraints and his quest for a psychophysical law did not allow him to pursue the solution to these problems in greater detail.

LESSONS OF CLASSICAL PSYCHOPHYSICS

A human being is not a perfect measuring instrument, infinitely sensitive to changes in external stimulation. The variability of the threshold and the statistical nature of ΔS attest to this fact. In addition, the threshold variability is not constant; it depends on the intensity of stimulation in a linear way according to Weber's law. Moreover, sensitivity is variant across stimulus continua. The Weber fractions for different continua, such as light, sound, and weight, range at least from 0.02 to 0.24. And finally, Fechner's logarithmic law states that humans are systematically nonlinear compared to physical instruments. According to this law, geometric increases in physical intensity are required to produce arithmetic increases in sensation (for instance, to cause an increment of 1 on the sensation scale, the physical intensity may need to be doubled or tripled), suggesting the following mind bender: As measuring instruments, humans are not calibrated the same as the instruments used to measure human responses.

A second lesson is of more direct theoretical importance. The key assumption in classical psychophysics is that the sensation scale is unitary and is not distorted by various laboratory conditions. Without evidence to the contrary, such faith is necessary if one is to make any sense at all out of psychophysical data. Just as an organism must first attribute a fixed structure to its own nervous system before it is able to distinguish between external and internal changes, so too must psychophysical theorists assume constancy somewhere in the system if they are to infer something about sensory transformations.

Several investigators have sought to verify this assumption by recourse to physiological data (see, for example, Stevens, 1972). But we have reason to pause here, because this time-honored theoretical pastime can easily lead us astray. Unless we exercise real caution, the search for relevant data in the physiological realm can turn into a self-fulfilling prophecy, where the investigator uncovers only those facts that agree with his or her preconceptions. This is one important lesson of classical psychophysics we would do well to recall as new techniques and data continue to proliferate in both the behavioral and physiological fields.

REFERENCES

Baird, J. C. "A cognitive theory of psychophysics: I. Information transmission, partitioning, and Weber's law." *Scandinavian Journal of Psychology*, 1970, *11*, 35–46.

Bock, R. D., and Jones, L. V. *The Measurement and Prediction of Judgment and Choice*. San Francisco: Holden-Day, 1968.

Bouguer, *Traité d'optique sur la gradation de la lumière*. Paris: 1760.

Burbeck, S. L. "A reexamination of Riesz's intensity discrimination data." *Journal of the Acoustical Society of America* (in press).

Cornsweet, T. N. "The staircase-method in psychophysics." *American Journal of Psychology*, 1962, *75*, 485–491.

Crozier, W. J. "On the law for minimal discrimination of intensities. IV. ΔI as a function of intensity." *Proceedings of the National Academy of Science*, 1940, *26*, 382–389.

Engen, T. "Psychophysics. I. Discrimination and detection." *Woodworth and Schlosberg's Experimental Psychology*. Vol. 1: *Sensation and Perception*, J. W. Kling and L. A. Riggs (Ed.). New York: Holt, Rinehart and Winston, 1972, pp. 11–46.

Gescheider, G. A. *Psychophysics: Method and Theory*. Hillsdale, N.J.: Lawrence Erlbaum Associates, 1976.

Guilford, J. P. *Psychometric Methods*. New York: McGraw-Hill, 1954.

Green, D. M. *An Introduction to Hearing*. Hillsdale, N.J.: Lawrence Erlbaum Associates, 1976.

Gulick, W. L. *Hearing: Physiology and Psychophysics*. New York: Oxford, 1971.

Jesteadt, W., Wier, C. C., and Green, D. M. "Intensity discrimination as a function of frequency and sensation level." *Journal of the Acoustical Society of America*, 1977, *61*, 169–177.

Luce, R. D., and Galanter, E. "Discrimination." In R. D. Luce, R. R. Bush, and E. Galanter, (Eds.), *Handbook of Mathematical Psychology*, Vol. I. New York: Wiley, 1963, pp. 191–243.

McGee, V. E. *Principles of Statistics: Traditional and Bayesian*. New York: Appleton-Century-Crofts, 1971.

Riesz, R. R. "Differential intensity sensitivity of the ear for pure tones." *Physical Review*, 1928, *31*, 867–875.

Stevens, S. S. "A neural quantum in sensory discrimination." *Science*, 1972, *177*, 749–762.

Teghtsoonian, R. "On the exponents in Stevens' law and the constant in Ekman's law." *Psychological Review*, 1971, *78*, 71–80.

Valter, V. "Deduction and verification of a quantum psychophysical equation." *Reports from the Institute of Applied Psychology, University of Stockholm*, no. 13, 1970.

Weber, E. H. "Der Tastsinn und das Gemeinfühl." In R. Wagner (Ed.), *Handwörterbuch der Physiologie*, Vol. 3. Braunschweig: Vieweg, 1846, pp. 481–588.

Weissmann, S., Hollingsworth, S., and Baird, J. C. "Psychophysical study of numbers: III. Methodological applications." *Psychological Research*, 1975, *38*, 97–115.

Wier, C. C., Jesteadt, W., and Green, D. M. "A comparison of method-of-adjustment and forced-choice procedures in frequency discrimination." *Perception & Psychophysics*, 1976, *19*, 75–79.

CHAPTER

$$\boxed{4}$$

DERIVATION
OF
PSYCHOPHYSICAL LAWS

It is universally acknowledged that Weber's law in its unmodified form is valid for the middle range of stimulus intensities but not for the very extremes near the lower and upper thresholds. This has been clear from the start, and Fechner considered Weber's law only as a first-order approximation to the law operating in the realm of inner psychophysics. If other functions later superseded Weber's law, it was argued, these new functions would be open to the same theoretical approach: Set up a differential equation and integrate to determine the psychophysical law. In this chapter we see that Fechner was not entirely justified in taking this stance. In fact, most alternatives to Weber's law produce Fechner scales that violate the very assumptions used in their construction! Although realization of this difficulty would have surely distressed Fechner, it probably would not have altered his philosophical view concerning the relation between sensation and physiological processes. It is clear from his writings that he was convinced of the truth of Weber's law as applied to *inner* psychophysics, regardless of its overall validity for *outer* psychophysics. Remember, the original logarithmic law was built on an intuitive hunch, not on an inductive argument from empirical data.

Nonetheless, deviations from Weber's law exist and deserve description. There are three primary types of distortions.

1.   As intensity (S) approaches zero, the jnd (ΔS) cannot continue to shrink proportionally because of the absolute threshold (according to the classical theory).

2.   A similar distortion occurs as intensity approaches the upper threshold. At some point near the upper end of the scale, the jnd must approach infinity—it becomes fruitless to coax a response from a burnt-out sense organ. Empirical results indicate that this deviation from linearity (if it could be measured completely) is a gradual one as intensity approaches either the lower or upper threshold.

3.   More significant departures from Weber's law occur for certain continua in all regions of their dynamic range. For instance, in the estimation of time duration, the jnd is not a constant proportion of length of time passed for any significant region of the continuum (Michon, 1964). A second counterexample is pitch perception. If sound frequency is thought of as a continuum, classical studies showed that the size of the jnd at any point is independent of frequency over a fairly extensive range (from 200 to ~2000 Hz). For these values the jnd is approximately constant (Gulick, 1971).

Just recently, an experiment by Wier, Jesteadt, and Green (1977) resulted in higher sensitivity measures over this region and a systematic change in the difference threshold as a function of the standard frequency (in the direction of Weber's law). However, the rate of increase of ΔF (frequency) as a function of F was much greater at higher frequencies than it was at lower ones, in accord with the classical findings of Shower and Biddulph (1931). In addition, the more recent investigation found that the jnd also depended on the intensity (amplitude) of the tone, implying once again that perception of differences in tonal frequency is a complex matter (see their paper for discussion of the implications of these results for various psychophysical models of auditory perception).

ALTERNATIVE WEBER FUNCTIONS

In order to more accurately mirror observed phenomena, several alternative equations have been suggested to replace Weber's law (see especially Guilford, 1954). Each, however, is designed to handle special experimental conditions, so none has gained universal favor. To facilitate discussion, let us first call the relation between ΔS and S a *Weber function* regardless of its compliance with Weber's law.

A shrinking jnd near the lower threshold can be represented by adding a constant to Weber's original formulation—a possibility noted by Fechner and Helmholtz in the last century (Miller, 1947). Thus we have

$$\Delta S = kS + a \qquad (4.1)$$

In this equation a may be considered proportional to the absolute threshold. When S is zero, $\Delta S = a$, which can be considered a correlate of the first step on the sensation scale. Since stimulus continua have diverse thresholds that vary with experimental conditions, Weber's law will be strictly true only for intensities above these effective thresholds. In any event, Eq. 4.1 must do *at least* as well as Weber's law, because a can take on the value of zero. Equation 4.1 has also provided better fits to data in several studies. Miller (1947) demonstrated its adequacy for auditory noise, as did Ono (1967) for judgment of line length.

Equation 4.1 also is a more realistic model of the sound intensity results discussed in the previous chapter (Fig. 3.7). Although the jnd for sound grows linearly with intensity over a wide range, the function has a positive y intercept (a) that varies with tonal frequency. That is, the perceptual system seems to require a little boost before it begins to operate in accord with the unmodified form of Weber's law.

By replotting the data from Fig. 3.7 we can obtain a more detailed view of what is happening around the absolute threshold and why an additive constant is required to faithfully describe matters. Before embarking on this venture, however, let us deal with some hypothetical jnd's to help lay the

Table 4.1   Hypothetical results
for jnd experiment

S	ΔS	$\Delta S/S$
1	.85	.85
2	.90	.45
5	1.05	.21
10	1.30	.13
100	5.80	.058
1,000	50.80	.0508
10,000	500.80	.05008
100,000	5000.80	.050008

basis for understanding the empirical results. Table 4.1 gives jnd size (ΔS) for a series of intensities, evaluated by the following equation:

$$\Delta S = .05S + .8$$

Imagine that an experimenter knows S, measures ΔS, and believes Weber's law, but doesn't know k and a. Then he might well try to summarize his findings by computing the Weber fractions listed in the right column of the table. True to psychophysical practice, he then might graph the Weber fraction as a function of S. Before doing this, however, he notes the huge values of S and realizes that a compression of that scale is desirable to save paper and still maintain the essentials of the relationship. So, he computes the logarithms of S and plots them along the x axis, as shown in Fig. 4.1. There are three points of interest about this graph.

1.   As S approaches 1, $\log_{10} S$ approaches 0 and $\Delta S/S$ approaches .85.
2.   The function flattens out very neatly as S increases beyond 100 ($\log_{10}(100) = 2$). Weber's law holds in this region.
3.   The logarithmic scale has the effect of magnifying activity at the low end and smoothing activity at the high end.

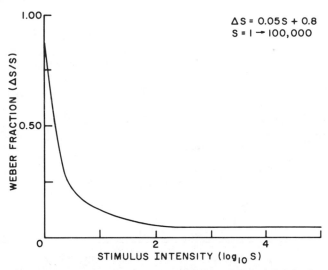

Figure 4.1.   Hypothetical function between the Weber fraction and the logarithm (base 10) of stimulus intensity. The function summarizes data from Table 4.1 obtained by an evaluation of Weber's law with an additive constant (Eq. 4.1).

Note that the logarithmic scale is used here for convenience only. The scale has no deeper theoretical meaning. It is a good idea to be aware of the implications (or lack thereof) of such transformations, since they influence interpretations of the graphed results. One must be ever alert to the diverse ways in which psychophysicists push numbers around!

So Fig. 4.1 is a picture of what occurs when data modeled by Eq. 4.1 are plotted as though one expected to obtain a straight horizontal line across the entire stimulus range (as in Fig. 3.6). Returning now to the findings on sound intensity, we can plot the points in the same fashion. First, Weber fractions were calculated from the results given in Fig. 3.7 for a 1000-Hz tone (Jesteadt, Wier, and Green, 1977; Riesz, 1928). Second, the hypothetical Weber fractions from Table 4.1 were plotted as the dashed function in Fig. 4.2 together with the empirical findings. A logarithmic transformation of S was not necessary to secure a good description of the general trend. It is clear that the hypothetical function is quite similar to the Riesz data. Therefore, an additive constant would greatly improve the fit of Weber's law to these results. The set of results determined more recently by Jesteadt et al. are not as readily accommodated. The curvature near threshold is less pronounced than for either the Riesz data or the hypothetical function. Nonetheless, some improvement of the fit would also be gained here by adding a constant to the basic Weber function.

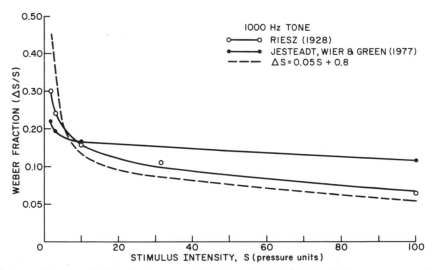

Figure 4.2. The Weber fraction as a function of sound intensity in pressure units (proportional to a reference value; e.g., .0002 dyne/cm²). The empirical data are from Fig. 3.7. The dashed function is an evaluation of Eq. 4.1 with the parameter values given on the graph, but with the resulting Weber fraction ($\Delta S/S$) plotted against S.

Figure 4.2 appears to signal a resounding defeat for the original formulation of Weber's law. Caution is advised, however. In actuality, the Weber fraction is reasonably constant once the stimuli are clearly above the absolute threshold. The function begins to flatten out at fairly weak intensities. To take a rural example, the intensities at which the curve begins to level off might be comparable to the ambient sound in an empty Vermont farmhouse. It is rather quiet.

Although the additive constant definitely improves the fit in the neighborhood of the absolute threshold, there also appears to be a little curvature in the data when ΔS is plotted as a function of S (Fig. 3.7). An alternative equation of general use that deals explicitly with curvature is the power function suggested by Guilford (1932, 1954):

$$\Delta S = kS^g \tag{4.2}$$

When fitting data, the exponent g may vary between 1 and .5 and might even exceed 1 for some conditions. When g is 1, Eq. 4.2 reduces to Weber's law, and when g is .5, ΔS is a square root function of S in agreement with an early proposal by Fullerton and Cattell (1892). Guilford and others have demonstrated the usefulness of the power function for studies of line length, sound intensity, and judgments of muscular tension (Guilford, 1932; Hovland, 1938; Fitts, 1947). One of the potential drawbacks of this function is its nonlinearity in the middle range. This is unfortunate because most writers recognize the legitimacy of a constant Weber fraction in the middle range of intensities. However, the problem is not severe when the exponent is near 1.

The generality of the power function should be explored more fully. To stay with our current examples in the auditory realm, the data of Riesz, Jesteadt et al., and others (Harris, 1963; McGill and Goldberg, 1968; Luce and Green, 1974) on the jnd for sound intensity are fit quite well by a power function with an exponent of approximately .9. That is,

$$\Delta S = kS^{.9}$$

In order to see what this means when $\Delta S/S$ is plotted as a function of S (as in Fig. 4.2), we divide both sides of the above equation by S and obtain

$$\frac{\Delta S}{S} = kS^{.9-1}$$

or

$$\frac{\Delta S}{S} = kS^{-.1}$$

If Weber's law held exactly, the exponent would be 0. So we are really talking about a discrepancy of $-.1$. This small difference has led McGill and Goldberg (1968) to talk about the "near miss to Weber's law." Green (1976) gives a thorough review of the auditory literature on this point together with a discussion of the importance of this result for the formulation of neural and psychophysical models of intensity discrimination.

None of these theories has much to say about the upper threshold. Indeed, it is possible to write equations describing both the upper and lower thresholds as well as the middle region of the scale. However, these equations quickly become messy and invariably contain four or five parameters to be estimated from the data. This is especially true of Valter's (1970) work, which is the most ambitious recent attempt to describe the relationship between intensity and the size of the jnd. Because of the number of free parameters in his model, it is even possible to fit nonmonotonic functions with special added twists at the lower and upper thresholds. By nonmonotonic we mean that the size of the jnd may go up and down as stimulus intensity increases. Other models with the same number of parameters might do as well (for example, the combination of two hyperbolas), and it is probably necessary to introduce such complications if the entire Weber function is to be accurately described. Nonetheless, for a considerable range of intensities, Weber's law (with an additive threshold constant) is usually adequate.

Of course, it is possible to construct a wide array of theoretical Weber functions in order to observe the consequences for psychophysical laws based on Fechnerian integration. One thing seems apparent in this regard. Since Weber's law holds tolerably well in the middle range, the integral of any type of Weber function that purports to fit empirical results will be approximately logarithmic with sufficiently large values of S. Hence, it is unlikely that any significant deviations from Fechner's law can be expected if one grants the assumption of equal steps along the sensation scale (W).

HOW LEGITIMATE IS FECHNERIAN INTEGRATION?

Recent mathematical developments have questioned the legitimacy of Fechnerian integration, because it does not seem appropriate for all types of Weber functions. The most extensive work on this topic was done by Luce and Edwards (1958), Krantz (1971), and Falmagne (1971, 1974). We will focus on the paper by Luce and Edwards.

We begin by noting that Fechner's idea for measuring sensation is only one of many possible mathematical models relating stimulus intensity to an internal dimension. But all assume three things:

1. There exists a function relating the magnitude of sensation to a corresponding physical stimulus.

2. The function is monotonic. An increase in the stimulus intensity will never produce a decrease along the sensation scale.

3. The function is everywhere differentiable. Changes in the stimulus produce smooth transitions from one sensation level to the next.

Unfortunately, there is no direct way to monitor the sensation scale. Therefore, one may *arbitrarily define* values on this scale with respect to values on the stimulus scale. The oldest sensation scale, Fechner's, defines equal jnd's on the sensation side. With this view it is clear that the ultimate validity of the sensation scale may be neither proved nor disproved by empirical evidence.

As discussed previously, the jnd's on the stimulus dimension need not be equal. In fact, the Weber function defining the size of each jnd at any point on the stimulus continuum is increasing with S. In a similar vein, we define a *Fechner function* as the relation between cumulative jnd's on the stimulus dimension and cumulative jnd's on the sensation dimension. This is not to be equated with Fechner's law, which is a particular Fechner function. To reiterate, the Fechner function can be derived from any Weber function, assuming constant sensation jnd's. For example, if we assume Weber's law ($k = \Delta S / S$) and equal sensation jnd's ($\Delta W = 1$), we may write

$$k \Delta W = \frac{\Delta S}{S} \quad \text{or} \quad \frac{\Delta W}{\Delta S} = \frac{1}{kS}$$

Next, rewrite it as a differential equation:

$$\frac{dw}{ds} = \frac{a}{ks}$$

The correction constant a is a scaling factor needed to convert discrete values (ΔS and ΔW) to continuous values (ds and dw). Then we rearrange and integrate to obtain

$$W = C \ln \frac{S}{S_0} \tag{4.3}$$

where $C = a/k$ and S_0 is a threshold.

The crucial step in this formulation is the conversion to a differential equation. This was accomplished by Fechner's "mathematical auxiliary principle," which states that whatever is true for differences as small as jnd's is also true for all smaller differences. In other words, jnd intervals may be divided into infinitesimal differences and integrated without distorting the results. Unfortunately, the "principle" is generally erroneous and may be rigorously justified in only a limited number of cases, such as Weber's law.

Even if Fechner's "principle" were true, a contradiction arises in the formulation of Fechner functions. He assumed that any Weber function could be integrated to produce a Fechner function. Luce and Edwards show that this is not true. It does, however, work correctly for Weber's law and the generalized version including the additive threshold constant. Let us examine this case first. Its validity can be checked by the following argument. Fechner defined the sensation scale with equal intervals between adjacent scale values (ΔW = constant). This was done *before* integration secured the psychophysical function. The latter must also satisfy the original definition; that is, ΔW values must be equal for all points on the W scale *after* integration. Otherwise, we have a flat contradiction of the original premises. At this point it is convenient to use functional notation to emphasize that W varies as a function of S. Therefore,

$$W(S+\Delta S) = W(S) + \Delta W \qquad (4.4)$$

states that the sensation (W) produced by the stimulus plus stimulus increment ($S+\Delta S$) equals that produced by the stimulus [$W(S)$] plus one sensation increment (ΔW). Stated another way, a single stimulus increment (ΔS) results in a single sensation increment (ΔW). Now consider two stimuli separated by one jnd according to Fechner's law. For the first stimulus,

$$W(S) = C \ln \frac{S}{S_0} \qquad (4.5)$$

and for the second,

$$W(S+\Delta S) = C \ln \frac{(S+\Delta S)}{S_0} \qquad (4.6)$$

Using the equality in Eq. 4.4 and subtracting 4.5 from 4.6 yields one sensation jnd (the larger stimulus minus the smaller).

$$\Delta W = C \ln \frac{S+\Delta S}{S_0} - C \ln \frac{S}{S_0} \qquad (4.7)$$

$$\Delta W = C \ln \frac{S+\Delta S}{S} \qquad (4.8)$$

$$\Delta W = C \ln \left(1 + \frac{\Delta S}{S}\right) \qquad (4.9)$$

Since both C and $\Delta S/S$ are constants, ΔW is a constant in compliance with the original definition. So Weber's law and Fechner's law satisfy this equal-ΔW requirement.

One slight problem remains. We initially defined $\Delta W = 1$, but Eq. 4.9 will not satisfy this for all values of $\Delta S/S = k$. The source of the problem seems to arise in going from discrete to continuous values via the constant a. This smoothing factor must change somewhat to accommodate different k values if Eq. 4.9 is to satisfy the initial definition that $\Delta W = 1$. Substituting a/k for C and k for $\Delta S/S$, and rewriting Eq. 4.9, we obtain

$$\Delta W = 1 = \frac{a}{k}\ln(1+k)$$

$$a = \frac{k}{\ln(1+k)}$$

Substituting the values of k into this equation reveals that a changes about 12% between $k = 0.02$ and $k = 0.24$ (see Table 3.1). This effect is relatively small but may prove important as more accurate measures become available for determining psychophysical functions (especially with regard to the power law discussed in the succeeding chapter).

For other types of Weber functions, we get into more serious difficulty, as pointed out by Luce and Edwards. For example, in the case where ΔS increases by the square of S:

$$\Delta S = kS^2; \qquad k = \frac{\Delta S}{S^2} \tag{4.10}$$

If we define $\Delta W = 1$, we can use the first of these equations and state

$$\frac{\Delta W}{\Delta S} = \frac{1}{kS^2}$$

Applying the "mathematical auxiliary principle" and rearranging:

$$dw = \frac{a\,ds}{ks^2}$$

where a is the correction constant mentioned previously. Integrating and using the functional notation to define sensation magnitude as a function of stimulus intensity:

$$W(S) = -\frac{a}{kS} + b \tag{4.11}$$

where b is a constant. Next, remember that each additional stimulus jnd adds a constant ($\Delta W = 1$) to the count of sensation jnd's:

$$W(S + \Delta S) - W(S) = \Delta W = 1$$

In words: the sensation aroused by a stimulus of intensity $(S + \Delta S)$ minus the sensation aroused by a stimulus one jnd less intense (S) is equal to a single sensation step (ΔW). Substituting for ΔS (Eq. 4.10),

$$W(S + kS^2) - W(S) = \Delta W = 1$$

Next we substitute from Eq. 4.11 for the two stimuli $S + kS^2$ and S to obtain:

$$W(S + kS^2) - W(S) = \left[-\frac{a}{k(S + kS^2)} + b \right] - \left[-\frac{a}{kS} + b \right] = \Delta W = 1$$

which reduces to

$$\Delta W = 1 \overset{?}{=} \frac{a}{1 + kS} \tag{4.12}$$

The question mark in the equation represents our skepticism about the relation expressed. Since a is a constant, k must equal zero for the equality in Eq. 4.12 to hold for all values of S. But Weber fractions of zero are not very interesting, so the "principle" may not be applied to define a Fechner function with constant-sensation jnd's. It may also be shown that very few Weber functions, aside from Weber's law, produce Fechner functions satisfying the constant-ΔW requirement.

Functional Equation Solution

Luce and Edwards then show that accumulating jnd's one at a time is an alternative to using the "mathematical auxiliary principle." In fact, this can always be accomplished by graphical techniques once the Weber function is known. Starting from an arbitrary stimulus level S_0, the ΔS_0 at that intensity is plotted in two dimensions (stimulus intensity, sensation intensity) at the coordinates $(\Delta S_0, 1)$. Next, stimulus intensity $S_0 + \Delta S_0 = S_1$ is plotted at the point $(\Delta S_0 + \Delta S_1, 2)$ and so on. Once the points are known, the equation for the curve of best fit may be used as the Fechner function. The solution of the analogous mathematical accumulation of jnd's, called a *functional equation* (see Aczél, 1966), may be used to derive the Fechner function from the Weber function. Often it is computationally difficult to obtain a solution, and in some instances it is impossible to derive a Fechner function. On the other hand, when such a function does exist it is automatically consistent with the definition of constant-sensation jnd's. The complete Luce-Edwards argument is involved and will not be presented here.

The difficulties encountered by these authors has resulted in a reformulation of Fechnerian integration by Krantz (1971). He states that integration produces meaningless results unless single steps along the stimulus dimension produce constant increments on the sensation scale. Existence of a solution may be determined by integrating the Weber function and checking the results in the manner of Luce and Edwards. In addition, Krantz explores the effects of an error term in the sensation dimension:

$$W(S + \Delta S) - W(S) = \text{constant} + \text{error}$$

In some cases, the difference between the functional equation and integration solutions including the error term are small enough to justify either approach.

In conclusion, Luce and Edwards demonstrate the inadequacies in the initial formulation of Fechnerian integration and the incompatibility of an equal-interval sensation scale with most Weber functions (that is, Weber's law is a special case). Fechnerian integration and the mathematical auxiliary principle are discarded and replaced by functional equation solutions. Unfortunately, it may be excessively difficult to derive a functional equation solution from experimental data. If one is after a Fechner function without all the associated mathematical niceties, the best policy is simply to sum jnd's by a graphical procedure and fit a function to the data. This will be adequate for empirical formulations as well as for all but the most rigorous theoretical approaches. For most experimentalists this is the natural way to proceed anyway, with or without the blessing of mathematical consistency. Consequently, the discovery of a weakness in Fechner's argument, although theoretically important, has had little impact on laboratory practice.

Alternative Definitions of ΔW

If one entertains different assumptions about the nature of the sensation scale (W), different psychophysical laws will be derived. Until now we have assumed that ΔW is a constant. We have also noted that under certain conditions ΔS is sometimes constant, independent of S, whereas Weber's law states that ΔS is a linear function of S over the middle range of most continua. It is natural to propose a parallel Weber-type law for the sensation scale, where ΔW is a linear function of W (Ekman, 1959; Treisman, 1964). Other assumptions and empirically determined Weber functions are also possible, but the four alternatives just mentioned cover the basic conditions we expect to encounter in classical psychophysics.

THE FOURFOLD WAY[1]

Ignoring the objections to the mathematical auxiliary principle, a psycho-physical function is derived on theoretical grounds by treating $\Delta W/\Delta S$ as a derivative and integrating. If we concentrate only on the two major possibilities for Weber functions (constant and linear), and for assumed sensation functions (constant and linear), four possible combinations exist.

$$
\begin{array}{lll}
\text{I.} & \Delta W = c & \Delta S = b \\
\text{II.} & \Delta W = c & \Delta S = kS \\
\text{III.} & \Delta W = hW & \Delta S = b \\
\text{IV.} & \Delta W = hW & \Delta S = kS
\end{array}
$$

Each case can be set up as a differential equation and integrated to predict the psychophysical law. All of the cases satisfy the strictures of Luce and Edwards (1958) and Krantz (1971).

CASE I

The fundamental formula is constructed as

$$\frac{\Delta W}{\Delta S} = \frac{c}{b}$$

Then,

$$dw = \frac{c\,ds}{b}$$

Integrating both sides from their respective absolute thresholds (W_0 and S_0):

$$\int_{W_0}^{W} dw = \frac{c}{b}\int_{S_0}^{S} ds$$

$$W - W_0 = \frac{c}{b}S - \frac{c}{b}S_0$$

$$W = \frac{c}{b}S - \left(\frac{c}{b}S_0 - W_0\right)$$

If we now set $C_1 = (c/b)S_0 - W_0$, then

$$W = \frac{c}{b}S - C_1 \tag{4.13}$$

---

[1]The following is in the spirit of formulations proposed by Ekman (1959) and especially Eisler (1963), although their approaches are more nearly akin to the one offered in the next chapter, where we dispense altogether with the sensation scale.

The prediction is a linear function between W and S where C_1 is a constant.

CASE II

This case was Fechner's favorite.

$$\frac{\Delta W}{\Delta S} = \frac{c}{kS}$$

$$dw = \frac{c}{k} \frac{ds}{s}$$

$$\int_{W_0}^{W} dw = \frac{c}{k} \int_{S_0}^{S} \frac{ds}{s}$$

$$W = \frac{c}{k} \ln\left(\frac{S}{S_0}\right) + W_0$$

$$W = \frac{c}{k} \ln S - \left(\frac{c}{k} \ln S_0 - W_0\right)$$

Now set $C_2 = (c/k) \ln S_0 - W_0$. Then,

$$W = \frac{c}{k} \ln S - C_2 \qquad (4.14)$$

CASE III

The outcome of this case is similar to Fechner's law (Case II), except that the stimulus intensity is a logarithmic function of the sensation magnitude. That is,

$$\frac{\Delta W}{\Delta S} = \frac{hW}{b}$$

$$\frac{b}{h}\left(\frac{dw}{w}\right) = ds$$

$$\frac{b}{h} \int_{W_0}^{W} \frac{dw}{w} = \int_{S_0}^{S} ds$$

$$\frac{b}{h} \ln\left(\frac{W}{W_0}\right) = S - S_0$$

$$\ln\left(\frac{W}{W_0}\right) = \frac{h}{b}(S - S_0)$$

$$\frac{W}{W_0} = e^{(b/h)(S - S_0)}$$

$$W = W_0 e^{-(b/h)S_0} \cdot e^{(b/h)S}$$

Setting $C_3 = W_0 e^{-(b/h)S_0}$, we have

$$W = C_3 e^{(h/b)S} \tag{4.15}$$

So W is an exponential function of S.

CASE IV

If Weber's law holds and we assume a parallel law in operation for the sensation scale, a power function results upon integration.

$$\frac{\Delta W}{\Delta S} = \frac{hW}{kS}$$

$$\frac{dw}{hw} = \frac{ds}{ks}$$

$$\frac{1}{h} \int_{W_0}^{W} \frac{dw}{w} = \frac{1}{k} \int_{S_0}^{S} \frac{ds}{s}$$

$$\frac{1}{h} \ln\left(\frac{W}{W_0}\right) = \frac{1}{k} \ln\left(\frac{S}{S_0}\right) \tag{4.16}$$

Then

$$W = W_0 \left(\frac{S}{S_0}\right)^{h/k}$$

$$W = W_0 \left(\frac{1}{S_0}\right)^{h/k} \cdot S^{h/k}$$

Setting $C_4 = W_0(1/S_0)^{h/k}$, we see that

$$W = C_4 S^{h/k} \tag{4.17}$$

and therefore

$$\ln W = \frac{h}{k} \ln S + \ln C_4$$

It is interesting to note at this point that the slope relating $\ln W$ to $\ln S$ (the exponent in Eq. 4.17) is composed of two parts. The constant h is the Weber fraction associated with the sensation continuum, and the constant k is the Weber fraction associated with the stimulus continuum. Hence, the rate of change in W is directly related to h and inversely related to k. It is

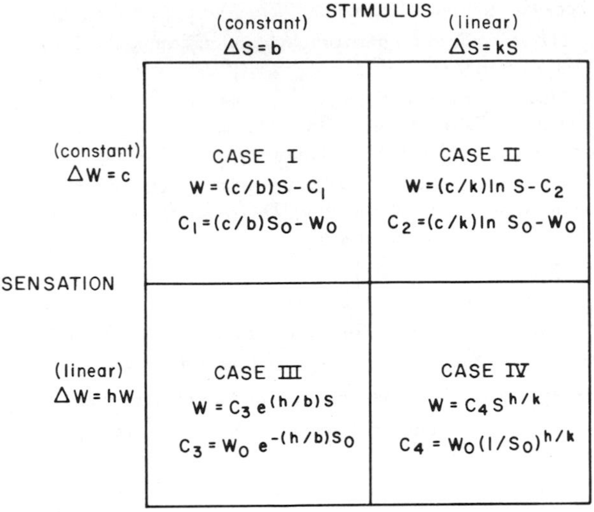
STIMULUS
(constant)
$\Delta S = b$
(linear)
$\Delta S = kS$
SENSATION
(constant)
$\Delta W = c$
CASE I
$W = (c/b)S - C_1$
$C_1 = (c/b)S_0 - W_0$
CASE II
$W = (c/k)\ln S - C_2$
$C_2 = (c/k)\ln S_0 - W_0$
(linear)
$\Delta W = hW$
CASE III
$W = C_3 e^{(h/b)S}$
$C_3 = W_0 e^{-(h/b)S_0}$
CASE IV
$W = C_4 S^{h/k}$
$C_4 = W_0 (1/S_0)^{h/k}$

Figure 4.3. The fourfold way. The marginal conditions lead to the derivation of four Fechner functions (I, linear; II, logarithmic; III, exponential; IV, power).

impossible to determine h by empirical means, but the value of k can be found. Therefore, the local sensitivity along the stimulus scale as measured by the Weber fraction becomes translated into a molar sensitivity measure for the relation between W and S over the entire effective stimulus range. The smaller the Weber fraction, the greater the sensitivity and the larger the exponent, assuming the value of h *is* constant.

The four derived laws are summarized in Fig. 4.3. It is obvious by now that the predicted psychophysical law depends on the nature of the Weber function on the stimulus side and on the nature of the internal sensation scale one defines. If an objective definition of the W scale could be obtained, it would be possible to test the predictions of the fourfold way by securing matching functions between W and S. Alas, this is impossible. By shifting our philosophical ground to observable stimuli and responses, however, we can reformulate the fourfold way into a testable model. This reformulation is discussed in the next chapter.

REFERENCES

Aczél, J. *Lectures on Functional Equations and Their Applications*. New York: Academic, 1966.

Eisler, H. "A general differential equation in psychophysics: derivation and empirical test." *Scandinavian Journal of Psychology*, 1963, *4*, 265–272.

Ekman, G. "Weber's law and related functions." *The Journal of Psychology*, 1959, *47*, 343–352.

Falmagne, J. C. "The generalized Fechner problem and discrimination." *Journal of Mathematical Psychology*, 1971, *8*, 22–43.

Falmagne, J. C. "Foundations of Fechnerian Psychophysics." In *Contemporary Developments in Mathematical Psychology*, D. H. Krantz, R. C. Atkinson, R. D. Luce, and P. Suppes (Eds.), Vol. 2. San Francisco, Calif.: W. H. Freeman, 1974, pp. 127–159.

Fitts, P. M. "Psychological research on equipment design." *Army Air Forces Aviation Psychology Program Research Reports*, no. 19. Washington, D.C.: Government Printing Office, 1947.

Fullerton, G. S., and Cattell, J. McK. "On the perception of small differences." *Philosophical Series*, (*University of Pennsylvania*) 1892, no. 2.

Green, D. M. *An Introduction To Hearing*. Hillsdale, N.J.: Lawrence Erlbaum Associates, 1976.

Guilford, J. P. "A generalized psychophysical law." *Psychological Review*, 1932, *39*, 73–85.

Guilford, J. P. *Psychometric Methods*. New York: McGraw-Hill, 1954.

Gulick, W. L. *Hearing: Physiology and Psychophysics*. London: Oxford, 1971.

Harris, J. D. "Loudness discrimination." *Journal of Speech and Hearing Disorders*, Monograph Supplement II, 1963.

Hovland, C. I. "A note on Guilford's generalized psychophysical law." *Psychological Review*, 1938, *45*, 430–434.

Jesteadt, W., Wier, C. C., and Green, D. M. "Intensity discrimination as a function of frequency and sensation level." *Journal of the Acoustical Society of America*, 1977, *61*, 169–177.

Krantz, D. H. "Integration of just-noticeable differences," *Journal of Mathematical Psychology*, 1971, *8*, 591–599.

Luce, R. D., and Edwards, W. "The derivation of subjective scales from just noticeable differences." *Psychological Review*, 1958, *65*, 222–237.

Luce, R. D., and Green, D. M. "Neural coding and psychophysical discrimination data." *Journal of the Acoustical Society of America*, 1974, *56*, 1554–1564.

McGill, W. J., and Goldberg, J. P. "Pure-tone intensity discrimination and energy detection." *Journal of the Acoustical Society of America*, 1968, *44*, 576–581.

Michon, J. A. "Studies on subjective duration: I. Differential sensitivity in the perception of repeated temporal intervals." *Acta Psychologica*, 1964, *22*, 441–450.

Miller, G. A. "Sensitivity to changes in the intensity of white noise and its relation to loudness and masking." *Journal of the Acoustical Society of America*, 1947, *19*, 609–619.

Ono, H. "Difference threshold for stimulus length under simultaneous and nonsimultaneous viewing conditions." *Perception & Psychophysics*, 1967, *2*, 201–207.

Riesz, R. R. "Differential intensity sensitivity of the ear for pure tones." *Physical Review*, 1928, *31*, 867–875.

Shower, E. G., and Biddulph, R. "Differential pitch sensitivity of the ear." *Journal of the Acoustical Society of America*, 1931, *3*, 275–287.

Treisman, M. "Sensory scaling and the psychophysical law." *Quarterly Journal of Experimental Psychology*, 1964, *16*, 11–22.

Valter, V. "Deduction and verification of a quantum psychophysical equation." *Reports from the Institute of Applied Psychology*, *University of Stockholm*, 1970, no. 13.

Wier, C. C., Jesteadt, W., and Green, D. M. "Frequency discrimination as a function of frequency and sensation level." *Journal of the Acoustical Society of America*, 1977, *61*, 178–184.

CHAPTER

$$\boxed{5}$$

DIRECT SCALING METHODS AND STEVENS'S LAW

Much of classical psychophysics concerns the relation between environmental stimuli and internal sensations—Fechner functions. Fechner's law is one such function, and strictly speaking it is not a 'law" since it cannot be verified or falsified by empirical test. On the other hand, Weber's law may be empirically tested. In this chapter we trace the more recent history of attempts to empirically determine stimulus-response functions.

The derivation of Fechner functions from Weber functions requires manipulation of data and the definition of a sensation scale. This has been termed the "indirect" approach to scaling (Ekman and Sjöberg, 1965). Of course, in this sense, all theoretical models are indirect since they represent best guesses about hypothetical processes. In psychophysics the words "indirect" and "direct" have more specialized meanings: The indirect (classical) approach determines a stimulus-sensation function by summing jnd's, whereas the direct methods fit functions to stimulus-response pairs. This distinction has given rise to some confusion in the literature. The important point to note is that *all* psychophysical methods for collecting data are "direct." The dichotomy between direct and indirect has meaning only with respect to the way one constructs a sensation or response scale from empirical data.

There are two opinions concerning the importance of fitting functions to stimulus-response pairs. The narrow view is that they afford the *only* avenue to psychophysical laws; consequently, the derivations of the previous chapter are irrevelant to this goal. The more charitable view is that direct methods can provide an independent test of classical derivations.

Quite naturally, after expending so much effort on the classical approach we are inclined to emphasize its role in guiding modern research. In particular, we explore here the congruence between results obtained with direct methods and the laws obtained by integrating Weber functions. By identifying the sensation scale with an overt response scale, the Fechner functions categorized by the fourfold way (Chapter 4) become stimulus-response models. In particular, one of the four cases will receive special emphasis. This case is the power function, which is commonly referred to as *Stevens's law*.

OPERATIONISM

The direct methods took root in a philosophical milieu that differed from the one created and nurtured by Fechner. A new atmosphere had developed along with the behavorist revolution (just after the turn of the century), and its peak of influence was reached in the 1930s. During this time, inner psychophysics was rejected as metaphysical dualism, and outer psychophysics was redefined. Instead of studying the link between stimuli and sensations, psychologists recast the psychophysical problem in behaviorist terms. The search for a psychophysical law between observable stimuli and observable responses was an acceptable enterprise, but the search for a law between stimuli and private sensations was considered futile. This view was incorporated in the position known as *operationism*.

Operationism was the result of three converging fields of inquiry: physics, philosophy, and psychology. In 1927, P. W. Bridgman wrote an influential book entitled *The Logic of Modern Physics* where he argued that concepts have meaning only when defined by observable operations (possible now or at some future date). In particular, the revolution fostered by relativity theory and quantum mechanics demanded a reformulation of measurement theory. Absolute space and time were not "entities," but concepts defined by the operations used to measure them. Psychologists were quick to generalize these ideas to psychophysics by demanding an operational definition of Fechner's sensation scale.

The attempt to purge physics of meaningless concepts was also echoed in the logical positivism associated with the Vienna Circle of philosophers. This group contended that science is separable into two parts: observational and formal. The formal (mathematical, logical) concepts have empirical meaning only when defined by concrete operations, either in fact or in theory. For example, in the 1930s it was legitimate to postulate "man-made canals on Mars" because it seemed reasonable that direct observations would someday verify or disprove their presence. On the other hand, a statement such as "private experience is the subject matter of psychophysics" was meaningless unless operations were stated to define "private" and "experience." Most people agreed that this was impossible in 1930 and would remain so in 3019. Behaviorism or physicalism was, then, a scientific attitude for defining concepts unambiguously (Ayer, 1935; Carnap, 1937; Feigl, 1934; Neurath, 1931). The widespread influence of this opinion signaled the demise of hypothetical sensations as the subject matter of psychophysics.

Beside the influence of physics and philosophy stood pressure from the behaviorist movement, especially within the field of comparative psychology (Tolman, 1932). Those engaged in the study of human and animal behavior diligently strove to eliminate the introspective methods used by the founding fathers, who attempted to study private sensations. Subsequently, psychophysics was remodeled along behavioristic lines.

The strongest spokesman for operationism vis-á-vis psychophysics was S. S. Stevens (1935, 1939, 1966a). While retaining Fechner's experimental approach, he rejected statements about private sensation (the W scale) as meaningless. Psychophysics, according to Stevens and others of his persuasion (for example, Boring, 1950) had absolutely nothing to say about private experience even though its existence was not denied. Science was a public enterprise where observations could be repeated. The old psychophysics prohibited this, because a public "private" sensation was a flat contradiction. If psychophysics were to gain scientific respectability, it had to adhere to the operational procedures used in physics.

The foregoing may sound as though major changes were on the immediate horizon. Not so! What happened was that sensation and subjective magnitude were redefined in terms of *response* measures. Outer psychophysics became the study of S-R relations, where both S and R as well as the experimental setting (including instructions, nature of the observer, etc.) were determined objectively. Stevens neatly summarized this position as follows: "Under this view, the meaning of sensation rests in a set of operations involving an observer, a set of stimuli, and a repertoire of responses" (1966a, p. 218).

So in fact the impact of operational thinking was not immediately apparent. There were perhaps two reasons for this. In the first place, although psychophysicists fully embraced the new philosophy, they did little or nothing to alter their scientific language. They continued to speak of sensations, subjective magnitudes, and sensory scales, and thus some psychologists (for example, Pratt, 1939) concluded that operationism offered nothing new. Since the same type of experiments were conducted and described in the same terms, it made hardly any difference if one were or were not an operationist. There is little doubt that adherence to the Fecherian language did lead to confusion in later years. For instance, Stevens continued to express his ideas in the language of subjectivism, and hence many people concluded that his research goals were indistinguishable from Fechner's (see, for example, Baird, 1970a; Savage, 1966; Treisman, 1964). Although Stevens saw things differently (1971), it is perhaps unfortunate that the Fechnerian language was not discarded in the 1930s together with its philosophical source. Indeed, then, Pratt had a valid point.

What Pratt failed to foresee was the long-term effect of operationism on methodology. This is where direct scaling enters the picture. Fechner thought that a person could not estimate the absolute magnitude of sensations. As long as the W scale was *defined*, attempts to empirically verify its existence were fruitless. Once psychophysics sidestepped the mind-body problem, however, it was possible to ask whether a person could give responses whose magnitudes were related to stimulus intensity in an orderly fashion. The mathematical relation between stimulus and response intensity then constituted a psychophysical law. This amounted to a substitution of observable responses for unobservable sensations. Approaches of this sort were in use by the turn of the century, but they were refined and publicized within an atmosphere created by the operationist movement (the early work is reviewed by Marks, 1974).

THE FOURFOLD WAY REFORMULATED[1]

Substitution of the R scale for the W scale does not change the structure of the fourfold way (Chapter 4). Everything that was said about the W scale is open to empirical test for the R scale. In Fig. 5.1, theoretical predictions of S-W laws are recast as S-R laws.[2] Direct scaling methods provide a means to test these predictions.

---

[1] Unless otherwise indicated, base 10 logarithms will be used throughout this chapter.

[2] The essential arguments in this chapter concerning psychophysical laws were written before the appearance of S. S. Steven's book (1975), which offers a comprehensive review of his position.

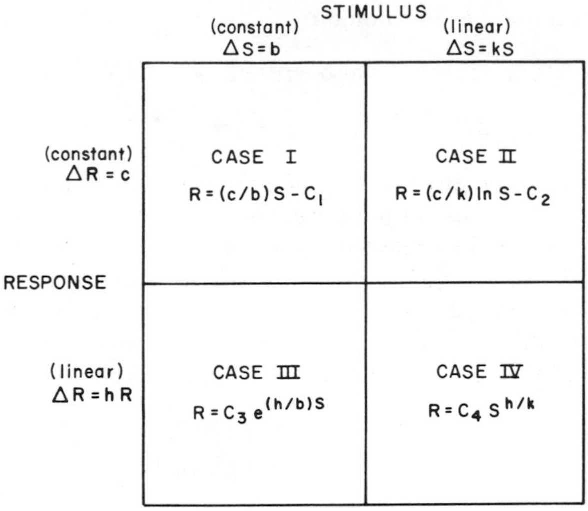

Figure 5.1. The fourfold way reformulated. The marginal conditions lead to the derivation of four Stevens functions (I, linear; II, logarithmic; III, exponential; IV, power). C_1, C_2, C_3, and C_4 are constants.

Operational Measures

There are four terms to be operationally defined: S, R, ΔS, and ΔR. The intensity of the stimulus, S, is measured by physical instruments, as is the size of the jnd, ΔS, at some particular intensity S. Both of these measures are central to classical psychophysics. In contrast, modern theory accepts the response continuum as equally amenable to physical measurement. Response intensities such as sounds and lights under control of the subject (or the experimenter) can also be gauged by physical instruments. So R is the response intensity and ΔR is the jnd at R. Often, the designation of which continuum is the stimulus and which is to be manipulated for the response is a matter of experimental convenience. Theoretically, at least, all perceptually meaningful continua can be used either as a stimulus or as a response.

Two relations of ΔS and ΔR to S and R are of special concern: (1) When Weber's law holds for both:

$$\Delta S = kS \quad \text{also written} \quad g(S) = kS \tag{5.1}$$

$$\Delta R = hR \quad \text{and} \quad f(R) = hR \tag{5.2}$$

and (2) when ΔS or ΔR are constants:

$$\Delta S = b \qquad \text{also written} \quad g(S) = b \qquad\qquad (5.3)$$

$$\Delta R = c \qquad \text{and} \quad f(R) = c \qquad\qquad\qquad (5.4)$$

Weber's law is generally valid in the middle range of intensities for most continua, whereas a constant jnd is sometimes found for low sound frequencies (Gulick, 1971) and for selected regions of continua such as time duration (Michon, 1964). In addition, continua such as position of a point on a line and azimuth position of a line (orientation) yield constant jnd's (Stevens and Galanter, 1957). However, it appears that most continua obey the general form of Weber's law, at least for intensities well above threshold.

A Mathematical Model

The cell entries in Fig. 5.1 were secured by applying a mathematical model. It is assumed by this model that ΔS and ΔR can be treated as derivatives, and hence dr/ds is the local slope of the function between R and S:

$$\frac{dr}{ds} = \frac{f(R)}{g(S)} \qquad\qquad (5.5)$$

$$\frac{dr}{f(R)} = \frac{ds}{g(S)} \qquad\qquad (5.6)$$

where $g(S)$ and $f(R)$ are given by Eqs. 5.1 through 5.4. Integrating both sides of Eq. 5.6 with the various combinations of $g(S)$ and $f(R)$ yields the fourfold way (see Chapter 4). These predictions rely upon the assumption that local differences (ΔS and ΔR) can be obtained in successive steps beginning at absolute threshold and continuing over the effective range of the relevant stimulus and response dimensions. By summing successive jnd's along each dimension, families of psychophysical relations are derived. We will call these *Stevens functions* (stimuli and responses) to distinguish them from Fechner functions (stimuli and sensations).

At this point one may ask if it is necessary to measure S and R, given that the fourfold way reflects the empirical facts on jnd's. The answer is yes. The operations for the measurement of jnd's and scale values (S and R) are different, thereby allowing for the possibility that they are drawn from two distinct realms; that is, jnd's measured by classical methods may bear no relation whatsoever to the values resulting from direct scaling methods. The two will be complementary if the mathematical derivation is appropriate and if we have the correct empirical procedures for measuring ΔS, ΔR, S, and R. The derivation will produce invalid predictions if the assumptions or measuring procedures are inappropriate.

A Psychological Theory

The problem, then, is to measure S and R and compare the result with predictions from a psychological theory. The following are the major assumptions of one possible theory:

1. The jnd is an appropriate unit of magnitude.
2. To find the scale value for a stimulus or response, count the number of jnd's needed to go from absolute threshold to current intensity.
3. People can match scale values on the R and S continua.

Now we ask what procedure will incorporate these assumptions. The somewhat surprising answer is that any of the classical methods will do. The methods of adjustment, limits, or constant stimuli each permit us to measure S and R. Figure 5.2 diagrams the underlying processes for the method of

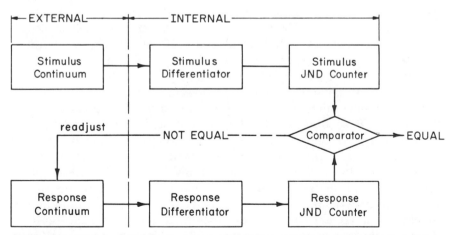

Figure 5.2 Model of judgment process for *S-R* matching tasks. The differentiators separate their respective inputs into jnd units. These are counted on the S and R continua and compared until a match (equal) is obtained. When unequal values exist, the response intensity is adjusted to reduce the difference between counts.

adjustment as predicted by this theory. The standard (S) first enters the system and is mapped into jnd units. The number of jnd's is counted and the total is passed to a comparator. In the method of adjustment the response has the same role as the comparison stimulus, so it too is processed by a differentiator and the count of jnd's is passed to the comparator. At this junction, two outcomes are possible. If the values of R and S do not match, the subject changes the intensity of R in an appropriate direction. When a match is finally secured, the trial ends. The mean (PSE) obtained over a number of trials is taken as the R value perceived to match the S value, and the relation between matched S-R pairs over a range of S is the Stevens function.

We must be clear about how this procedure compares with the classical method of adjustment for obtaining jnd measurements. In the latter situation only one continuum is employed; the standard (S) and comparison (R) are both luminances, or sound pressures, or line lengths, etc. The standard deviation of a large number of adjustments defines the jnd for each standard, and the relation between jnd and intensity of the standard constitutes the Weber function. The point of subjective equality (PSE) is always in close agreement with the standard used in the method of adjustment (to obtain a jnd). Therefore, if S is the standard, and R is taken as the PSE, the relation between the two will always approximate a linear function with a slope of 1.0. That's not very interesting.

On the other hand, the size of the jnd increases at different rates as intensities are increased on different continua—Weber fractions differ from one modality to another. For example, the approximate value for line length is .04, and for loudness of a 1000-Hz tone it is .10. After setting a calibration standard for each continuum, an increment of one jnd in loudness will be larger than an increment of one jnd in line length when each is measured in terms of relative physical intensity. Plotting mean (PSE) responses against standard stimulus intensities now makes sense theoretically because the two modalities will be linearly related with a slope of 1 only if the Weber fractions are equal. The limiting case occurs when two stimuli (standard and comparison) on the same continuum are matched, as in the classical method of adjustment. In every case, the Stevens function can be checked against predictions from the appropriate Weber functions inserted in the mathematical model. We are really trying to find whether we can sum local jnd's to obtain an accurate prediction of the S-R function. That is, if we determine the intensities corresponding to the addition of equal numbers of jnd's along two continua, are these intensities paired in a cross-modality match?

Cross-Modality Matching

When the method of adjustment is applied in the way just described, it is called *cross-modality matching* (CMM), even though both continua may be processed by the same sense modality (Stevens, Mack, and Stevens, 1960; Stevens and Marks, 1965; Stevens, 1966b). In CMM an experimenter selects a series of stimuli (say sounds) and measures each by physical means (for example, with a sound meter). The subject might then adjust the intensity of a light to match each sound and the experimenter measures the responses (for instance, with a photometer).

Surprisingly, most people do not balk (although some do hesitate) at matching values from diverse continua, despite the bizarre nature of the task and the lack of relevant experience. In the course of everyday events one is seldom asked to adjust the loudness of a radio to match the brightness of a desk lamp! In the laboratory, many subjects perform a related task with apparent ease.

The quantitative relation between S and R is then found by fitting a function to the pairs of meter readings. Usually, arithmetic means are used to summarize data from multiple responses by individual subjects, and geometric means or medians are used on data from a group of subjects. Any measure of central tendency may be used in place of the arithmetic mean, but the geometric mean is taken across subjects for reasons we will discuss later in the chapter. These measures of central tendency are analogous to the PSE obtained by classical methods with a single stimulus dimension. The Stevens functions can then be compared with the prediction based on summation of jnd's found by classical methods. A thorough study of different continua where both CMM and jnd's are obtained under similar conditions, same subjects, and so forth would provide a good test of the fourfold way. Such a study has never been reported.

One of the methodological problems that has cropped up in direct matching is the "regression effect" (Stevens and Greenbaum, 1966). It seems that subjects constrict the range of intensities for the continuum under their control. This creates a discrepancy in the two S-R functions when the role of stimulus and response continua are reversed. A possible solution to this difficulty would be to have *both* continua under the subject's control in a modified method of limits or adjustment. The intensity of one continuum could be set well above the other in respect to a match. If the subject's response now leads to a decrease in the high intensity while *simultaneously* increasing the low, the arbitrary separation of stimulus and response (continua) vanishes. That is, arrange the experimental apparatus so that the intensity of one continuum cannot be changed without also changing the other. With proper initial spacing between intensities, a point of equality would eventually be reached. Different starting positions would allow one to map S-S (or R-R?) pairs over the entire dynamic range. It's anybody's guess as to how the results from this procedure would compare with results from traditional methods, but the regression effect might be eliminated. Of course, this double adjustment technique could also be used to obtain intracontinuum matches.

The resulting S-R relation from CMM is usually a power function (Case IV in Fig. 5.1). This is not surprising, from the standpoint of the psychological theory discussed a few pages back, since most continua employed thus far in CMM generally obey Weber's law at the jnd level. In addition, much of this research was conducted by people who seemed convinced that the power law was the most appropriate psychophysical function. It is not unreasonable to assume that these investigators did not spend a great deal of time fitting alternative functions. One quarter of the predictions of the fourfold way have been verified, and three quarters have not been tested by CMM. However, another line of research involving the number continuum as an R scale offers further insight into the validity of these predictions.

NUMBERS AS A PHYSICAL CONTINUUM

It would be a formidable undertaking to secure matching functions for all possible pairs of continua. Practically speaking, it would be convenient if a standard continuum were established that could be matched to all others. The number scale serves this purpose. Most functioning adults are familiar with numbers, no special apparatus is needed, and numbers can be matched to all continua. Over the past 20 years thousands of "eager" undergraduates and a smaller number of professors have rendered numerical estimates of stimulus magnitudes in the psychophysical laboratory. From an operationist viewpoint, these responses can be treated like any other physical continuum (Stevens, 1966b). In this situation, no physical instrument is required to measure scale values. The numbers emitted are accepted at face value, as though the experimenter and subject are in agreement as to the intrinsic value of any specific number. They are viewed as if governed by rules of a subjective arithmetic.

Because of their flexibility, numbers can be handled in alternative ways, and different psychophysical methods stress different alternatives. Basically, there are two methods: category estimation and ratio estimation.

Category Estimation Methods

In category estimation, the subject uses a limited range and type of number. Usually, the response set consists of the integers from 1 to N, where N ranges from 5 to 10. Fractions are not permitted, nor are numbers outside the range. Most importantly, the subject is told to construct equal-width categories. Usually this is referred to as equal spacing between adjacent categories, as though a category were identified with its lower boundary. The subject is urged to keep in mind the equal-spacing requirement, even though the number of stimuli may greatly exceed the number of response categories. In other words, the subject partitions the stimulus continuum (length, light, sound, or whatever) into a set of N equally spaced response bins. This procedure can serve as an operational definition of Fechner's W scale, translated by modern psychophysics into an observable R scale. The numbering of categories is arbitrary (for example, $10, 20, 30, \ldots, 100$ would do as well as $1, 2, 3, \ldots, 10$ or even $-2, -1, 0, 1, 2$), but a constant width category ($\Delta R = 10$, or $\Delta R = 1$, etc.) is the critical feature of the R scale. This method, then, attempts to operationally define the number continuum with $\Delta R = c$ (Cases I and II in the fourfold way; Fig. 5.1). It is assumed that subjects follow instructions and that the R scale is fixed up to a linear transformation, so it is commonly thought that category estimation produces an interval scale (Chapter 1).

Ratio Estimation Methods

The ratio methods permit any numbers, including fractions, for responses, and nothing is mentioned about equal intervals between scale values. Instead, the subject is told to concentrate on ratios; for example, if one stimulus were judged to be three times as intense as another, this judgment could be represented either by assigning them the numbers 1 and 3, or 100 and 300, or 55 and 165, but not -1 and 2, since the latter involves an inadmissible transformation of the ratio scale (Chapter 1). The numbers chosen depend partly on the particular estimation technique.

The most common technique is *magnitude estimation*. Here, one stimulus is presented as a standard and assigned a numerical value (modulus) by the experimenter. The subject assigns numbers to subsequent stimuli (which sometimes include the standard) so as to represent their judged ratio with respect to the standard. In a popular variation called *free ratio estimation*, no standard is presented and the subject assigns any numbers, with the restriction that they reflect judged ratios among stimuli. Hence, any number whatever may be given to the first stimulus presented, but judgments of subsequent stimuli are constrained by this initial numerical calibration. The most thorough approach is to present all possible stimulus pairs for judgment. This is known as *complete ratio estimation*. Not many researchers have the stamina required to test all pairs, but it is often done in European laboratories (most notably in Stockholm).

Since all these methods emphasize the ratio of judgments, the operations (instructions) are different from those used in category estimation. Hence, the type of R scale is also different. If ratios among R values are equal, irrespective of intervals, then values along the R scale are spaced geometrically and $\Delta R = hR$ (Cases III and IV). Therefore, it should not surprise us if the psychophysical functions obtained by the two methods were not the same. Indeed, we would be surprised if they were the same, since the fourfold way predicts otherwise. The chief difference between them is that in category estimation the equality of intervals is emphasized, while in ratio estimation the equality of ratios is stressed (Torgerson, 1960). The implication here is that equal intervals define an arithmetic series of scale values and equal ratios a geometric series. (Of course, the ability of subjects to follow these instructions is another matter, which probably doesn't receive the attention it deserves.) We now turn to a brief examination of the empirical results bearing on this proposal of an operational distinction between category and magnitude estimation.

Case I: The Linear Function

If category estimation ($\Delta R = c$) is employed with a stimulus dimension yielding constant jnd's ($\Delta S = b$), the $S\text{-}R$ function should be linear. Stevens and Galanter (1957) report experiments where linear functions were found for position of a point on a line, azimuth position, and inclination of a line. Although evidence was not given on the associated Weber functions, it seems reasonable that $\Delta S = b$ for these continua. For example, suppose the method of adjustment is employed to determine the jnd for the position of a point on a line. A point is fixed as a standard along the line, and a variable point is moved along a second line to match the position of the standard. It seems likely that the standard deviation (defined as a jnd) of the adjustments would be independent of standard location.

Empirical results bearing on this are given in Fig. 5.3 for judgments of the position of a point along a line. The filled circles are for category judgments (1–15) reported by Stevens and Galanter (1957). The other two sets of points are results obtained by Baird and Vernon (1965) from magnitude estimates

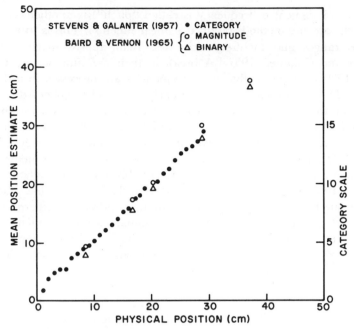

Figure 5.3. Mean estimate (in centimeters) of the position of a point along a line as a function of the physical position of the point (in centimeters). Results are given for three methods; category estimation, magnitude estimation, and binary estimation.

of the position of a point (open circles), and for binary estimates of the same points (open triangles). In the latter task, the subject rendered a sequence of binary judgments about the locations of the point relative to the ends of the line or relative to imagined boundaries defined by previous responses. Specifically, the subject first stated "one" if the point appeared to be in the right half of the line, and "zero" if it was perceived as being in the left half. Without stimulus alteration, the subject then bisected (in his or her mind's eye) the half containing the point and again rendered a judgment as to the point's location (left or right). On the average, about five sequential judgments were possible; that is, the point was put into one of $2^5 = 32$ categories along the line. The binary numbers (a series of five ones and zeros) were converted into decimal notation, and the mean values are shown in Fig. 5.3. Of special interest here is that both category methods yield the same results: a linear relation between judged and actual location of points, in agreement with the Case I prediction of the fourfold way.

The same prediction holds for visual inclination and other continua defined by "positional" or "locational" criteria (Stevens, 1951). Sound frequency (judgment of frequency is called "pitch") is another continuum for which category methods produce a linear function. This is true for short stimulus ranges and for frequencies less than approximately 1500 Hz (Stevens and Galanter, 1957). A break in their S-R function at approximately 1500 Hz suggests that high frequencies are processed in a different manner. This makes sense in terms of early studies of frequency discrimination where the jnd was relatively constant up to about this point and then increased according to Weber's law (Gulick, 1971; Shower and Biddulph, 1931; Wever, 1949). Hence, one would expect separate S-R functions for low and high frequencies. On the other hand, more recent experiments do not reveal a break in the function—it is reasonably linear throughout a wide range of frequencies (Harris, 1952; Nordmark, 1968). It has also been pointed out by Green (1976) that substantial individual differences exist among subjects in their ability to discriminate sound frequencies, thus further complicating the interpretations of data based on a small sample. This entire problem area has not been thoroughly researched within the framework of the fourfold way.

Case II: The Logarithmic Function

Category estimation of stimuli whose jnd's follow Weber's law should produce a logarithmic function. Since Weber's law is steady over the middle range of most continua, the log function should be quite prevalent. The facts generally support this. The trend of the data points, however, sometimes does not bend over enough on a linear plot to satisfy a perfect log function (Stevens and Galanter, 1957; Marks, 1974). In several casual experiments we found that one of the critical factors, in addition to instructions, is the number of response categories. Others report that the log function becomes less likely as the number of response categories exceeds seven (Gibson and Tomko, 1972). In any event, whenever a log function is found, it is correctly referred to as "Fechner's law," since it is an empirical relation and merely requires the substitution of observable responses for private sensations. Fechner might not have opposed this substitution if he had been aware of the data showing that subjects can give numerical estimates of stimulus intensities.

An example is provided by an unpublished experiment from our laboratory at Dartmouth. We had 30 subjects use category estimation to judge the luminance (brightness) of 13 light intensities, each presented in the form of a circular patch. The findings are shown in Fig. 5.4, where the mean category estimates are plotted against the logarithm of the stimulus intensity (given in arbitrary units). The function is a straight line, in excellent agreement with the prediction based on Case II of the fourfold way.

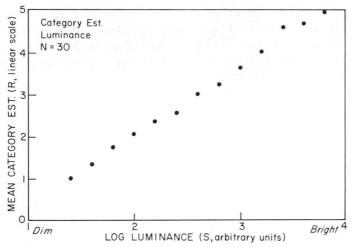

Figure 5.4. Mean category estimates as a function of luminance intensity (on a logarithmic scale). Data are based on 30 subjects who used the integer categories 1 through 5.

Case III: The Exponential Function

This function has never been seriously considered in the context of direct scaling—and with good reason. There seem to be few data to support this prediction, although some relevant studies have been reported. What we need are ratio estimates of stimuli whose jnd is constant. Such continua are scarce, but probably include (as mentioned previously) position of points, visual inclination, and low-frequency sounds. When category methods are applied to these continua, linear functions result, in agreement with Case I. When ratio estimates are secured for these stimuli, linear functions also seem to occur (except for frequency) rather than the exponential (Stevens and Galanter, 1957). For instance, magnitude estimation of the position of points along a line produces the same results as category estimation (Fig. 5.3). More research is needed to resolve this discrepancy between theory and data.

Case IV: The Power Function

The power function has rapidly become the most celebrated of all psychophysical laws. Although it is theoretically limited to results from ratio methods, Marks (1968) and Stevens (1971) have suggested that the power function applies as well to category estimates (the exponent is lower). We concentrate here on the ratio techniques.

The power function describes the situation where a geometric increase along the S scale corresponds to a geometric increase along the R scale. The exponent reflects the relative rate of increase along the two scales. These facts are often summarized by stating that "equal stimulus ratios produce equal response ratios." That is, if

$$R_i = \lambda S_i^n \tag{5.7}$$

and

$$R_j = \lambda S_j^n \tag{5.8}$$

then

$$\frac{R_i}{R_j} = \left(\frac{S_i}{S_j}\right)^n \tag{5.9}$$

regardless of the absolute values of S_i and S_j. As long as their ratio stays the same, so does the response ratio. Therefore, by dividing each stimulus in a series by a standard intensity, the need for λ is eliminated (at least theoretically). This constant can be thought of as a way to change the units of measure. Just as we multiply by 100 in converting from meters to centimeters, units of R can be changed by multiplying by $1/\lambda$.

Returning to Eq. 5.7, it is often convenient to rewrite matters by taking logarithms.

$$\log R = n \log S + \log \lambda \tag{5.10}$$

Note that Eq. 5.10 is a standard linear equation:

$$y = ax + b$$

where $y = \log R$, $x = \log S$, $a = n$, and $b = \log \lambda$. For this reason, a linear function is fit to pairs of logarithms of S and R to determine the slope (exponent) and y intercept (log λ). It is also common practice to plot R against S on double logarithmic paper (base 10) so that a straight line can be drawn through the points, allowing the slope and y intercept to be found directly.

In the study of brightness perception just discussed, we also had subjects render magnitude estimates of 13 light intensities. The log of the geometric mean (GM) of the responses for each stimulus was calculated as a measure of central tendency, where

$$\log(GM) = \frac{\sum_{i=1}^{N} \log R_i}{N}$$

In this formula N is the number of subjects, i is a particular subject, and R_i is the magnitude estimate. The results are shown in Fig. 5.5 (log-log coordinates). The best-fitting straight line has a slope of .4, which we take as the exponent n in Eq. 5.7. The fit is not great at the low end of the scale, however, where a slight curvature is apparent. We will return to this matter momentarily.

The power function is ubiquitous. It has been verified in hundreds of experiments for a wide variety of continua. Because much of this research was conducted or inspired by S.S. Stevens, Eq. 5.7 is called Stevens's law. The exponent is the key term here because it is sensitive to changes in continua and other experimental manipulations. In this regard, the exponent has the same role as the Weber fraction. It is an *index* of perceptual sensitivity. Unlike the Weber fraction, however, the exponent can be interpreted only if two scales are specified. If the R scale is always the number continuum, we are justified in comparing exponents for different stimulus dimensions (see Table 5.1). With this in mind, note that sensitivity is directly related to the size of the exponent. An exponent of 1.0 means that the power function reduces to a linear relation between R and S with a slope of λ.

$$R = \lambda S$$

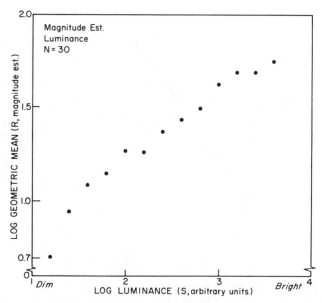

Figure 5.5. Geometric means of magnitude estimates as a function of luminance intensity (log-log coordinates).

Taking logarithms,

$$\log R = \log S + \log \lambda$$

It is interesting to note, then, that slopes of linear functions map as parallel lines with different y intercepts on the log-log plot. According to this analysis, these functions all reflect the same sensitivity (slope of 1.0). The lower the exponent, the less the relative sensitivity, so exponents less than 1.0 indicate that perceptual sensitivity is less than sensitivity to the number continuum, whereas exponents greater than 1.0 indicate the reverse. In brief, the exponent reflects the *relative* sensitivity of the subject to the R and S dimensions.

Examples of power functions on logarithmic coordinates are given in Fig. 5.6, and some representative exponents are listed in Table 5.1. References for the relevant studies can be found in Baird (1970b) and Teghtsoonian (1971). From the table we see, for example, that high sensitivity is exhibited to electric shock and low sensitivity to luminance. The exponent of 1.0 for line length means that sensitivity is identical to that for the number continuum.

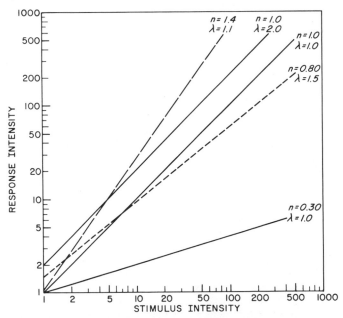

Figure 5.6. Response intensity as a function of stimulus intensity on double logarithmic coordinates. Power functions are straight lines on this plot, where the exponent n and multiplicative constant λ are shown for a variety of hypothetical cases.

Table 5.1 Representative exponents for common continua

Continuum	Exponent
Electrical (skin)	3.5
Saturation (red)	1.7
Finger span	1.3
Heaviness	1.1
Length of lines (visual)	1.0
Position of points (visual)	1.0
Taste (salt)	0.9
Area (visual)	0.8
Skin vibration (250 Hz)	0.6
Taste (sweet)	0.6
Smell (coffee, benzene)	0.5
Loudness (1000 Hz)	0.3
Brightness	0.3

ADDITIVE CONSTANTS

The simple power function does not always accurately describe data because of slight departures from linearity (in the log-log plot) near the low end of the scale. On purely pragmatic grounds, these departures can be remedied by subtracting or adding a small constant to each stimulus value (noted, among others, by Ekman, 1956). Hence, one often encounters the modified version of Stevens's law written as

$$R = \lambda(S - s)^n \tag{5.11}$$

where s can be either positive or negative but is usually positive. Attempts to relate s to absolute threshold have been largely unsuccessful on an empirical level, although the connection is often assumed theoretically. At present, we should be honest about our lack of understanding and consider the additive constant a "fudge" factor. In other words, we simply vary s until it works, without worrying too much about the underlying theory. Such fudge factors have their place in science because they allow us to withdraw gracefully until reinforcements arrive in the form of new data and theory. One special problem arising in the present case is that the exponent with the additive constant will not equal the exponent without it (unless the constant does not improve the fit) (Baird and Stein, 1970). For this reason, it is risky to attach significance to the size of an exponent without due attention to the other parameters in the equation as well as to the nature of the R scale induced through instructions. One set of data that would be straightened out through judicious use of the constant s are the brightness results in Fig. 5.5. The function could be straightened by subtracting a constant from each stimulus before plotting.

According to the fourfold way, the exponent of the power function is the ratio between the Weber fractions for the response and stimulus dimensions. A good plan, then, is to compare exponents with Weber fractions to see if the predicted connection between them is valid. The best way to do this is to secure all measures under comparable conditions. Very few studies of this sort have been reported (Graf, Baird, and Glesman, 1974), and therefore we must settle for indirect routes. We focus here on magnitude estimation, which allows us to tap the storehouse of information on Stevens's law. Since this method employs numbers as the R scale, the task is to estimate the Weber fraction for numbers under these circumstances. This can be done as follows.

Suppose first that the assumptions of the fourfold way are correct. Then, the exponent n for the power function is

$$n = \frac{h}{k} \tag{5.12}$$

where h and k are the Weber fractions for numbers and the S continuum, respectively. An exponent of 1 will occur whenever $k = h$. Since it is well established empirically that the exponent for line length is 1, the Weber fraction for numbers, h, equals that for line length. Therefore, to determine the Weber fraction for numbers, one need only find the Weber fraction for line length. The most recent determination of the latter value was made by Ono (1967), who reports a fraction between .03 and .05. If we take the average of these two values, $h = .04$ for numbers. Armed with a list of Weber fractions for different stimulus dimensions, we can now divide each value into .04 (Eq. 5.12) to obtain a prediction of the exponent. This prediction can then be compared with the empirical exponent for different continua. This has already been done (Baird, 1970b) in a slightly altered context, and results suggest that n is inversly related to k, as predicted by Eq. 5.12 and the fourfold way.

Another way to determine h is to use all the available data on Weber fractions and exponents and substitute the appropriate values in Eq. 5.12 which can be rewritten as

$$h = nk \tag{5.13}$$

The product of the exponent and Weber fraction yields a single estimate of *h*. The average of these values over many continua (different *k*) is an even better estimate (assuming variability is small). Teghtsoonian (1971) used a strategy that reduces to an evaluation of Eq. 5.13 and found a mean *h* of .03. This line of attack has an advantage over the one just mentioned because more data points are involved. On the other hand, line length is a very stable continuum (we have faith in the exponent and Weber fraction), so we might want to weight matters in that direction. Both strategies have special advantages. But the empirical data are variable, obtained under diverse conditions, and certainly do not warrant hair-splitting arguments (We discuss variability of exponents in the next chapter.) So let us not compromise, and instead assume that $h = .04$. Then, taking the Weber fractions listed in Table 3.1 (Chapter 3), we substitute each for *k* in Eq. 5.12 to secure a prediction of the exponent. The relation between predicted and actual exponents is shown in Fig. 5.7. Considering the theoretical machinations, the fit is not bad, but there is probably more going on here (in terms of psychological processes) than is suggested by the fourfold way. That is, a perfect match between exponents derived from Weber fractions and exponents obtained by direct methods may not occur even under the most favorable conditions (Marks, 1974).

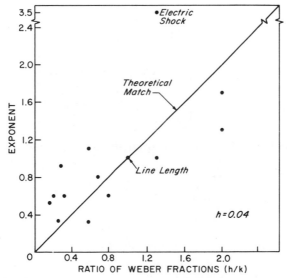

Figure 5.7. Empirical exponents as a function of predictions based on the ratio of two Weber fractions. The fraction ($h = .04$) for the number continuum was theoretically determined. The *k* values for the various stimulus continua are listed in Table 3.1. The empirical exponents for the same continua are listed in Table 5.1. For more details, see the text.

RELATIONS AMONG RESPONSE SCALES

If the fourfold way is correct, the discrepancies between category and ratio estimation revolve around Torgerson's (1960) distinction between equal-interval and equal-ratio scales. In category estimation the R scale is arithmetic; there are equal intervals between adjacent scale values. In ratio estimation the R scale is geometric; ratios are equal between adjacent scale values. It necessarily follows that the relation between these two R scales is logarithmic. An arithmetic increase along the category scale is accompanied by a geometric increase along the magnitude scale. More formally, if the same stimulus continuum is used in category and ratio estimation, the respective Stevens functions can be written as

$$R_{cat} = m \log S + \kappa \qquad (5.14)$$

$$R_{rat} = \lambda S^n \qquad (5.15)$$

Transforming Eq. 5.15 and taking logs, we obtain

$$\left(\frac{R_{rat}}{\lambda}\right)^{1/n} = S$$

$$(1/n) \log\left(\frac{R_{rat}}{\lambda}\right) = \log S$$

Multiplying both sides by m and adding κ, we obtain

$$\frac{m}{n} \log\left(\frac{R_{rat}}{\lambda}\right) + \kappa = m \log S + \kappa \qquad (5.16)$$

The right-hand side of Eq. 5.16 is equal to the right-hand side of Eq. 5.14, and therefore,

$$R_{cat} = \frac{m}{n} \log\left(\frac{R_{rat}}{\lambda}\right) + \kappa \qquad (5.17)$$

The category scale is a logarithmic function of the magnitude scale. Now substitute the appropriate Weber fractions for m and n. From Fig. 5.1, Cases II and IV,

$$m = \frac{c}{k} \quad \text{and} \quad n = \frac{h}{k}$$

where c is a constant for the category scale (Eq. 5.4), h is the Weber fraction for the ratio scale (Eq. 5.2) and k is the Weber fraction for the stimulus scale (Eq. 5.1). Therefore,

$$\frac{m}{n} = \frac{c}{h}$$

Substituting in Eq. 5.17,

$$R_{cat} = \frac{c}{h}\log\left(\frac{R_{rat}}{\lambda}\right) + \kappa \qquad (5.18)$$

the coefficient c/h is a constant independent of S. There is ample support for both the logarithmic relation between category and magnitude scales and the constant coefficient (references in Baird, 1970b; Stevens and Galanter, 1957; Torgerson, 1960).

Speaking more generally, a logarithmic function is predicted whenever values increasing arithmetically along one scale are mapped into values increasing geometrically along another, whether we are considering S or R variables. In addition to the example just given, the fourfold way contains three other such relations. The R scale in Case I is logarithmically related to the R scale in Case III. Similarly, on the stimulus side, the S scale in Case I and the S scale in Case II are logarithmically related, as are the two S scales from Cases III and IV. Discovery of a logarithmic relation between two response scales (say category and ratio) for a given stimulus continuum does not imply that the jnd's of the stimulus obey Weber's law. The same function occurs whether the S scale is arithmetic (Cases I and III) or geometric (Cases II and IV). Understanding of this fact undercuts the rationale behind an often-quoted theoretical paper by Stevens (1966c) in which he attempted to show the applicability of direct scaling (and in particular, the power function) for judgments of stimuli that do not lend themselves to convenient physical measurement (for example, excellence of handwriting, seriousness of crimes, popularity of Swedish monarchs). Although direct scaling may be used for these stimuli, their associated Weber functions cannot be uniquely determined by Stevens's theoretical argument. That is, the results do not allow us to distinguish between $\Delta S = b$ and $\Delta S = kS$.

TRANSITIVITY OF SCALES

Stevens (1953) first introduced magnitude estimation (originally called absolute judgment) in a brief note to *Science*. In the same paper, the power function was suggested as a good description of the resulting S-R function. This statement came *well before* enough data were collected to justify designation of an empirical power law. Once again (remember Fechner) we see that scientific intuition may precede empirical evidence by a wide margin. The danger, of course, is that simply stating a "law" in a prestigious journal may induce a selective search for supporting data.

In any event, from a modest beginning in 1953 came a flood of experiments and controversy. At issue was the acceptance of numbers as data to be added, averaged, and plotted in the manner usually reserved for numbers read from physical instruments (Graham and Ratoosh, 1962). To counter these criticisms, cross-modality matching was developed as an independent check on the validity of the exponents. Basically, CMM is a test of scale transitivity, in which $a = b$ and $a = c$ imply $b = c$. In functional notation, if S_a and S_b are two continua matched by R, the traditional test of transitivity can be illustrated for Stevens's law. Let

$$R = f(S_a) \quad \text{and} \quad R = g(S_b)$$

Then,

$$f(S_a) = g(S_b)$$

Using this argument, let

$$R = S_a^{n_a} \quad \text{and} \quad R = S_b^{n_b}$$

be the power functions for S_a and S_b obtained by magnitude estimation. Then, if a subject adjusts S_a to match S_b, it is predicted that

$$S_a^{n_a} = S_b^{n_b}$$

Taking the n_ath root,

$$S_a = S_b^{n_b/n_a} \tag{5.19}$$

The exponents n_a and n_b are empirically determined by separate tests using magnitude estimation. The cross-modality match also yields an exponent, say, m. If transitivity holds, $m = n_b/n_a$. According to the fourfold way, $n_a = h/k_a$, and $n_b = h/k_b$. The ratio n_b/n_a cancels the effect of h, the Weber fraction for numbers in ratio estimation. If the prediction works, numbers can be treated as a physical dimension. Stevens (1966b) and others have presented data in support of transitivity, although Mashhour and Hosman (1968) raise questions as to its empirical universality.

Some investigators feel that evidence from CMM does not necessarily prove the truth of the power law (Ekman, 1964; Treisman, 1964), because the log function (Case II) yields the same result. That is, suppose

$$R = n_a \log S_a \quad \text{and} \quad R = n_b \log S_b$$

Then

$$\log S_a = \frac{n_b}{n_a} \log S_b$$

Taking antilogs,

$$S_a = S_b^{n_b/n_a} \tag{5.20}$$

which is the same as Eq. 5.19.

This argument is valid if grounded in the theoretical derivation leading to the fourfold way. However, the argument is misleading when applied to experimental results, for the reasons discussed in Chapter 1 on scale types. Recall that the response scale secured by ratio estimation (Eq. 5.7) is invariant under the operation of multiplication; λ is merely used to change units of measure. The exponent, on the other hand, *means something* inasmuch as it depends on the responses to a specific set of stimulus conditions. Therefore, the predicted exponent n_b/n_a also has meaning in an empirical sense. The same cannot be said about n_a and n_b in Eq. 5.20, if it is assumed that category estimation yields an interval scale. In this case, both the multiplicative constant (n) and the additive constant in Fechner's law are arbitrary—in that they are conventions of the measurement procedure (for example, categories $1, 2, 3$ yield one set of values, while $-10, 0, 10$ yield another.) For this reason, the predicted exponent n_b/n_a in Eq. 5.20 does not have the empirical validity it does in Eq. 5.19. Hence, the success of cross-modality matching as a test of transitivity does indeed offer support for the power law over the log law, when both are based upon empirical results.

For completeness, we present without further comment the transitivity tests for Cases I and III.

Case I:

$$R = n_a S_a$$

$$R = n_b S_b$$

$$S_a = \left(\frac{n_b}{n_a}\right) S_b \tag{5.21}$$

Case III: For the exponential,

$$R = e^{n_a S_a}$$

$$R = e^{n_b S_b}$$

$$e^{n_a S_a} = e^{n_b S_b}$$

Taking logarithms to the base e and rearranging,

$$S_a = \left(\frac{n_b}{n_a} \right) S_b \tag{5.22}$$

Hence, on a purely theoretical plane, transitivity tests cannot be used to uniquely infer the nature of individual S-R functions (cf. Eqs. 5.21 and 5.22). On the other hand, empirical considerations of scale type help us decide the practical validity of the different tests (for example, tests of the power law hold more weight than tests of the log law).

CONCLUDING COMMENT

The majority of results on direct scaling support the fourfold way. There appears to be some connection between classical measures of the just-noticeable-difference and Stevens functions. Most minor departures from this theoretical link are probably due to the variety of experimental conditions under which the data were collected. In certain instances, however, departures are more striking and seem to involve a deeper violation of the assumptions underlying direct scaling. These instances are discussed in Chapter 6.

REFERENCES

Ayer, A. J. *Language, Truth and Logic*. London: Gollantz, 1935.

Baird, J. C. *Psychophysical Analysis of Visual Space*. London: Pergamon, 1970a.

Baird, J. C. "A cognitive theory of psychophysics: II. Fechner's law and Stevens' law." *Scandinavian Journal of Psychology*, 1970b, *11*, 89–102.

Baird, J. C., and Stein, T. "When power functions fail: A theoretical explanation." *Perceptual and Motor Skills*, 1970, *30*, 415–525.

Baird, J. C., and Vernon, C. W. "Binary estimation." *Psychonomic Science*, 1965, *3*, 469–470.

Boring, E. G. *A History of Experimental Psychology*. New York: Appleton-Century-Crofts, 1950.

Bridgman, P. W. *The Logic of Modern Physics*. New York: Macmillan, 1927.

Carnap, R. *Logical Syntax of Language*. London: Routledge & Kegan Paul, 1937.

Ekman, G. "Subjective power functions and the method of fractionation." *Report from the Psychological Laboratories, University of Stockholm*, 1956, no. 34.

Ekman, G. "Is the power law a special case of Fechner's law?" *Perceptual and Motor Skills*, 1964, *19*, 730.

Ekman, G., and Sjöberg, L. "Scaling." *Annual Review of Psychology*, 1965, *16*, 451–474.

Feigl, H. "Logical analysis of the psycho-physical problem." *Philosophy of Science*, 1934, *1*, 420–445.

Gibson, R. H., and Tomko, D. L. "The relation between category and magnitude estimates of tactile intensity." *Perception & Psychophysics*, 1972, *12*, 135–138.

Graf, V., Baird, J. C., and Glesman, G. "An empirical test of two psychophysical models." *Acta Psychologica*, 1974, *38*, 59–72.

Graham, C. H., and Ratoosh, P. "Notes on some interrelations of sensory psychology, perception, and behavior," In S. Koch (Ed.), *Psychology: A Study of a Science*, Vol. IV. New York: McGraw-Hill, 1962.

Green, D. M. *An Introduction To Hearing*. Hillsdale, N.J.: Lawrence Erlbaum Associates, 1976.

Gulick, W. L. *Hearing: Physiology and Psychophysics*. London: Oxford, 1971.

Harris, J. D. "Pitch discrimination." *Journal of the Acoustical Society of America*, 1952, *24*, 750–755.

Marks, L. E. "Stimulus range, number of categories, and form of the category scale." *American Journal of Psychology*, 1968, *81*, 467–479.

Marks, L. E. *Sensory Processes: The New Psychophysics*. New York: Academic, 1974.

Mashhour, M., and Hosman, J. "On the new psychophysical law: a validation study." *Perception & Psychophysics*, 1968, *3*, 367–375.

Michon, J. A. "Studies on subjective duration: I. Differential sensitivity in the perception of repeated temporal intervals." *Acta Psychologica*, 1964, *22*, 441–450.

Neurath, O. "Physicalism: The philosophy of the Vienesse circle." *Monist*, 1931, *41*, 618–623.

Nordmark, J. O. "Mechanisms of frequency discrimination." *Journal of the Acoustical Society of America*, 1968, *44*, 1553–1540.

Ono, H. "Difference threshold for stimulus length under simultaneous and nonsimultaneous viewing conditions." *Perception & Psychophysics*, 1967, *2*, 201–207.

Pratt, C. C. *The Logic of Modern Psychology*. New York: Macmillan, 1939.

Savage, C. W. "Introspectionist and behaviorist interpretations of ratio scales of perceptual magnitudes." *Psychological Monographs*, 1966, *80* (19), 1–32.

Shower, E. G., and Biddulph, R. "Differential pitch sensitivity of the ear." *Journal of the Acoustical Society of America*, 1931, *3*, 275–287.

Stevens, J. C., Mack, J. D., and Stevens, S. S. "Growth of sensation on seven continua as measured by force of handgrip." *Journal of Experimental Psychology*, 1960, *59*, 60–67.

Stevens, J. C., and Marks, L. E. "Cross-modality matching of brightness and loudness." *Proceedings of the National Academy of Science*, 1965, *54*, 407–411.

Stevens, S. S. "The operational definition of psychological concepts." *Psychological Review*, 1935, *42*, 517–527.

Stevens, S. S. "Psychology and the science of science." *Psychological Bulletin*, 1939, *36*, 221–263.

Stevens, S. S. "Mathematics, measurement, and psychophysics." In S. S. Stevens, (Ed.), *Handbook of Experimental Psychology*. New York: Wiley, 1951, pp. 1–49.

Stevens, S. S. "On the brightness of lights and the loudness of sounds." *Science*, 1953, *118*, 576 (ABSTRACT).

Stevens, S. S. "Quantifying the sensory experience." In K. Feyerabend and G. Maxwell (Eds.), *Mind, Matter and Method: Essays in Philosophy and Science in Honor of Herbert Feigl*. Minnesota: University of Minnesota Press, 1966a, pp. 215–233.

Stevens, S. S. "Matching functions between loudness and ten other continua." *Perception & Psychophysics*, 1966b, *1*, 5–8.

Stevens, S. S. "A metric for the social consensus." *Science*, 1966c, *151*, 530–541.

Stevens, S. S. "Issues in psychophysical measurement." *Psychological Review*, 1971, *78*, 426–450.

Stevens, S. S. *Psychophysics: Introduction to its Perceptual, Neural and Social Prospects*. New York: Wiley, 1975.

Stevens, S. S., and Galanter, E. H. "Ratio scales and category scales for a dozen perceptual continua." *Journal of Experimental Psychology*, 1957, *54*, 377–411.

Stevens, S. S., and Greenbaum, H. B. "Regression effect in psychophysical judgment." *Perception & Psychophysics*, 1966, *1*, 439–446.

Teghtsoonian, R. "On the exponents in Stevens' law and the constant in Ekman's law." *Psychological Review*, 1971, *78*, 71–80.

Tolman, E. C. *Purposive Behavior in Animals and Men*. New York: Appleton-Century-Crofts, 1932.

Torgerson, W. S. "Quantitative judgment scales." In H. Gulliksen and S. Messick. (Eds.), *Psychological Scaling: Theory and Applications*. New York: Wiley, 1960, 21–31.

Treisman, M. "Sensory scaling and the psychophysical law." *Quarterly Journal of Experimental Psychology*, 1964, *16*, 11–22.

Wever, E. G. *Theory of Hearing*. New York: Wiley, 1949.

CHAPTER

$$\boxed{6}$$

EFFECT OF CONTEXT ON SCALE INVARIANCE

The paradigm of human as measuring instrument is at the heart of theoretical psychophysics. Without this belief it makes very little sense to speak of Stevens functions, to say nothing about determining their form. Without this paradigm we would also be forced to treat each situation as unique with no hope of finding any patterns of behavior. This would be unfortunate and puzzling since there is ample evidence that people perceive their environment in consistent ways over time. On the other hand, for the paradigm to be useful, it must be applied to specific situations by making assumptions as to what processes can be measured and as to what we mean by "consistency." To determine the form of a Stevens function, several assumptions must be made. First, the results produced by the measurement tools must be independent of whether the stimulus or response is being measured. Second, the subject must be able to follow the directions and ignore all "irrelevant" parts of the environment such as location, time of day, and order of stimulus presentation.

These assumptions are part of the theoretical base that permits one to state that the Stevens function for a particular set of experimental conditions obeys the power law. Inconsistencies with regard to this law due to "irrelevant" factors in the environment do not mean that the concept of the human as a measuring instrument is false. Rather, it indicates that the assumptions used to make the paradigm operational are too strong. The issue, then, is whether these empirical deviations are sufficiently large to cause us to reject the assumptions. To a certain extent, the answer to this question is one of personal opinion having to do with how much deviation a particular scientist requires before rejecting a model. On the other hand, we can at least all agree on the nature and amount of the deviations from clearly stated models.

PSYCHOLOGICAL MEASUREMENT

Assume for the moment that there are certain contextual effects linked to experimental conditions. That is, the response pattern from magnitude estimation (for instance) will vary due to the particular sequence of stimuli, range of numbers used as responses, and so on. The question then becomes, what variations in the results are contrary to those predicted by theoretical mechanisms? (For example, intensity judgments are expected to be independent of factors such as presentation order.) Also, do these deviations (if they occur) present sufficient evidence to question the assumption of an internal sensation scale?

To gain more insight into the first question, a review of some of the predictions of the direct scaling theory is in order. The basis for scaling magnitude estimates is that exponents in the power law may vary somewhat over subjects but must remain constant for a given subject regardless of the experimental conditions. So, for example, changing the modulus (number assigned to the standard stimulus) should only multiply all responses by a constant. If the standard were paired with a modulus of 10 on one set of trials and with 30 on the second set, then a stimulus receiving a rating of 20 on the first set should receive a 60 on the second. In other words, the numbers form a ratio scale, as defined in Chapter 1, where numbers assigned to stimuli are unique up to multiplication by a constant.

For scaling category estimates, the considerations are similar to those for magnitude estimation. Since the numbers for each category are specified, the range of responses is limited. (If the categories run from 1 to 10, a response of 27.5 is not allowed.) We would hope, however, that responses for different sets of categories would be comparable. Responses in categories 1 to 10, for example, can be mapped into responses in categories 30 to 120 by multiplying by 10 and adding 20. So, a stimulus eliciting a response of 3 on the first set should elicit a response of 50 on the second. Invariance up to a constant multiplier and addition of a constant means that we have an interval scale.

Therefore, each set of responses must satisfy certain invariances but need not satisfy others. Category estimates over several sets of trials may vary by the addition of a constant and still be consistent with the requirements of an interval scale, while magnitude estimates that showed the same results would be in violation of the required ratio scale.

By examining responses made in various contexts, the adherence to the various scale types may be examined. This leads us to ask about the theoretical significance of these results. The answer ultimately depends on one's philosophy of measurement. Three major philosophical alternatives can be identified: behaviorism, subjectivism, and conventionalism (Baird, 1970a). These are idealized viewpoints—it would be difficult at the present time in psychology's development to find a scientist who steadfastly adheres to only one. Nonetheless, the ideals are useful referents for the evaluation of a number of problems related to contextual effects.

Behaviorism

The strict behaviorist treats Stevens functions as a summary of the effects of experimental conditions. The particular results are useful in identifying invariances in the processing of stimulus information, but no inferences are made about the nature of this processing. The person is considered to be a black box, where input/output functions simply reflect orderly behavior in the context of psychophysical experiments. In other words, the strict behaviorist has little interest in the internal workings of the human. Therefore, the consistency of the data across different psychophysical methods is best "explained" as mere coincidence. This position is the outcome of an excessive brand of operationism, believed by a diminishing number of scientists, most of whom are not doing psychophysics.

Subjectivism

There are two versions of this viewpoint, but both assume that the subject is performing as a measuring instrument capable of generating data consistent with a particular scale type.

The first version is epitomized by Fechner, who distinguished between physical and subjective measurement. The experimenter measured stimuli, but the subject measured sensations. For the subjectivist, the *scale of sensation* is simply defined outright. Therefore, Fechner's law (as originally stated) can never be proven or disproven using *S-R* functions based on objective measures of the input and output sides of the psychophysical equation. Failure to appreciate this fact has often led to confusion and heated argument over the "correct" psychophysical law.

The second (and more popular) version of subjectivism is represented in the later work of Stevens (1951, 1961, 1971), who seemed to accept a mediating sensation scale as an essential postulate for understanding the main goal of psychophysics: the objective measurement of stimulus and response. Although Stevens was in the forefront of the operationist movement during the 1930s, this position evolved to the point where in later writings his arguments became very similar to those of Fechner. The two were alike in claiming that (1) psychological measurement is conducted by the subject; (2) internal jnd scales are defined independently of observable operations; and (3) there is one psychophysical law. Points (2) and (3) deserve further comment.

Even though both Stevens and Fechner defined unique internal scales, Stevens spoke of two classes of scales—*metathetic* continua in which internal jnd's are constant (Fechner's definition) and *prothetic* continua in which internal jnd's follow Weber's law (Stevens, 1951; Stevens and Galanter, 1957). These two classes were described in the fourfold way in Chapter 4. In order to derive a power function through summation of jnd's, it is necessary to assume that the internal continuum is prothetic. This definition of an internal Weber function was called *Ekman's law* by Stevens (1966), because Gösta Ekman, the late head of the Stockholm laboratories, was one of the first to note that stimulus and response continua should be treated identically in the development of psychophysical theory (Ekman, 1959).[1] One can, of course, avoid discussion of internal jnd's entirely. In fact, the advent of operational definitions (based on observable jnd's for stimuli and responses) eliminates much of the confusion that has surrounded the use of the terms prothetic and metathetic, because they need not then be defined as internal scales (Chapter 5).

---

[1]Ekman actually tried to secure *objective* measures of response jnd's, although his approach was inadequate because the contribution of the stimulus continuum was not identified and parceled out of the measures. If we are talking about objectively determined jnd's for a response continuum, we should be referring to Weber's law. In our opinion, that is what Ekman was really after.

The most crucial similarity between the approaches of Fechner and Stevens was that both believed in a single psychophysical law, although there is evidence that Fechner was more flexible in this regard (Fechner, 1966, p. 212). This may explain Stevens's many attacks on the logarithmic law, his relegation of certain continua (metathetic) and scale types (interval) to a low status, and his proselytizing for the power function as "the" psychophysical law (thus repealing Fechner's law).

Stevens's position was unlike Fechner's in several respects. Most important, he stressed objective measurement of stimuli and responses, thus fostering a family of S-R models. Second, the type of response scale was always seen, at least in part, as an empirical question. Whereas psychological measurement was defined, scale types were open to empirical verification. These steps toward objectifying S-R functions led eventually to what can be termed conventionalism.

Conventionalism

The conventionalist approach is to look at psychophysics within the larger scope of psychological theory. The subjectivist's definitions of scales and measurement rules are treated as working models. There is nothing inappropriate about attempts to explain S-R functions by postulating such models. This is a viewpoint capable of empirical test. In short, the objectivity of the behaviorist is retained while his or her attendant aversion to the construction of a theory is not. The major difference between the conventionalist and the subjectivist lies in their opinions about the utility of a model. The conventionalist sees theory and model merely as first approximations to "reality." If evidence runs contrary to certain predictions, the model still retains its usefulness until a more comprehensive one is developed. For example, although the conventionalist may not believe in the existence of sensations, the concept is retained because of its heuristic value (cf. Luce, 1972). This seems to be the dominant view among theorists today, and it is a view that we will encounter regularly in the chapters to follow.

CONTEXTUAL EFFECTS

The stability of Stevens functions depends on the experimental context in which they are secured. If the subjectivist approach is valid, response scales should be relatively invariant under a variety of circumstances. These include alterations in stimulus and response properties, instructions, and psychophysical method. For the supersubjectivists in the Fechnerian tradition, the internal scale type is true by definition, so it cannot be shaken by the results of experiments. From a conventionalist viewpoint, a scale that is useful must be applicable to a fairly wide range of conditions to permit generalizations to be made. Otherwise, the measurement framework should be discarded in favor of alternative views (for example, information processing) of the judgment process. For the strict behaviorist, tests of scale invariance merely extend the conditions for which we have data. With no overview of how these data should fit together in a larger pattern, the behaviorist cannot be contradicted, and for that reason, his occasional philosophical statements are usually ignored by theoreticians. This treatment is cheerfully reciprocated in the behaviorist's dealings with theoretical models of judgment and sensory processes.

Stimulus Context

A large number of response scales have emerged from the method of magnitude estimation, where the exponent of the power function is supposed to be an index of a subject's sensitivity to different continua. A representative list of exponents was presented in Table 5.1. This list is somewhat misleading since it implies that there is a single scale for line length, a single scale for luminance, and so on. In fact, there are multiple scales for each of these dimensions. The exponent varies systematically with such factors as stimulus exposure time, adaptation level of the sensory system, and details of stimulus composition [for example, loudness exponents vary with frequency (Marks, 1974)].

What does this imply about the subjectivist definition of psychological measurement? Well, as long as the scales fulfill the necessary criteria (equal stimulus ratios produce equal response ratios, Chapters 1 and 5), the measurement definition of a ratio scale is intact. But something is still awry. For what good are the scales if we require a separate one for each new set of stimulus conditions? The importance of physical scales is that they are few in number and can be used as standards against which the properties of unknown objects can be evaluated. The notion of a standard scale with fixed units implies invariance of operation under a variety of conditions. We would not be very pleased with a ruler whose scale values depended on whether it was used to measure the length of a desk or the height of a chair! Similarly, if the organism (measuring instrument) is attending to "irrelevant" factors, we have a shaky foundation for constructing scales. A set of responses at one instant in time occurring under a restricted set of conditions may fulfill all the requirements of a ratio scale and yet be the result of a useless measuring instrument (Cliff, 1973). The instability of the scale over time and physical context renders it useless as a standard against which other objects can be compared.

We have arrived at a point in psychophysics where a few hundred "sensory scales" exist, some with their own units of measurement. (There are sones, maks, mels, gusts, dols, etc. suggested as units for responses to different stimulus continua.) The scientific merits of the scaling model fade under these circumstances, and much might be gained by abandoning it altogether. In this eventuality, neutral terms such as "relation" and "function" should be more appropriate than "scale" for describing results from the direct methods.

Instructions and Subject Strategies

Direct scaling can easily suggest a mechanistic attitude toward psychophysics. The assumed processes are all so automatic. The stimulus arrives at the sensory system, becomes located neatly along some common scale, and is simply transformed into a response and read out for the experimenter's benefit. One has the feeling that all the experimenter must do is plot the S-R function, and the understanding of underlying sensory processes will follow immediately. But where do psychological variables enter into this scheme? The subject's sensory processes are admittedly important in determining a response, but so are his or her strategies in dealing with the task set out by the instructions. The problem with a mechanistic theory is that psychological variables are omitted or considered of secondary importance. With this view, there is little reason to discriminate and classify Stevens functions. But how can this approach explain consistent differences among Stevens functions associated with various procedural differences? Let us explore this question with the aid of the fourfold classification scheme.

ALTERNATIVE PSYCHOPHYSICAL LAWS

The difference between category and magnitude estimation is surely linked with instructions. It is reasonable to believe that the logarithmic and power functions depend on the subject's attempts to follow instructions, as he or she understands them. Since numbers can be used in alternative ways, more than one Stevens function is possible with the same stimulus continuum, even when stimulus context is held constant. The category scale is assumed to be interval; the magnitude scale, ratio. This much, then, is apparent: On separate occasions the human being is capable of giving responses that satisfy more than one scale type. One scale is as valid as the next, and hence, arguments to the effect that there is a single psychophysical law (for example, a power function) are simply not in keeping with the data.

The behaviorist accepts this conclusion, as does the conventionalist who further attempts to identify the underlying psychological processes. In response to such evidence the subjectivist may either stick to his definition of a unitary scale and take the consequences in criticism, broaden the definition of internal scales to include effects of instructions, or find means to discredit research showing more than one Stevens function. All three reactions have been expressed in the literature, but on balance, none has been well received by other investigators.

ONE LAW—MULTIPLE SCALES

Even when a single Stevens function is found, the parameters of that function depend on instructions and, by inference, the strategies of the subject. A variety of exponents can be obtained for ratio judgments of the same continuum. If nothing else, this leads one to question the wisdom of reporting a single exponent (or even several) for a stimulus continuum. We will now offer three lines of evidence to illustrate the extent of, and conditions leading to, individual variation in exponents.

The first line is the most direct. We can simply look at the variability of exponents determined for a group of subjects who judged a series of intensities under the same conditions. In one such study (Baird, Kreindler, and Jones, 1971), 80 subjects made magnitude estimates of line length; in another (unpublished), 80 different subjects gave estimates of length under comparable stimulus conditions. Individual power functions were fit to each subject's data, yielding 160 exponents. The frequency distribution of these exponents is shown in Fig. 6.1 (top). The mean exponent is .93 with a standard deviation of .11. (The region covered by one standard deviation below the mean is indicated on the graph.) Although the distribution is not too broad, the variability cannot be passed off as "experimental error." Exponents as far apart as .7 and 1.2 would suggest substantial differences in perceptual sensitivity.

The bottom graph in Fig. 6.1 presents analogous results for judgments of luminance with $N = 158$ subjects. Thirty of these subjects participated in an experiment previously reported (Feldman and Baird, 1971); the remaining individuals participated in experiments (unpublished) employing the same optical system and general procedure. The mean exponent is .34 with a standard deviation of .08 (as indicated on the graph). As with line length, the frequency distribution is fairly symmetrical around the mean, but

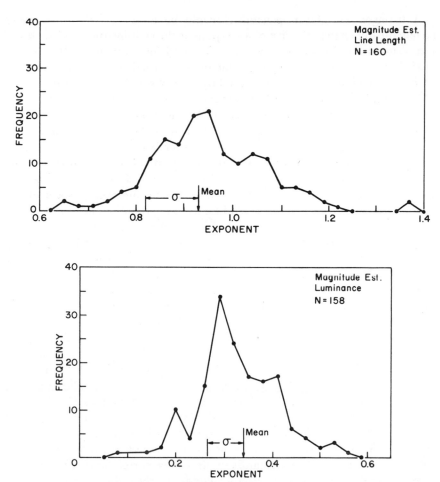

Figure 6.1.   Frequency distribution of exponents for individual subjects (top graph, line length; bottom graph, luminance). Data are from Baird et al., 1971; Feldman and Baird, 1971; and several unpublished experiments.

individual variation cannot be ignored. It should be noted that the power function fits were excellent for most of the individual functions. Such a pattern naturally raises the question as to the underlying cause of a particular exponent. Could such variability simply be attributed to individual differences in sensory mechanisms? Perhaps, but we should entertain the possibility that the exponent is influenced by cognitive (psychological) factors as well. For example, there could be clear individual differences in the use of the number scale in magnitude estimation.

A stronger test of this possibility would be to see whether one could systematically change the size of an exponent through instructions about the use of numbers. Such a test has been reported for estimates of line length (Baird et al., 1971). The cognitive factor was varied by providing subjects with anchor numbers assigned to the largest and smallest lines in the series. Different subjects received different numerical anchors for the largest stimulus; the smallest was always called 1. Seven groups were run with the identical stimulus series. The upper numerical anchors for the groups were either 29577, 956, 97, 31, 13, 5.5, or 3.1. After being told that the experimenter had a certain relation in mind between the line lengths and the number scale used for responses, the subject's task was to assign numbers to the lengths in accordance with this relation. The interesting aspect of the results was that power functions could be fit to the data for each of the seven groups, except that the fits were only fair for the groups receiving the two largest anchors. For the others, however, the exponent ranged from .31 to 1.71 (depending systematically upon the size of the anchor; that is, low anchors led to low exponents). Subjects generated *what looked to be* power functions, and hence different ratio scales, for the same stimulus continuum. Although the anchor may have induced somewhat different judgment strategies than are usually employed in magnitude estimation, the fact remains that a wide variety of exponents were obtained through rather minor changes in instructions. This clearly suggests that individual differences in the use of numbers could be responsible for the variety of exponents shown in Fig. 6.1. The literature abounds with similar examples that illustrate this point. Experiments by Jones and Marcus (1961), Rule (1966), and Ekman et al. (1968) all reveal that the same individual differences in exponents are present for different stimulus continua; that is, a significant positive correlation is found among individual exponents secured for different continua. It seems unlikely that these correlations are a result of some general "perceptual sensitivity" factor. Rather, they suggest a more psychological interpretation—subjects have unique ways for dealing with the number scale in estimating magnitudes.

Direct experimental evidence for the hypothesis that individual differences in subjects' use of the response scale are more salient than differences in their perceptual sensitivity is provided in a study by Rule and Curtis (1977). Their model assumes that the exponent is comprised of both stimulus (input) and response (output) factors. By having subjects judge differences between paired stimuli they were able to statistically separate the two components. Estimates of each were obtained for the continua of visual area and numerousness of dots on a screen. A correlation of .51 was found between the two output factors determined separately for area and numerousness when judged by the same subjects, whereas the correlation for the input factor was only .07.

Further support for the presence of enduring individual differences in the judgment of stimulus intensity is evident in experiments where the same subjects were tested on the same stimuli after periods of time ranging from a week to a year. In most instances, significant positive correlations were obtained among the exponents determined on different occasions for line length, area, and sound amplitude (Logue, 1976; Engeland and Dawson, 1974; Baird and Noma, 1975). One exception to this was a study by Teghtsoonian and Teghtsoonian (1971), who found positive but nonsignificant correlations for line-length judgments. However, their sample of subjects was small ($N = 10$), making it difficult to draw conclusions about the stability of exponents over long time intervals. In sum, the fact that one obtains a power function should not be taken to imply that sensory mechanisms are solely responsible. Both the power law and its exponent are under the control of instructions.

As a final example of the crucial role of psychological factors in the estimation of magnitude, consider the following experiment on visual size judgment in a more naturalistic setting. Suppose that under natural, full-cue conditions (say, in someone's back yard) a comparison rod is placed upright at a distance of 2 meters from a subject, and a series of standards, all the same physical size, are placed at different distances beyond the comparison. The subject adjusts the size of the variable to match each standard (for discussion of these tasks, see Baird, 1970a or Carlson, 1977). One way to conceptualize matters is this. The distance relations, the cues in the environment, and the instructions provide a complex criterion that the subject attempts to meet in adjusting the comparison. It is possible to have more than one criterion, so it is possible to obtain more than one type of size match. For example, if the instructions stress an "objective" match, the subject usually overestimates the size of the standard rod, and the amount of deviation from accuracy increases with distance from the comparison. Instructions to match "apparent" size usually result in a physical size match, whereas instructions to match "projective" or "angular" size at the eye yield adjustments that are less than physical equality. For our purposes, it is sufficient to know that size adjustments as a function of standard distance depend in a critical way upon instructions. A power function can always be fit to these data,[2] but the exponent varies with instructions. Therefore it is difficult to say which exponent (response scale) is correct for the size continuum.

Some people think that the "correct" scale is the one indicating a physical Euclidean match (size constancy). This belief rests upon a loose application of the theory of biological evolution and goes something like this. The

[2]The most useful (theoretical) way to plot these results, if one is after generality, is somewhat complicated and would take us too far afield. A theoretical visual angle ratio of comparison to standard targets is compared with a produced (adjusted) ratio (Baird, 1970a).

everyday physical world is Euclidean. Correct perception of physical size in this environment is adaptive. Since the ability of the perceptual system to maintain size constancy implies an adaptive response to the environment, the scale indicating a physical (Euclidean) match of size is the correct one. The slippery key to this argument is the definition of adaptive behavior. If size constancy is defined as the *true* or *best* state of nature, there are no grounds for quarrel or experiments. In fact, however, most scientists in this tradition would find it difficult to be explicit about what they mean by adaptive behavior without becoming hopelessly mired in tautologies. Of course, one can always say "*x*" is whatever I choose to call "*x*" and thereby stop all further discussion![3]

An alternative opinion is that one *cannot* decide on a single ratio scale to represent responses to size or any other continuum. The multiple functions are interesting in their own right, and the task is to devise models to explain this diversity. This is a difficulty that has barely been touched upon in the size constancy and space perception literature. Such an approach excludes references to evolution, adaptive behavior, and the like, on the basis that such concepts are operationally vague and theoretically misleading.

Finally, we should mention that several investigators have been forced to abandon the power law altogether when dealing with the data of individual subjects (Freides and Phillips, 1966; Luce and Mo, 1965; McGill, 1960). This certainly signals a serious problem with the formulation of Stevens functions based on aggregate data from groups of subjects. On the other hand, we are unlikely to see the demise of these descriptive functions until a more satisfactory explanation for their failures is suggested and experimentally verified. The only general theory of this type has been proposed (but not tested) by Baird (1975a,b). This approach is touched upon at a later point in the chapter.

Effects of Procedural Factors

One of the advantages of a good physical scale is its range of application. A ruler can be used to measure small and large objects in any sequential order,

---

[3]To quote an eminent operationist:

"When I use a word", Humpty Dumpty said,..., "It means just
   what I choose it to mean—neither more nor less".
"The question is", said Alice, "Whether you *can* make words
   mean so many different things".
"The question is", said Humpty Dumpty, "Which is to be
   master—that's all".

(Lewis Carroll, 1923, p. 124)

and the results are the same for measurements taken with any section of the scale. A one-meter rod will be recorded as such (within limits of random error) irrespective of the size and number of objects previously measured. If human response scales are to "enjoy" the status afforded physical scales, they also must be impervious to "minor" procedural changes. Admittedly, this is a matter of degree, since it would be unreasonable to expect the invariance of humans to match that of physical instruments, even under the most controlled circumstances. Nonetheless, we should be wary of any model of the person as a measuring instrument if "irrelevant" procedural factors lead to systematic or random variations in response scales.

The compelling evidence is that response scales depend on the context in which they are obtained. It is generally agreed that this is true for category estimation and related techniques that require the subject to partition the stimulus continuum into a fixed number of response bins. There is less agreement about the importance of context in determining ratio judgments. To some researchers, the effects here are of secondary interest and consequently are treated as a nuisance to be ignored, eliminated, or kept in check (Stevens, 1971; Marks, 1974). This position is justified by arguing that the primary business of psychophysics is to understand sensory processes, uncontaminated by procedural variables. But can pure sensory factors be sifted out by these methods? Many think not.

Two years after Stevens first proposed the power law, Engen and Levy (1955) showed that the exponents for brightness and weight depend on the position of a standard in the stimulus series. That is, an invariant S-R relationship was not found for the same stimulus continuum tested with a slightly different procedure. This means that the responses did not behave in the manner required by a ratio scale. Recall from Chapter 1 that multiplication by a constant is the only legitimate transformation for a ratio scale. That is, if

$$R = \lambda S^n \tag{6.1}$$

is the power function obtained with one standard, an admissible transformation of the R scale into R' would be

$$R \to R', \qquad R' = aR \tag{6.2}$$

where a is the multiplicative constant. Contrary to this picture Engen and Levy reported that the transformation took place in the exponent n; the responses did not obey a ratio scale. In fact, a power transformation of this sort implies a log-interval scale (Chapter 1; Krantz et al., 1971), which is defined as a scale restricted to the transformation

$$R \to R', \qquad R' = aR^m$$

$$\log R' = m \log R + \log a \qquad (6.3)$$

Equation 6.3 is in the same form as an interval scale, except that log values are being transformed. In any case, if Eq. 6.3 holds we do not have a ratio scale of the sort required by Stevens's law. In the present situation, both m and $\log a$ can vary while still maintaining the same scale. It is interesting to note that the difficulties encountered here by the power law parallel those faced by the log law when one attempts to explain the success of transitivity tests involving cross-modality matching (Chapter 5). In both instances the empirical data force us to relax the scale type requirements, thus resulting in a corresponding loss of explanatory power.

In subsequent studies by Engen and others, an array of procedural effects were uncovered with ratio methods, including the range of stimulus intensities, the position of the standard target in the series, the number assigned to the standard, and whether the response was a multiple or a fraction of the standard. The role of these and related variables has been thoroughly reviewed by Poulton (1968). Although their influence is not always pronounced, contextual effects exhibit a regularity that demands attention. Because models have not been proposed to account for the quantitative details (though see Helson, 1964), we will consider only the direction of such effects, and not their amounts. The major results are summarized in Table 6.1. In this table and in what follows, it is assumed that (1) a ratio method is used (usually, magnitude estimation), (2) the stimulus continuum is fixed, and (3) the power law holds.

Range. The exponent depends on the range of stimulus intensities. As the range of comparison stimuli increases, the exponent decreases somewhat (Poulton, 1968).

Table 6.1   Summary of procedural effects on exponents of the power function.[a]
For details, see text

Procedural Variables

	Range (S_c)		Position (S_{st})			(S_c)		Modulus (S_{st}) small		large	
	narrow	wide	low	med.	high	mult.	frac.	mult.	frac.	mult.	frac.
High Exponent	*			*		*		*			*
Low Exponent		*	*		*		*		*	*	

[a]S_c and S_{st} refer to comparison and standard, respectively. mult = multiplies; frac = fractions.

Position of the Standard. Consider a series of stimuli spanning a fixed range. When either of the end stimuli is designated as a standard, the exponent will be lower than when the standard is taken from the middle of the series. This effect is probably related to that of range, since a target in the middle of a series splits it into two subranges, each influencing matters toward a higher exponent (Engen and Ross, 1966).

Multiples vs. Fractions. Stimuli below the standard are judged as fractions (of the standard), while those above are multiples (Poulton, 1968). The size of the exponent depends partly on the location of the standard and partly on the number assigned to it (known as the modulus). In general, the exponent is higher for multiples than it is for fractions (Svenson and Åkesson, 1967; Poulton, 1968).

Modulus. It is not completely clear how the modulus (the number assigned to the standard) interacts with the stimulus range and the position of the standard. If a standard is fixed at the lower end of a series, increasing the size of the modulus tends to decrease the exponent (Wong, 1963). However, there is a problem here because the small moduli used in this study had only one significant digit (2, 4, and 6), whereas the larger moduli had more than one (e.g., 81, 182, 273). This difference may also affect the exponent.

When the standard is in the middle of the series, the effect of the modulus is asymmetrical in respect to multiples and fractions (Poulton, 1968). A small modulus will produce a high exponent for multiples and a low one for fractions. This may occur because of differences in the number of viable responses perceived by the subject. A small modulus does not leave much room for judging stimuli less intense than the standard, because of the zero point and because subjects are reluctant to respond with fractions. Theoretically, of course, the room is there. Ratios are being expressed, and they can be of any fractional size. At the same time, the subject may perceive a greater range of multiples, choose comparatively larger values for responses, and thus raise the exponent. The same line of reasoning can be applied to the situation where the modulus is a large number. Now the subject perceives a wide range of responses when judging stimuli less than the standard, but a more restricted range when judging multiples. Consequently, the exponent for fractions will be steeper than for multiples. Robinson (1976) has gone one step further by showing that the sample numbers used in the instructions for magnitude estimation can affect the exponent, and Macmillan et al. (1974) found different exponents depending upon whether a single standard was present (magnitude estimation) or absent (complete ratio estimation). These and other results viewed in this chapter have forced theorists to treat the exponent of the power function as a parameter with multiple determinants. At a minimum, both sensory (stimulus) and psychological (response) factors must be seen as responsible for the differences in exponents obtained under diverse experimental conditions. Such considerations are apparent in several models (for example, Curtis, Attneave, and Harrington, 1968; Baird, 1970c).

Sequence Effects

Recently, Ward (1972, 1973) investigated sequence effects in both category and magnitude estimation. In his procedure, the previous stimulus (on trial $N-1$) was considered the standard, with a modulus taken as the subject's response. The response to the stimulus on trial N was then a judgment of the ratio of that stimulus to the previous one. It was found that the response on trial N was assimilated toward the response on trial $N-1$. That is, if an intense stimulus were judged on trial $N-1$, the response on trial N would tend to be higher than if a weak stimulus were presented on trial $N-1$.

More recently, Jesteadt, Luce, and Green (1977) have shown that such sequence effects do not extend back over more than one trial. That is, a subject's response on trial $N-1$ is positively correlated with the response on trial N, but none of the earlier trials need be considered. This makes construction of a theory *much* easier. However, this simplification of the problem was offset somewhat by their additional finding that the degree of influence of the preceding stimulus (trial $N-1$) depends upon its intensity separation from the current stimulus (trial N). This was clear for 1000-Hz tones, judged by several ratio-estimation procedures. The correlations between the response on trial N and that on trial $N-1$ ranged from approximately .8, when the same intensity was repeated, to approximately .10 when stimulus separation was large.

These, then, are the major procedural effects associated with ratio methods. Although the power function can adequately describe the results for a *particular* set of conditions, the exponent changes in a manner more suggestive of human beings than of the permanence of physical instruments. In brief, it is not the scaling results that are controversial but their interpretation.

Number Bias

In early research with direct methods it was implicitly accepted that numbers were used according to the rules of arithmetic. The number scale was an unbiased standard against which all other continua could be matched. Over the past 20 years the validity of this assumption has been gradually eroded. The prevalent view nowadays is that people exhibit systematic biases in their use of numbers. Some of these biases (for example, the difference between the use of numbers in ratio and category estimation) can be derived from the fourfold way (Chapter 5), and hence they need not be discussed here. Other types of bias are more subtle.

It has been noted by many investigators that subjects give certain values much more frequently than others when generating or guessing numbers (Baird and Noma, 1975; Ross and Engen, 1959) or when judging physical intensities (Baird, Lewis, and Romer, 1970). Specifically, multiples of 1, 10, 100 and, to a lesser extent, multiples of 5, 50, and 500 are clearly preferred responses; whereas, numbers such as 17, 37.5, and 178 have a low frequency of occurrence.

MODEL OF NUMBER BIAS

Subjects' preferred numbers from 1 to 100 can be easily listed because there are not too many of them: 1, 2, 3, 4, 5, 6, 7, 8, 9, 10, 15, 20, 25, 30, 40, 50, 60, 70, 75, 80, 90, 100. All other numbers within this region (especially fractions) are emitted with very low frequency. A simple model can be proposed to explain this pattern (Noma and Baird, 1975). It turns out that these 22 values are the only ones created by the mathematical bases 10 and 5 when only one significant digit is allowed. An example of how this works is as follows. If B is the base, n is the integer exponent 0, 1, 2, etc., and k is the integer category (where k ranges from 1 to $B-1$), any preferred number N can be described by the exponential function

$$N = kB^n \tag{6.4}$$

The preferred numbers are summarized in Table 6.2. Multiplying the values of k (down the left margin) by the B^n values across the top produces the preferred numbers given in the table (decimal notation). For example, if $B=10$, $k=2$, and $n=3$, we have $N=2\times10^3=2000$; if $B=5$, $k=2$, and $n=3$, we have $N=2\times5^3=250$; and so forth. The reason we generate a restricted set of values with this model is that the exponent n can only be an integer. Note that the preferred numbers 15, 25, and 75 are produced by base 5 alone. The rest are produced by base 10 or by 10 and 5.

Since the spacing between preferred numbers is not constant throughout the scale, the effect of employing numbers in a judgment task will vary with stimulus and response magnitude. Higher numbers are separated by larger spacing. Obviously, such number bias should be considered in the discussion of scaling results. If the bias problem is restricted to the number domain, it can be avoided by employing cross-modality matching (Chapter 5). How-

Table 6.2   Preferred numbers N generated by base 10 and base 5, where $N = kB^n$. Entries are in decimal notation

k	10^3	10^2	10^1	10^0	5^3	5^2	5^1	5^0
1	1000	100	10	1	125	25	5	1
2	2000	200	20	2	250	50	10	2
3					375	75	15	3
4					500	100	20	4
⋮								
9	9000	900	90	9				

ever, the operation of similar biases in matching other continua such as lights, sounds, or length cannot be ruled out (Baird, 1975a,b; Banks, 1973). The empirical proof of such bias would have far-reaching implications for psychophysical theory.

CONCLUDING COMMENT

Nobody disputes the fact that direct methods lead to reliable psychophysical functions. Once the stimulus, procedure, and instructions are specified, we can derive an accurate prediction of the shape of the function. It is the interpretation that provokes controversy. It is now apparent that humans are not strictly analogous to a physical measuring instrument yielding invariant scale values at the ratio level. As Luce (1972) implies, the time has come to discard this view in favor of models more in keeping with the empirical results. Considering all the contextual effects mentioned in this chapter, one might conclude that direct scaling methods yield measures only at the ordinal level (Mashhour, 1965), but this is a rather extreme position.

One way out of this difficulty is to downplay the direct scaling methods and develop sensitivity indices that require less stringent assumptions (say ordinal or nominal) about the level of the response scale. This is the tack of investigators who think of perception within the framework of statistical decision theory or in terms of information theory. These types of models are discussed in later chapters.

An alternative solution is to expand the traditional conception of scaling to include more dimensions. Here the subject's task is no longer seen as the matching of values from two unidimensional scales, but rather as the mapping of a multidimensional stimulus into a multidimensional response space. The particular response may represent the subject's attempt to satisfy a criterion with many determinants, including procedural variables (see, for example Ross and DiLollo, 1968). The tools for multidimensional analyses and the psychological models implied by their use are treated in Chapter 10. Full treatments of more complicated alternatives are beyond the scope of this work. One recent theory stresses a common physiological basis (interarrival time of neural impulses) for mediating intensity perception (Luce and Green, 1972); another emphasizes the cognitive strategies of subjects (Baird, 1970b,c). These approaches will be briefly treated in Chapter 13.

REFERENCES

Baird, J. C. *Psychophysical Analysis of Visual Space*. London: Pergamon, 1970a.

Baird, J. C. "A cognitive theory of psychophysics: I. Information transmission, partitioning, and Weber's law." *Scandinavian Journal of Psychology*, 1970b, *11*, 35–46.

Baird, J. C. "A cognitive theory of psychophysics: II. Fechner's law and Stevens' law." *Scandinavian Journal of Psychology*, 1970c, *11*, 89–102.

Baird, J. C. "Psychophysical study of numbers: IV. Generalized preferred state theory." *Psychological Research*, 1975a, *38*, 175–187.

Baird, J. C. "Psychophysical study of numbers: V. Preferred state theory of matching functions." *Psychological Research*, 1975b, *38*, 189–207.

Baird, J. C., Kreindler, M. and Jones, K. "Generation of multiple ratio scales with a fixed stimulus attribute." *Perception & Psychophysics*, 1971, *9*, 399–403.

Baird, J. C., Lewis, C., and Romer, D. "Relative frequencies of numerical responses in ratio estimation." *Perception & Psychophysics*, 1970, *8*, 358–362.

Baird, J. C., and Noma, E. "Psychological study of numbers: I. Generation of numerical responses." *Psychological Research*, 1975, *37*, 281–297.

Banks, W. P. "A new psychophysical ratio scaling technique: Random production." *Bulletin of the Psychonomic Society*, 1973, *1*, 273–275.

Carlson, V. R. "Instructions and perceptual constancy judgments." In W. Epstein (Ed.), *Stability and Constancy in Visual Perception*. New York: Wiley, 1977, pp. 217–254.

Carroll, Lewis. *Through the Looking Glass and What Alice Found There*. New York: Macmillan, 1923.

Cliff, N. "Scaling." *Annual Review of Psychology*, 1973, *24*, 473–506.

Curtis, D. W., Attneave, F., and Harrington, T. C. "A test of a two-stage model of magnitude judgment." *Perception & Psychophysics*, 1968, *3*, 25–31.

Ekman, G. "Weber's law and related functions." *The Journal of Psychology*, 1959, *47*, 343–352.

Ekman, G., Hosman, B., Lindman, R., Ljungberg, L. and Åkesson, C. A. "Interindividual differences in scaling performance." *Perceptual and Motor Skills*, 1968, *26*, 815–823.

Engeland, W., and Dawson, W. E. "Individual differences in power functions for a 1-week intersession interval." *Perception & Psychophysics*, 1974, *15*, 349–352.

Engen, T., and Levy, N. "The influence of standards on psychophysical judgments." *Perceptual and Motor Skills*, 1955, *5*, 193–197.

Engen, T., and Ross, B. M. "Effect of reference number on magnitude estimation." *Perception & Psychophysics*, 1966, *1*, 74–76.

Fechner, G. T. *Elements of Psychophysics*, Vol. 1. Translated by H. E. Adler. New York: Holt, Rinehart and Winston, 1966.

Feldman, J., and Baird, J. C. "Magnitude estimation of multidimensional stimuli." *Perception & Psychophysics*, 1971, *10*, 418–422.

Freides, D., and Phillips, P. "Power law fits to magnitude estimates of groups and individuals." *Psychonomic Science*, 1966, *5*, 367–368.

Helson, H. *Adaption-Level Theory*. New York: Harper and Row, 1964.

Krantz, D. H., Luce, R. D., Suppes, P., and Tversky, A. *Foundations of Measurement*, Vol. 1. *Additive and Polynomial Representations*. New York: Academic, 1971.

Jesteadt, W., Luce, R. D., and Green, D. M. "Sequential effects in judgments of loudness." *Journal of Experimental Psychology: Human Perception and Performance*, 1977, *3*, 92–104.

Jones, F. N., and Marcus, M. J. "The subject effect in judgments of subjective magnitude." *Journal of Experimental Psychology*, 1961, *61*, 40–44.

Logue, A. W. "Individual differences in magnitude estimation of loudness." *Perception & Psychophysics*, 1976, *19*, 279–280.

Luce, R. D. "What sort of measurement is psychophysical measurement?" *American Psychologist*, 1972, *27*, 96–106.

Luce, R. D., and Green, D. M. "A neural timing theory for response times and the psychophysics of intensity." *Psychological Review*, 1972, *79*, 14–57.

Luce, R. D., and Mo, S. S. "Magnitude estimation of heaviness and loudness by individual subjects: A test of a probabilistic response theory." *British Journal of Mathematical and Statistical Psychology*, 1965, *18*, 159–174.

Macmillan, N. A., Moschetto, C. F., Bialostozky, F. M., and Engel, L. "Size judgment: The presence of a standard increases the exponent of the power law." *Perception & Psychophysics*, 1974, *16*, 340–346.

Marks, L. E. *Sensory Processes: The New Psychophysics*. New York: Academic, 1974.

Mashhour, M. "Note on the validity of the power law." *Scandinavian Journal of Psychology*, 1965, *6*, 220–224.

McGill, W. "The slope of the loudness function. A puzzle." In H. Gulliksen and S. Messick (Eds.), *Psychological Scaling: Theory and Applications*. New York: Wiley, 1960, pp. 67–81.

Noma, E., and Baird, J. C. "Psychophysical study of numbers: II. Theoretical models of number generation." *Psychological Research*, 1975, *38*, 81–95.

Poulton, E. C. "The new psychophysics: Six models for magnitude estimation." *Psychological Bulletin*, 1968, *69*, 1–19.

Robinson, G. H. "Biasing power law exponents by magnitude estimation instructions." *Perception & Psychophysics*, 1976, *19*, 80–84.

Ross, B. M., and Engen, T. "Effects of round number preferences in a guessing task." *Journal of Experimental Psychology*, 1959, *58*, 462–468.

Ross, J., and DiLollo, V. "A vector model for psychophysical judgment." *Journal of Experimental Psychology*, 1968, *77*, No. 3, Pt. 2.

Rule, S. J. "Subject differences in exponents of psychophysical power functions." *Perceptual and Motor Skills*, 1966, *23*, 1125–1126.

Rule, S. J. and Curtis, D. W. "Subject differences in input and output transformations from magnitude estimation of differences." *Acta Psychologica*, 1977, *41*, 61–65.

Stevens, S. S. (Ed.). "Mathematics, measurement, and psychophysics." *Handbook of Experimental Psychology*. New York: Wiley, 1951, pp. 1–41.

Stevens, S. S. "To honor Fechner and repeal his law." *Science*, 1961, *133*, 80–86.

Stevens, S. S. "A metric for the social consensus." *Science*, 1966, *151*, 530–541.

Stevens, S. S. "Issues in psychophysical measurement." *Psychological Review*, 1971, *78*, 426–450.

Stevens, S. S., and Galanter, E. H. "Ratio scales and category scales for a dozen perceptual continua." *Journal of Experimental Psychology*, 1957, *54*, 377–411.

Svenson, O., and Åkesson, C. A. "A further note on fractional and multiple estimates in ratio scaling." *Report from the Psychological Laboratory, University of Stockholm*, 1967, No. 224.

Teghtsoonian, M., and Teghtsoonian, R. "How repeatable are Stevens's power law exponents for individual subjects?" *Perception & Psychophysics*, 1971, *10*, 147–149.

Ward, L. M. "Category judgments of loudnesses in the absence of an experimenter-induced identification function." *Journal of Experimental Psychology*, 1972, *94*, 179–184.

Ward, L. M. "Repeated magnitude estimations with a variable standard: Sequential effects and other properties." *Perception & Psychophysics*, 1973, *13*, 193–200.

Wong, R. "Effect of the modulus on estimates of magnitude of linear extent." *American Journal of Psychology*, 1963, *76*, 511–512.

CHAPTER

$$\boxed{7}$$

THURSTONIAN SCALING

Since the time of Fechner, psychophysics has developed along two major lines. One culminates in the direct scaling approach discussed in the last two chapters. The second branch, which focuses on perceptual variability as an index of resolving power or stimulus sensitivity, was treated in Chapter 3 and will be explored further in this and the succeeding two chapters.

The key person in this story is L. L. Thurstone (1887–1955), who was born in the same year that Fechner died. In his Dartmouth lecture as retiring president of the Psychometric Society, Thurstone expressed the intent "to encourage the development of psychology as a quantitative rational science" (1937, p. 228). His brilliant efforts in this regard helped lay the foundations for much of modern psychophysics, factor analysis, and multidimensional scaling.We will concentrate here on Thurstone's original contributions to scaling and psychophysics. The accumulated 50-year impact of Thurstone's ideas on modern psychophysical research is summarized in R. Duncan Luce's 1977 presidential address to the Psychometric Society. Some of this material will be covered in later chapters.

Thurstone (1927a,b,c, 1959) extended Fechner's classical approach by devising methods for finding psychological scale values for complex stimuli even if corresponding physical measurements were unknown. Specifically, he was interested in obtaining scale values for such items as excellence of handwriting, seriousness of crimes, and preference for nationalities. None of these concepts have obvious physical correlates, in contrast to stimuli such as light intensity, line length, and sound level. Nevertheless, one would hope that these complex stimuli could still be ordered as points along a continuum. Because both Thurstone and his students were more interested in scaling complex attitudes than in understanding sensory processes, psychophysics was reformulated to handle a wider spectrum of stimuli. The primary limitation of this approach is its restriction to the generation of values along a unidimensional continuum (problems caused by this restriction will be discussed in succeeding chapters). Despite this shortcoming, the approach has been relatively successful in many areas of psychology.

THE PSYCHOLOGICAL THEORY

The Thurstonian approach postulates a psychological scale onto which stimuli are mapped. The nature of this scale is left unspecified: it may be psychic, physiological, or both (Thurstone, 1927a). In this way we sidestep the mind-body controversy without going so far as to define a response scale. Remember, the operationist movement was barely off the ground in 1927 and had yet to exert an influence on psychology (Chapter 5). In effect, Thurstone asks only that a scale be granted. If we want to push further and identify its "true" composition, we are moving beyond Thurstone's concerns.

One way to conceptualize matters is this. Each time a stimulus is presented it is presumed to be represented by a point along the psychological scale. The location of the point is determined by an unknown *discriminal process* "by which the organism identifies, distinguishes, discriminates, or reacts to stimuli" (1927a, p. 368). Because of the uncertain nature of a person's perceptual state due to a multitude of factors (motivational, physiological, extrasensory, mystical, or whatever), the same stimulus does not always excite the same discriminal process.[1] It is assumed, moreover, that repeated occurrences of a stimulus produce a distribution (called a *discriminal dispersion*) of such processes along the psychological scale. A normal distribution is usually assumed since many different factors probably contribute to the inherent noise in the system. Reapplying the rationale used in the classical psychophysical measurement of jnd's (Chapter 3), these random events will tend to describe a normal distribution around a mean. Therefore

---

[1]Thurstone's terminology may be confusing to readers familiar with the language of information processing. In Thurstone's theory, *each* point on the psychological scale is associated with a *single* discriminal process (different from all others).

the mean is associated with the scale value of the stimulus, and the standard deviation is interpreted as the unit of measurement along the internal scale.

Up to this point the theory is conceptually indistinguishable from that of classical psychophysics (Chapter 3, Fig. 3.3). Moreover, as in the traditional approach, a person compares stimuli and the experimenter notes the percent of time one stimulus is perceived, preferred, or judged to be greater than another. Here the similarity between the two approaches pretty much ends. For example, in the classical method of constant stimuli, an internal distribution associated with a standard is probed by comparisons that are considered to act as cutoffs along the stimulus continuum. The resulting psychometric function (probability "greater than" plotted against comparison intensity, see Fig. 3.5) is then used to compute the difference limen or absolute threshold. One resultant stimulus measure (jnd) can be examined for a variety of standard intensities to obtain a Weber function. As far as the internal scale is concerned, we may *define* steps corresponding to each stimulus jnd. Integration of defined internal jnd's and empirical stimulus jnd's then produces the Fechner functions discussed in Chapter 4.

In Thurstone's theory, on the other hand, all the action takes place along a hypothetical psychological continuum, since no physical measures of the stimulus are obtained. Because there is no way to determine a stimulus jnd, one could view this analysis as defining equal stimulus jnd's and computing the corresponding size of the internal jnd's. For convenience, we represent each stimulus on the continuum by *the single* discriminal process corresponding to the mean of its discriminal dispersion. By using the standard deviations of the discriminal dispersions as units of measure, scale values are then established. Thus the means of the discriminal dispersions are the scale values measured on an interval scale in units of standard deviation. Pairs of stimuli are presented for judgment to obtain an empirical estimate of the distance along the psychological scale separating each stimulus from every other one.

In summary, then, four factors are needed to determine scale values. They are the means and standard deviations of the discriminal dispersions of a standard and a comparison stimulus. The quantitative model tells us how to recover scale values from the percent of time each stimulus is preferred, chosen, or judged to be greater than each other in a series.

Now let us become more specific by considering the theoretical situation shown in Fig. 7.1. External stimuli j and k are associated on the psychological scale with their respective normal discriminal dispersions with means u_j and u_k and standard deviations σ_j and σ_k. In this example, $\sigma_j = \sigma_k$, but they need not be equal. The hypothetical probability density of a discriminal process is represented as the vertical height.

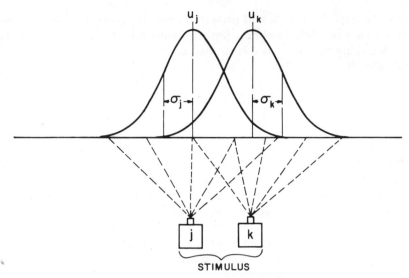

Figure 7.1. Discriminal dispersions for stimuli j and k. The means of the hypothetical distributions are u_j and u_k with standard deviations $\sigma_j = \sigma_k$. Intensity increases to the right along the x axis (psychological continuum).

Suppose we now present the stimulus pair (j,k) to a person on a large number of occasions. On each presentation a single discriminal process (one point along the psychological continuum) is excited from *each* distribution and the two are compared. On those occasions when the process associated with k is greater than the process for j the person will judge k to be greater than (or preferred to) j, and vice versa. Because the two distributions are normal, and therefore no value for a process is impossible (it may, however, be very, very improbable), the two distributions will overlap, and theoretically a stimulus will not be judged greater than another on 100% of the trials. For example, in Fig. 7.1, it is clear that k will be judged greater than j on most occasions since most of the distribution for k has higher values than the one for j. However, assuming random sampling from each distribution, once in a while there will be a reversal. On this occasion, j would be judged greater than k. In the analysis of stimulus pairs, we do not directly measure the variance and means of individual discriminal dispersions. Instead, we are actually receiving information on the distribution generated by all possible pairs of processes selected from the two discriminal dispersions. Fortunately, with the appropriate assumptions, which we discuss shortly, information on the individual dispersions is directly translated into information on the distribution of differences, and vice versa. That is really all there is to the theory. An experimenter would present all possible pairs of N stimuli on a large number of trials to obtain representative samples from the distributions. Assuming the theory is correct, we can recover meaningful scale values for all stimuli.

DATA ANALYSIS

The analysis starts with data collected on pairs of stimuli. We wish to estimate the distances between stimuli and use this information to locate the stimuli relative to each other along the unidimensional psychological scale. Each pair is associated with a *single* hypothetical distribution of differences generated by pairing all possible discriminal processes in j with all discriminal processes in k. Information about this distribution of differences accumulates over many presentations of the particular stimulus pair. The model says that the subject uses the differences in the magnitude of discriminal processes to make a decision concerning the dominance of one stimulus over another.

Statistics tells us that the difference between the means of two normal distributions is equal to the mean of their differences. Therefore, to find the differences in scale values for two stimuli (k and j), find the mean of their distribution of differences. This mean can be measured (arbitrarily) from a point representing those cases where the difference between two discriminal processes (one for each stimulus) is 0. For convenience we locate the zero point at the mean discriminal process for the stimulus j. This transformation may be done by subtracting the original mean u_j from all discriminal processes in both distributions. The mean of the discriminal dispersion of j is now $u_j - u_j = 0$, and the mean of the discriminal dispersion of k is now $u_k - u_j$. Shifting all discriminal processes a fixed amount is tantamount to admitting we have an interval scale, as discussed in Chapter 1. The zero point on the scale has no special meaning, so we need not be troubled that the ratios of scale values are not preserved by this transformation.

Let us now digress a moment to gain an intuitive understanding of why this value ($u_k - u_j$) is also the mean of the differences between all possible discriminal dispersions. Recall that the new distribution was created by taking differences between pairs of discriminal processes, one from each of the discriminal dispersions. Pick a discriminal process with value r from distribution k and calculate the mean difference between r and all discriminal processes in j. (It may help to refer to Fig. 7.1.) This average, however, is still r, since the discriminal dispersion of j is symmetric around zero (because we place it there). That is, for every discriminal process with value x there is one with value $-x$ with the same probability density defined by the discriminal dispersion of j. So their effects cancel. Repeating this procedure for all discriminal processes in k produces a symmetric distribution around $u_k - u_j$. Therefore, the mean of the difference of the discriminal dispersions is $u_k - u_j$.

A hypothetical distribution of differences is shown in Fig. 7.2, with a mean $u_k - u_j$ and a standard deviation σ_{kj} that depends on the standard deviations of the original distributions (j and k) in a manner we will get to later. Next, define d_i as an arbitrary discriminal process for stimulus i. The shaded area in the figure indicates the proportion of times the difference $d_k - d_j$ was positive, and the unshaded area indicates the proportion of times that $d_k - d_j$ was negative. As we saw in Chapter 3, probabilities corresponding to areas under the normal curve can be converted to z scores that mark off distances in standard deviation units. By converting the probability with which $k > j$ (shaded area) into a z score, we obtain a standardized measure of the difference between the discriminal processes ($u_k - u_j$). Therefore,

$$z_{kj} = \frac{u_k - u_j}{\sigma_{kj}} \tag{7.1a}$$

If we further assume that σ_{kj} is the same for all stimulus pairs, it can arbitrarily be set equal to 1. (This could be likened to establishing a unit of measure for an interval scale.) Therefore,

$$u_k - u_j = z_{kj} \tag{7.1b}$$

In this instance, u_k and u_j are the scale values for stimuli k and j, but at this point all we have is the difference between them. In fact, we have a difference (z) for each stimulus paired with every other stimulus.

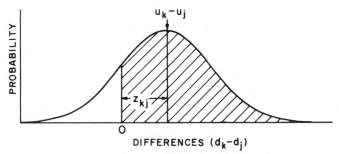

Figure 7.2. Hypothetical normal distribution of differences between discriminal processes ($d_k - d_j$). Data obtained by pairing stimuli j and k on many occasions.

To secure a scale value for a stimulus, we average the distances (z) across all pairs involving that stimulus. This approach locates all stimuli along the psychological scale; that is, each stimulus is assigned a single value u_j. (Such an averaging procedure is also a least squares solution, cf. Torgerson, 1958, p. 170.)

So far, the discussion has centered on pure theory. To summarize, if the subject bases his or her judgment of stimulus dominance upon the difference between two internal discriminal processes, then information on a distribution of such differences accumulates over a large number of trials (although the subject need not be aware of this). The probability with which one stimulus is judged to dominate another can then be converted into an estimate of the mean of this distribution of differences and consequently a measure of the distance separating the two along the psychological scale. The only evidence the experimenter has of these processes is the frequency with which one stimulus is said to dominate another in a specific experiment. But this is enough evidence to infer differences in scale values, as we have seen. Therefore, the scaling procedure starts with a matrix of all stimulus pairs containing the probability with which one stimulus is picked over (dominates) another, and uses these probabilities to measure distances (z scores). The distances are then averaged to compute scale values for each stimulus.

THE LAW OF COMPARATIVE JUDGMENT

Determination of differences between scale values in this manner is called Thurstone's Case V model (Thurstone, 1927b). As the reader may have guessed, other cases exist, but they are less widely employed because of computational difficulties. Specifically, Case V assumes that one can ignore the standard deviations associated with individual stimuli because they are constant and their discriminal processes are uncorrelated. That is, knowing the occurrence of a discriminal process from one distribution would not help us predict the discriminal process from another. High values from one distribution do not imply high values from the other, and so forth. The remaining cases relax these assumptions.

If we are unwilling to make the Case V assumptions, we must adjust the scale values obtained for each stimulus pair by considering the standard deviation of their differences as well as their mean difference (Fig. 7.2). The standard deviation of the differences between two normal distributions is

$$\sigma_{kj} = \sqrt{\sigma_j^2 + \sigma_k^2 - 2r_{kj}\sigma_j\sigma_k} \qquad (7.2)$$

where r_{kj} is the correlation coefficient (when the discriminal processes are uncorrelated, $r_{kj} = 0$). Rearranging Eq. 7.1a gives us

$$u_k - u_j = z_{kj}\sigma_{kj} \tag{7.3}$$

Substituting from Eq. 7.2 into 7.3, we obtain Thurstone's complete *law of comparative judgment*:

$$u_k - u_j = z_{kj}\sqrt{\sigma_k^2 + \sigma_j^2 - r_{kj}\sigma_j\sigma_k} \tag{7.4}$$

An experimental test of the complete law of comparative judgment has not been conducted because of the problems encountered in determining values for the unknowns σ_j, σ_k, and r_{kj}. Simplifying assumptions are usually made to reduce these difficulties (for example, in Case V, $r_{kj} = 0$ and $\sigma_j = \sigma_k$), and in fact Thurstone himself placed varying restrictions on the unknowns and came up with five different cases. Such variations are not treated here because they are peripheral to understanding the basic model (for more details, see Torgerson, 1958).

It would be possible to test the complete law of comparative judgment with numbers representing discriminal processes whose distributions and correlations could be determined exactly (as in Weissmann, Hollingsworth, and Baird, 1975). In the next chapter we will consider the theory of signal detectability, the most famous modern extension of Thurstonian scaling. The empirical tests appropriate for that theory could also be modified to test some of Thurstone's complex cases. Paradoxically, the theory of signal detectability was originally taken from engineering and statistical decision theory, and only later was the connection with Thurstone made perfectly clear. The close relationship between the law of comparative judgment and modern approaches is more apparent in Chapter 9, where we return to further adventures of Case V in the realm of decision theory.

A WORKED EXAMPLE

Now let us turn to an example of how Thurstone's Case V can be applied. Suppose we wish to scale a set of town facilities (for example, house, school, hospital, shopping center, factory) in terms of their relative importance in an ideal town. Each pair of facilities is presented to a group of subjects (individually tested) who have to indicate the dominant (most important) facility of the pair. A matrix is created of probabilities $p(j,k)$ from the group data, with each cell in the matrix corresponding to a pair of facilities. For each probability a z score is computed, and averaging techniques are employed to secure scale values for each facility located along an importance scale.

For the present illustration, only the five facilities just mentioned will be used. In point of fact, data were collected from only one subject, who indicated the *percent* dominance of one facility over the other in each pair. This percent was then treated as a probability in the computation of scale values.

This is done as follows. The matrix of assigned probabilities is organized as Table 7.1, and each entry is converted to a z score, which appears in the corresponding cell of Table 7.2. These z scores represent the psychological distances between a facility and every other facility. Given this set of distances, the problem now becomes one of spacing the facilities along a dimension so the obtained distances between facilities equals the z score distances; but unless we have perfect data, this cannot be done directly. The reason can be illustrated as follows. Suppose we cut strings to match the lengths indicated by the distances. Next tie the end of each string to its appropriate facility. Since each facility is tied to each other (separated by the lengths of the individual strings), its location along a straight line must satisfy $N-1$ distances where N is the total number of stimuli. In general, this will be impossible, and so some of the strings will have to be slackened, stretched, or somehow distorted in order to achieve the goal of a linear ordering. These unesthetic procedures are avoided by computing an average of all the distances between a stimulus and every other one, and then calling this average the scale value (position on the line).

The obtained averages (means) for the town facilities in our example are shown in the second to last column of Table 7.2. The priorities can be directly inferred from the resulting ordering and spacing of the facilities. Moreover, because we have an interval scale, adding a constant to each value leaves the scale intact. This has been done in the last column to set the least preferred facility at zero. A picture of the final linear ordering is shown in Fig. 7.3, which seems to represent the view of a hardened academic.

Table 7.1. Dominance matrix of priorities (probability that row facility dominates column facility)

Apartment	School	Hospital	House	Apartment	Factory
School	—	.60	.65	.75	.85
Hospital	.40	—	.60	.65	.65
House	.35	.40	—	.70	.70
Apartment	.25	.35	.30	—	.60
Factory	.15	.35	.30	.40	—

Table 7.2   Dominance matrix of *z* scores (values based on probabilities in Table 7.1

Apartment	School	Hospital	House	Apartment	Factory	Total	Mean	Adjusted Scale[a]
School	0	.25	.39	.67	1.04	2.35	.47	.91
Hospital	−.25	0	.25	.39	.39	.78	.16	.60
House	−.39	−.25	0	.52	.52	.40	.08	.52
Apartment	−.67	−.39	−.52	0	.25	−1.33	−.27	.17
Factory	−1.04	−.39	−.52	−.25	0	−2.20	−.44	0

[a]Mean +.44, to set least preferred facility at 0.

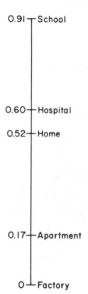

0.91 ─ School

0.60 ─ Hospital

0.52 ─ Home

0.17 ─ Apartment

0 ─ Factory

Figure 7.3. Scale values for the importance of town facilities. Data based on the application of Thurstone's Case V to the dominance matrices in Tables 7.1 and 7.2.

A BRIEF LOOK BACK

Through these seven chapters we have encountered a variety of scales that have been important in the historical development of psychophysics. The three most frequently discussed are the stimulus, response, and sensation (psychological) scales. In addition, a number of functions have been proposed to represent the theoretical transformation from one scale to another. The major candidates are Weber functions, Fechner functions, and Stevens functions; the law of comparative judgment merely describes scale values along a single psychological continuum. Thurstone did not attempt to relate this scale to either a stimulus or response scale determined by alternative measurement procedures. Nonetheless, he was well aware that such departure from traditional routes separated his approach from the one taken by his predecessors. In fact, in an early article (1927d), he contrasted the assumptions and formulation of the law of comparative judgment with Weber's law and Fechner's law.

The purpose of Thurstone's effort in this regard can now be extended to include other types of Weber and Fechner functions as well as Stevens functions. This is done in Table 7.3.

To recap the definition of these types:

1. *Weber functions* relate the stimulus jnd and the stimulus intensity at which it is measured.

2. *Fechner functions* relate the sensation or psychological scale (theoretically derived) and the stimulus scale.

3. *Stevens functions* relate observable response scales to stimulus scales.

4. *The law of comparative judgment* relates psychological scale values for different stimuli whose physical properties are of no consequence to the formal representation. That is, Thurstone's scales are not linked with any other types.

In Table 7.3 we have summarized these facts by showing the relevance ($+$) or nonrelevance ($-$) of each of the three general scales to each of the four relations. Consideration of these entries helps us to categorize the similarities and differences among the major psychophysical principles discussed so far.

Table 7.3   Relevance ($+$) or nonrelevance ($-$) of different scales for the statement of psychophysical functions and the law of comparative judgment (LCJ)

	Functions			
Scale	Weber	Fechner	Stevens	Thurstone (LCJ)
Stimulus	$+$	$+$	$+$	$-$
Response	$-$	$-$	$+$	$-$
Sensation (psychological)	$-$	$+$	$-$	$+$

REFERENCES

Luce, R. D. "Thurstone's discriminal process fifty years later." *Psychometrika*, 1977, 42, 461-489.

Thurstone, L. L. "Psychophysical analysis." *American Journal of Psychology*, 1927a, *38*, 368–389.

Thurstone, L. L. "A law of comparative judgment." *Psychological Review*, 1927b, *34*, 273–286.

Thurstone, L. L. "The method of paired comparisons for social values." *Journal of Abnormal and Social Psychology*, 1927c, *21*, 384–400.

Thurstone, L. L. "Three psychophysical laws." *Psychological Review*, 1927d, *34*, 424–432.

Thurstone, L. L. "Psychology as a quantitative rational science." *Science*, 1937, *85*, 228–232.

Thurstone, L. L. *The Measurement of Values*. Chicago: University of Chicago Press, 1959.

Torgerson, W. S. *Theory and Methods of Scaling*. New York: Wiley, 1958.

Weissmann, W. M., Hollingsworth, S. R., and Baird, J. C. "Psychophysical study of numbers. III. Methodological applications." *Psychological Research*, 1975, *38*, 97–115.

CHAPTER

$$\boxed{8}$$

THEORY OF SIGNAL DETECTABILITY

The theory of signal detectability (TSD) can be viewed as a natural outgrowth of classical psychophysics and Thurstonian scaling. Its conceptual innovation was to consider the effects of cognitive factors—such as a subject's expectations and desire to acquire wealth—in the analysis of judgments. For the first time in psychophysics, a judgment was seen as the end product of two mechanisms, one sensory and one cognitive. The early development of analyses for such two-stage systems was transplanted to psychology from engineering and statistical decision theory (Green and Swets, 1966; Swets, 1973; Tanner and Swets, 1954). It seems that only later did the founders of TSD fully realize the formal connection between what they were doing in the 1950s and what L. L. Thurstone had done in the 1920s.

TSD is similar to classical and Thurstonian models in that a single stimulus is usually assumed to evoke a normal distribution of internal events. It also assumes, as did Thurstone, that stimuli give rise to overlapping internal distributions, which form the basis for decisions concerning relative magnitude. Moreover, due to its wide applicability in sensory psychology, TSD has rekindled interest in classical (pre-1927) psychophysics.

TSD differs from previous approaches by emphasizing cognitive variables that act independently of the subject's sensory ability to distinguish stimuli. This is the most important aspect of the theory. The measure of *sensory discrimination* (resolving power) obtained is presumably uncontaminated by a subject's *response* (cognitive) *bias*.

An example of response bias might be this. Suppose the method of adjustment is employed to secure a jnd for sound intensity. On a number of trials a subject adjusts a comparison until it "equals" a standard. The size of the resulting jnd will depend on the subject's understanding of the word "equal" and the importance attached to fine-tuned sensory discrimination. For instance, one person may hold a loose criterion, so that a comparison stimulus anywhere near the standard is considered equal, whereas another person is more careful and responds "equal" within a narrower range of intensities around the standard. The jnd in the first case will be larger than in the second, even if the two subjects' sensory abilities are identical. Classical analyses are unable to establish this fact; TSD treats the matter by providing independent measures of sensory discrimination and response bias. Two hypothetical examples will introduce the spirit of the theory and its quantitative model.

AN ANECDOTAL EXAMPLE

You are listening to your stereo and think the phone is ringing.[1] TSD uses the followng terminology to describe this situation. You must distinguish a weak *signal* (phone ringing) from a background *noise* (stereo playing). Someone in the room asks you to decide "yes" (phone is ringing) or "no" (phone is not ringing). The response "maybe" is not allowed. There are four possible outcomes. If you say "yes" and are correct you have scored a *hit*. If you say "yes" and are incorrect, it was a *false alarm*. A correct "no" response is called a *correct rejection*; an incorrect "no" is a *miss*. In any case, your friend checks the phone and reports back to you about the actual state of the world. The particular response you make depends upon a number of factors.

1. *Signal-to-noise ratio*. If the stereo is turned way up (say, the walls are vibrating) it will be more difficult to detect the phone ringing (signal) than if the music (noise) is barely audible. This facility to distinguish signal from background noise depends on sensory (physiological) processes, that is, on the sensitivity of your auditory system.

2. *Expectations*. If you are expecting a call, it is more probable that you will say "yes" than if a call is unlikely. For example, for most people a call during the day is more likely than one at three in the morning (excluding irate neighbors). This internal coding of signal probability has nothing to do with sensory capacity. It is purely a cognitive process.

3. *Motivation*. Your answer will also depend on the relative importance and costs associated with each of the possible outcomes. You will be more

[1]We thank Nanci Zimble for suggesting this example.

inclined to say "yes" if a call is expected from a university official concerning your job application than if you expect to hear from a neighbor who has been selling raffle tickets on a perpetual motion machine. Also, if the cost of going to the phone is great (an exciting part of the music will be missed), you might be inclined to say "no," whereas if you have only one chance to receive a call from a friend (because he or she is leaving town), you might well say "yes" at the slightest provocation.

TSD specifies one way that signal strength, expectations, costs, and rewards might influence such binary decisions. We now introduce another example to help define terms more precisely.

A LABORATORY EXAMPLE

An ecology-minded government (say, on Jupiter) hires an unemployed local psychologist to determine the sensitivity of the citizenry to polluted air. Normal air is called noise (n). The signal (s) is air bottled in the streets of Jupiter's busiest city. The study is conducted in the laboratory, enabling the experimenter to randomly introduce puffs of polluted or normal air into a small enclosure that comfortably houses a Jovian's nose.

The experimenter decides to present the signal on 50% of the trials and the noise on 50% of the trials. Therefore, the subject is dutifully told that the probability of signal (pollution) is $p(s) = .5$ and the probability of noise (normal air) is $p(n) = .5$. It is assumed that this information is stored accurately in the subject's memory.

The experimenter also uses a *payoff matrix* to motivate the subject and influence decisions. The Jovian is told that a 10-unit reward will be issued for a hit: saying "yes, signal" when indeed the signal was present. The response "yes, signal" is represented by Y, and the outcome or value of a hit is defined as O_{Ys}. Similarly, the outcome of correct rejection (saying "no" to noise) is specified as $O_{Nn} = 10$, where N is the response "no, noise." Costs are also attached to incorrect responses. The subject is told that the cost of a false-alarm outcome (saying "yes" to noise) is $O_{Yn} = -5$ units and the cost of a miss (saying "no" to signal) is $O_{Ns} = -5$. These costs are the amounts to be *deducted from* the subject's existing wealth. The payoff matrix thus arrived at is shown in Fig. 8.1. Each of the four possible outcomes leads to an unambiguous monetary result that is known to the subject beforehand. The payoff matrix and stimulus probabilities are stored in memory for later use. The experiment proper now proceeds in two phases.

The first phase familiarizes the subject with the task and makes sure the payoff matrix and the signal and noise probabilities are known. This phase

Response

	Yes (Y)	No (N)
Signal (s)	$O_{Y_s} = 10$	$O_{N_s} = -5$
Noise (n)	$O_{Y_n} = -5$	$O_{N_n} = 10$

Stimulus

Figure 8.1. Hypothetical payoff matrix for Jupiter example. (O_{Y_s} = value of a hit, O_{N_n} = value of a correct rejection, O_{Y_n} = cost of a false alarm, O_{N_s} = cost of a miss.)

consists, say, of 100 trials on which the experimenter introduces a puff of signal or noise into the nose holder, and the Jovian responds "yes" or "no." The experimenter then announces "right" or "wrong" and the consequences (for example, "Right, it was a signal. You win 10 units of Earth yummies"). Phase 2 is identical to phase 1 except that we are now dealing with a "prepared" subject whose behavior in the task is recorded for further analysis.

THE TSD MODEL

TSD describes the conditions under which the prepared subject answers "yes" or "no." The theory assumes that on each trial the signal (plus noise)[2] or noise (alone) produces some internal event x, which is called the *evidence variable*. Following both Fechner and Thurstone, it is believed that the noise and signal generators are imperfect, as is the sensory system. Hence, over a long series of trials the noise and the signal each lead to their own normal distribution of the evidence variable. These two hypothetical distributions are shown in Fig. 8.2, which is structurally the same as Thurstone's model (Fig. 7.1, Chapter 7). The noise has a mean u_n and a standard deviation σ_n, and the signal has mean u_s and a standard deviation σ_s. We assume that $u_s = u_n + k$ but that $\sigma_s = \sigma_n$. That is, the signal and noise distributions are identical, except for displacement by an amount k along the evidence axis. One thing to bear in mind is that on any given trial either the noise is presented alone or the signal (superimposed on the noise) is presented alone. The subject is never asked to compare one stimulus with another as in the classical methods of adjustment, limits, and constant stimuli or as in

[2]When the term "signal" is used alone it refers to signal superimposed on background noise. In many experiments, external noise is purposely introduced to avoid the technical difficulties involved in producing and controlling very weak stimuli.

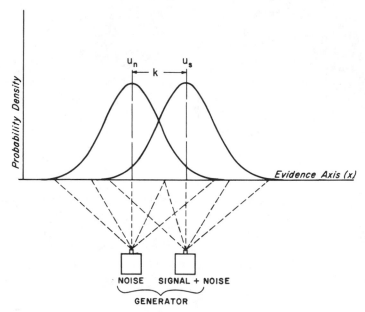

Figure 8.2. Hypothetical probability distributions produced by noise and signal+noise. The mean of the signal+noise distribution (u_s) is equal to the mean of noise (u_n) plus a constant k. The two distributions have the same standard deviation.

Thurstone's pair-comparison technique. That is to say, the two distributions in Fig. 8.2 are depicted together for convenience; just one is appropriate to describe the parent stimulus distribution on a single trial. A related procedure, called the two-alternative forced-choice design, will be described later in the chapter. It is more similar to the classical methods.

The physiological basis of the evidence axis is unimportant to the model. However, it sometimes helps in conceptualizing matters if it is thought to represent amount of neuronal firing. Then, looking at either distribution, we interpret as follows: Occasionally the external stimulus (noise or signal) leads to relatively small or relatively large amounts of neuronal firing (the two tails of the normal curve), but most trials lead to intermediate levels of activity. The overlapping nature of the two distributions implies that the same amount of neuronal firing (same x) can be obtained from presentation of either the signal or the noise. In fact, because the normal distribution extends from minus infinity to plus infinity, there is always a nonzero (but sometimes tiny) probability density associated with a given x for both the signal and the noise curves. The importance of this fact will become clear in a moment. For now it is sufficient to realize that this probability is different from the probability of signal or noise presentation $[p(s),p(n)]$. The latter refer only to the probability of a signal or noise trial—that is, which stimulus generator is turned on. One can think of the density functions as distributions of neuronal firings over many occasions, conditional upon activation of the stimulus generators in Fig. 8.2.

Measure of Sensitivity, d'

According to TSD, the separation of the signal and noise along the evidence axis is an indication of the level of sensory discrimination possible. The term "sensitivity" will refer here to how well two stimuli can be discriminated. Thus, high sensitivity means "easy to distinguish," which implies that the stimuli are far apart on the evidence continuum. This use of the term is not the one encountered in classical psychophysical theory, where high sensitivity connotes the resolution of small stimulus differences (jnd's). It is important to keep in mind the TSD meaning of sensitivity in the following discussion. Take, for example, the case of determining the Jovian's sensitivity to a very weak odorant. When none is present there is still noise in the sensory system, giving rise to an internal distribution. And with very weak odorants added to the background, it will be difficult for the subject to distinguish noise from signal. In this instance, a measure of sensitivity would be a small value. As the intensity of the signal increases, however, discrimination improves and the sensitivity measure should increase. At no point in the course of changing the intensity of the signal need we speak of an absolute threshold for smell. This is an interesting and rather important point. Recall that the models for the classical methods (for example, the method of constant stimuli) assume that the stimuli gradually become more discriminable from the standard as their intensity difference widens. A somewhat arbitrary percentage point was assumed to mark the intensity of a just discriminable stimulus. So, even the classical theory predicts that any comparison stimulus (no matter how close to the standard) will be at least slightly discriminable. The difference between classical methods and TSD, therefore, lies in the interpretation of what is important in defining and determining "sensitivity." In this chapter we are interested in finding a continuous measure of discrimination, not a single number to serve as a lower threshold. In brief, TSD does not share the concern of classical psychophysics with measuring absolute and difference thresholds.

The sensitivity measure suggested by TSD is known as d' (d prime) distance. Intuitively, the separation between the signal and noise distributions can be seen as the distance between their means. To operationalize d', we introduce the following notation.

σ_n = standard deviation of the noise distribution

σ_s = standard deviation of the signal distribution

u_n = mean of the noise distribution

u_s = mean of the signal distribution

$z_n(x) = \dfrac{x - u_n}{\sigma_n}$ = distance of x in z-score units from the mean of the noise distribution

$z_s(x) = \dfrac{x - u_s}{\sigma_s}$ = distance of x in z-score units from the mean of the signal distribution

We also assume that the signal and noise standard deviations are equal; that is, $\sigma_n = \sigma_s$.

For any x on the evidence axis, the following formula holds:

$$d' = z_n(x) - z_s(x)$$

To bolster our intuitive notion of d', consider the special case in which $x = u_s$. Then,

$$d' = z_n(u_s) - z_s(u_s) \qquad (8.1)$$

By substitution (remember the assumption that $\sigma_s = \sigma_n$), we obtain

$$d' = \frac{u_s - u_n}{\sigma_n} - \frac{u_s - u_s}{\sigma_n}$$

or

$$d' = \frac{u_s - u_n}{\sigma_n}, \qquad u_s \geqslant u_n \qquad (8.2)$$

So d' is the distance between the two means in units of standard deviation. Multiplying both sides by σ_n,

$$d' \cdot \sigma_n = u_s - u_n \qquad (8.3)$$

Note the similarity between this formula and Thurstone's law of comparative judgment (Eq. 7.3, Chapter 7).

Ideal Detector

When elevated to the lofty status of a psychological theory, TSD specifies the processes underlying judgment in a decision task. If we postulate that a subject is attempting to maximize monetary payoff, the best decision strategy would be that followed by an *ideal detector*.

In order to behave as an ideal detector, the subject must have stored in memory the signal and noise distributions or have some other way to gain access to them. In particular, the ideal detector maps the external stimulus (noise or signal) onto a value x on the evidence axis and determines the probability of obtaining x from the noise and signal distributions, independently. If the two distributions were not available, the theory would not apply, and psychophysics would be minus some very fascinating results and explanations. Returning to the problem at hand, the ideal detector computes the conditional probabilities: probability of x given noise, written as $p(x|n)$, and probability of x given signal, $p(x|s)$. These probabilities are in fact the heights of the two normal curves (see Fig. 8.3) at the particular x value. In symbols this means

$$h_s(x) = p(x|s)$$

and

$$h_n(x) = p(x|n)$$

Recall that the formula for the normal curve is

$$h_a(x) = \frac{1}{\sqrt{2\pi}} e^{-(1/2)[z_a(x)]^2} \tag{8.4}$$

where $z_a(x)$ is the normal deviate (z score) of x, and $h_a(x)$ is the height of the curve for the given x. The symbol a is replaced by either n for noise or s for signal. According to TSD, the subject (acting as an ideal detector) can compute (know, fathom, or otherwise determine) the heights of the noise and signal distributions associated with each x. Plug in an x and you get out $h_n(x)$ for noise and $h_s(x)$ for signal (the formula has to be applied twice). Once these are determined, their ratio or some other parameter monotonically related to the ratio (for example, log likelihood ratio) is computed. By definition, the likelihood ratio is

$$l(x) = \frac{h_s(x)}{h_n(x)} = \frac{p(x|s)}{p(x|n)} \tag{8.5}$$

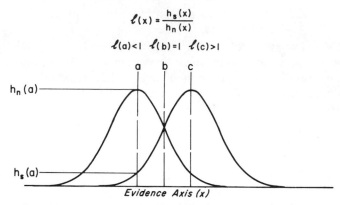

Figure 8.3.   Illustration of three cutoffs (a,b,c) along the evidence axis. The likelihood ratio $l(x)$ associated with each cutoff is calculated by taking the ratio between the heights of the signal + noise and noise curves at the cutoff value for x. These heights are designated on the graph for cutoff a.

The gist of the matter is this: With fixed probabilities of noise and signal $[p(n)$ and $p(s)]$, as $l(x)$ increases, so does the probability that x was caused by the signal. In other words, as x increases along the evidence axis in Fig. 8.3, the likelihood ratio increases monotonically. For example, in the case where $p(n)=p(s)$, $l(x)>1$ means that it is more likely that a signal was presented and $l(x)<1$ means that it is more likely that x was caused by noise alone. Examples of the three major types of likelihood ratio (in Fig. 8.3) are indicated by the ratio of the heights of the two curves at the points of intersection with the sample cutoffs a, b, and c.

Response Bias, β

Let us return to our example from outer space. When the Jovian senses x and computes a likelihood ratio, it still must decide whether a signal or a noise was presented on that trial. At this juncture the probabilities of stimulus presentation and the payoff matrix enter the picture. The manner in which they influence matters depends on what it is the subject wishes to maximize. A number of different criteria can be applied, and in each case statistical decision theory describes the ideal strategy to accomplish the goal (Green and Swets, 1966).

A realistic goal would be to maximize the amount of monetary gain (or Earth yummies). Given this goal, we wish to define a cutoff, β, of the likelihood ratio $l(x)$ such that if $l(x) \geqslant \beta$, one should respond "yes"; if

$l(x) < \beta$, then one should respond "no" to maximize the long-run gains. In a moment we will show that β is a function of the values of the payoff matrix and the experimenter-determined probabilities of signal and noise:

$$\beta = \frac{p(n)}{p(s)} \times \frac{O_{Nn} - O_{Yn}}{O_{Ys} - O_{Ns}} \tag{8.6}$$

For the Jupiter experiment, then, we have $p(n) = .5$, $p(s) = .5$, and the values and costs (outcomes) in the payoff matrix (Fig. 8.1). When these numbers are substituted in Eq. 8.6, β is seen to be 1. In general, the denominator in Eq. 8.6 reflects the importance of the signal and the numerator the importance of the noise. Various combinations will of course yield a range of β's. For example, if $p(s)$ is high, the subject will be very tempted to say "yes" often, and β will be small. If the penalty of a false alarm (O_{Yn}) is disproportionately costly, β will be large, and so on.

As the story goes, for any fixed set of experimental conditions the subject employs a single β as a criterion or cutoff to decide whether to say "yes" or "no." To do this, the current β is compared with the likelihood ratio obtaining on a trial, and if

$$l(x) \geqslant \beta$$

the response is "yes," and if

$$l(x) < \beta$$

the response is "no." Each β can be located along the evidence axis, indirectly, since it is really just a likelihood ratio associated with a particular x. In Fig. 8.4 the connection between β, the likelihood ratio, and the evidence axis is depicted. On the graph a single hypothetical β is shown. Below this point the subject answers "no"; above it "yes." For convenience, the log likelihood ratio is plotted. Note that this value grows systematically (linearly) with increasing x and that β could fall anywhere along the linear function, depending on the particular probabilities and payoffs effecting the position of the cutoff.[3]

The remainder of this section is a derivation of the response bias β as a cutoff along a dimension of likelihood ratio $l(x)$. We start with the assumption that the subject wants to maximize his or her expected payoff given a stimulus represented as an x on the evidence axis. That is, for the given x, the subject responds "yes" if the expected winnings for saying "yes" are

---

[3]The linearity of log likelihood ratio with increasing x can be demonstrated by substituting Eq. 8.4 for $h_s(x)$ and $h_n(x)$ into Eq. 8.5 and taking logarithms.

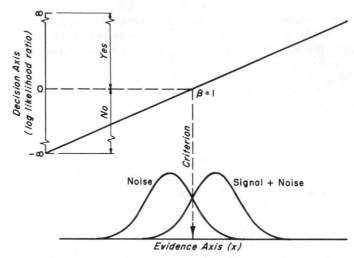

Figure 8.4.　Illustration of a fixed cutoff rule in the binary task (in this case, $\beta=1$). It is assumed that for ratios greater than or equal to this value (associated with a particular x), the subject responds "yes, signal" and for ratios less than this value the subject responds "no, noise." For convenience in graphing, log likelihood ratio is plotted to produce a linear function as values increase along the decision axis.

greater than the expected winnings for saying "no":

$$E(Y|x) \geqslant E(N|x)$$

Since the expected value is defined as the sum of the payoff (Fig. 8.1) for an event times the probability that such an event occurs, we can write

$$E(Y|x) = O_{Ys}\big[\,p(s|x)\,\big] + O_{Yn}\big[\,p(n|x)\,\big]$$

and

$$E(N|x) = O_{Ns}\big[\,p(s|x)\,\big] + O_{Nn}\big[\,p(n|x)\,\big]$$

From this we get

$$O_{Ys}\big[\,p(s|x)\,\big] + O_{Yn}\big[\,p(n|x)\,\big] \geqslant O_{Ns}\big[\,p(s|x)\,\big] + O_{Nn}\big[\,p(n|x)\,\big]$$

and, using a little algebra,

$$(O_{Ys} - O_{Ns})\,p(s|x)\,p(x) \geqslant (O_{Nn} - O_{Yn})\,p(n|x)\,p(x)$$

By applying a well-known result in probability theory called Bayes' theorem,

$p(s|x)p(x) = p(x|s)p(s)$, to both sides of the inequality, we get

$$(O_{Ys} - O_{Ns})p(x|s)p(s) \geqslant (O_{Nn} - O_{Yn})p(x|n)p(n)$$

All "reasonable" signal detection payoffs have $O_{Ys} \geqslant O_{Ns}$ (when a signal trial is given, the subject is paid more for a "yes" response than for a "no" response), so

$$\frac{p(x|s)}{p(x|n)} \geqslant \frac{p(n)}{p(s)} \times \frac{O_{Nn} - O_{Yn}}{O_{Ys} - O_{Ns}}$$

Note that the left-hand side of this formula is a likelihood ratio (Eq. 8.5) and the right-hand side is the response bias (Eq. 8.6). Hence, $l(x) \geqslant \beta$. Using a similar argument, we could prove that responding "no" is equivalent to the relation $l(x) < \beta$. This completes the derivation of the relation between the likelihood ratio and the response bias. (For further details, see Coombs, Dawes, and Tversky, 1970, pp. 169–171.)

DATA ANALYSIS

We finally come to the reasons for introducing all this theoretical machinery. The important result is that the subject and experimenter, between them, have all the information necessary to determine sensory discrimination d' and response bias β. This information is combined in a two-by-two matrix in which the relative frequency (probability) of a response is entered for occasions of signal and noise presentation. The symbols and names for the probabilities are shown in Fig. 8.5. The following equality holds there.

$$p(Y|s) + p(N|s) = 1$$

		Response	
		Yes	No
Stimulus	Signal	$p(Y\|s)$ hit	$p(N\|s)$ miss
	Noise	$p(Y\|n)$ false alarm	$p(N\|n)$ correct rejection

Figure 8.5. Probability matrix to summarize data from a binary task, analyzed according to TSD.

A subject must say something on all signal trials, so the sum of the two probabilities is 1. Similarly,

$$p(Y|n) + p(N|n) = 1$$

Therefore,

$$p(N|s) = 1 - p(Y|s)$$

$$p(N|n) = 1 - p(Y|n)$$

Only two of the entries in the matrix are necessary to convey all the available information. By convention, hits, denoted by $p(Y|s)$, and false alarms, denoted by $p(Y|n)$, are tabulated from the responses over a large number of trials. Now let us see how this matrix leads to estimates of d' and β.

Calculation of Empirical d' and β

Until now we have been discussing a theory according to which subjects are supposed to perform in a binary task. Both d' and β are hypothetical, gaining substance only from theoretical argument. As is always true, one must accept a psychological argument on faith before knowing how to analyze the data according to a quantitative model. The purpose of the present analysis is to obtain empirical estimates of d' (the larger d', the greater the sensitivity) and β (the larger β, the less willing the subject is to say a signal occurred).

The key to this analysis is a familiar theme: Relative response frequencies are equated with probabilities, and these reflect areas under a normal curve. Consider Fig. 8.6. The two distributions have been displaced vertically to facilitate viewing and to emphasize the fact that we deal with each distribution separately (almost as though data were collected from two experiments). The criterion or cutoff c is associated with a β, splitting the evidence axis into two parts. All $x \geqslant c$ is equivalent to $l(x) \geqslant \beta$, and the subject claims that a signal occurred. The probability of saying "yes" when there is a signal is the area under the signal curve to the right of the cutoff. This is the probability of a hit. The area under the noise curve to the right of the cutoff is the probability of a false alarm (saying "yes" when noise occurred). With these two probabilities we can work backward and calculate the position of the cutoff in z score units from the means of each distribution and the height of each curve at the cutoff. The first calculation yields an estimate of d', the second, an estimate of β. At this stage we are dealing only with a mathematical model.

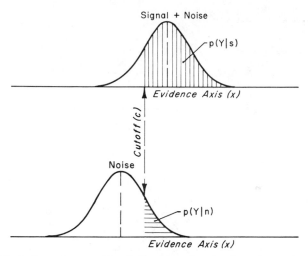

Figure 8.6. Illustration of a cutoff splitting both the signal+noise and noise distributions. The striped region under the top curve represents the probability of "yes" responses when the signal+noise were presented together [$p(Y|s)$=hits]. The striped region under the bottom curve represents the probability of "yes" responses when the noise was presented alone [$p(Y|n)$=false alarms].

The following steps are performed to calculate d'. Area under the normal curve can be used to determine the z score of the cutoff. Since we have two curves (signal and noise) and two areas (hits and false alarms), we find two z scores. The z value of cutoff c in terms of the noise dispersion σ_n is a measure of the distance between the mean u_n and the cutoff. It is based on the false alarm rate. Similarly, a z score indicates the distance from the mean (u_s) of the signal distribution and the cutoff. It is based on the hit rate. It was previously stated (Eq. 8.1) that for any value c along the evidence axis,

$$z_n(c) - z_s(c) = d' \qquad (8.7)$$

yielding the perceptual sensitivity index of the TSD model.

To convince yourself that Eq. 8.7 works no matter where the cutoff is located, examine Fig. 8.7. We want to show that d' is always the distance between the means of the two distributions. In the case of the top graph, $z_n(c)$ is positive, $z_s(c)$ is negative (because it is assessed from u_s), and therefore their difference (Eq. 8.7) gives the correct d'. In the second case (middle graph), $z_n(c)$ and $z_s(c)$ are both positive because the cutoff is to the right of u_s. Obviously, Eq. 8.7 works correctly here also, since it is necessary to subtract an amount $z_s(c)$ to obtain a measure of the distance between the

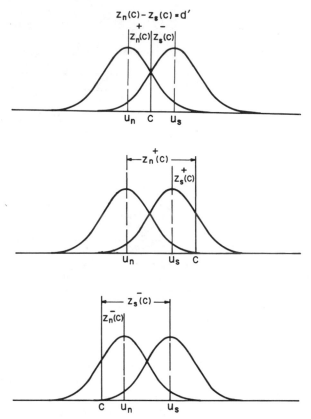

Figure 8.7 Calculation of d' with different positions of the cutoff (c). The dashed vertical lines are at the means (u_n and u_s) of the two distributions and are fixed. The solid vertical line gives an example of the cutoff located between the means (top), higher than u_s (middle), and lower than u_n (bottom). The particular z values [$z_n(c)$ and $z_s(c)$] required to calculate d' are shown for each of the three cases. Substitution of these values into the equation at the top of the graph always yields the same distance, d', between the means.

means. To satisfy skeptics, the bottom graph shows the successful application when $z_n(c)$ and $z_s(c)$ are both negative.

Now we can easily calculate β. Since the z scores of the cutoff relative to the signal and noise distributions are known from the calculations of d', the height h of the normal curve can be found by applying the formula in Eq. 8.4. A separate h is determined for the signal and noise distributions, and the ratio of these two heights is an estimate of β, since

$$\frac{h_s(c)}{h_n(c)} = \beta \qquad (8.8)$$

Summary of the TSD Model for Yes-No Tasks

The course of events on a trial in a binary task is highlighted in Fig. 8.8. Time extends from left to right. We do not distinguish between types of memory (for example, short-term, long-term), although it is possible that a subject who calculates β can forget the payoff matrix and stimulus probabilities. From then on, only the signal and noise distributions and β need be kept in long-term storage. A similar diagram of this process was suggested by Tanner (1961).

A more concise summary is shown in Table 8.1, where the course of events occurring on a trial is outlined in terms of the roles of the experimenter and the subject.

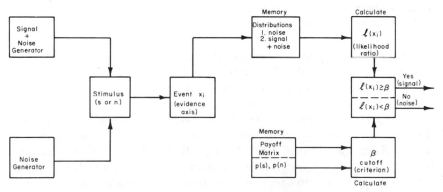

Figure 8.8. Schematic diagram of the processes assumed to occur on a single trial of a binary task according to TSD. Time extends from left to right.

Table 8.1　One trial in the yes-no task

Time	Experimenter	Subject
1	signal or noise presented	receives stimulus
2	waits	codes stimulus as evidence variable (x)
3	waits	calculates likelihood ratio $l(x)$
4	waits	compares $l(x)$ with criterion (β)
5	waits	responds yes, signal or no, noise
6	feedback right or wrong plus payoff	receives feedback
7	records response	waits for next trial

This concludes discussion of the basic theory. The remainder of the chapter extends the treatment to a variety of stimuli, instructions, and motivation conditions.

GRAPHING ROUTINES

The Isosensitivity Curve

The foregoing analysis is appropriate for an experiment involving:

1.   a single signal intensity
2.   a single set of stimulus probabilities
3.   a single payoff matrix

On a plot of hit rate versus false alarm rate, we get one data point for each experiment satisfying these three conditions. By varying the conditions we secure other points on this function. Of particular interest is the set of points found by systematically varying conditions 2 and 3. The curve passing through all such points is called an *isosensitivity function* (Luce, 1963). Another, more common name for the curve is *receiver operating characteristic* (ROC) (Green and Swets, 1966; Swets, 1973). The term ROC was taken from its original use in engineering, although in our opinion Luce's term is more appropriate for psychophysics, as we shall see in a moment.

Changing either the stimulus probabilities or the payoff matrix changes β (at least in theory) and hence the position of the cutoff along the evidence axis. This in turn leads to a change in the areas under the normal curve to the right of the cutoff. Hence, the hit and false alarm rates depend on the location of the cutoff. As the cutoff moves to the right, both rates diminish, because the subject says "yes" less often to both signal and noise—assuming they are both of fixed intensity (as measured by the reading on the stimulus generators).

This is demonstrated in Fig. 8.9, where we have plotted hits $p(Y|s)$ along the ordinate and false alarms $p(Y|n)$ along the abscissa. These are hypothetical data. One point on the graph represents one set of experimental conditions—a single data matrix (Fig. 8.5) with single hit and false alarm rates, assuming the underlying distributions shown at the lower right of the figure $(d'=1)$. Note that as the cutoff increases along the evidence axis (a,b,c,d), the data points on the isosensitivity curve approach the point $(0,0)$, since there are fewer "yes" responses. Each d' is associated with a unique isosensitivity function, and each point on that function represents a

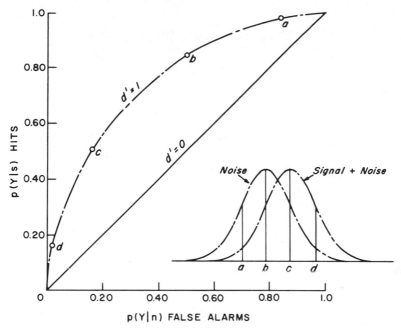

Figure 8.9. Hypothetical isosensitivity curve for the noise and signal+noise distributions shown ($d'=1$). The open circles on the curve indicate the mapping of hits and false alarms for different positions of a cutoff (a,b,c,d). The solid diagonal line represents the case where $d'=0$ (when the noise and signal+noise distributions are identical).

unique measure of response bias (β). Hence, perceptual sensitivity and response bias are separate and independent within the framework of TSD.

TSD is supported by an impressive array of empirical data, samples of which are presented in Figs. 8.10 and 8.11. These results were secured by having a single subject attempt to detect a tone burst embedded in a background of auditory noise (Tanner, Swets, and Green, 1956; as described in Green and Swets, 1966, pp. 88–93). Each point is based on 600 trials with a unique set of stimulus probabilities and monetary outcomes in the payoff matrix.

Figure 8.10 shows how β changes systematically with changes in the signal probability (with constant entries in the payoff matrix). The solid line represents the prediction of TSD with $d'=0.85$, as determined from the data. The shape of the theoretical curve corresponds very nicely to the empirical trend accompanying shifts in the obtained β, as reflected in the relative proportion of hits and false alarms.

Further results from the same study are plotted in Fig. 8.11, but in this case the signal probability was fixed at .50. Here, the shift in β was

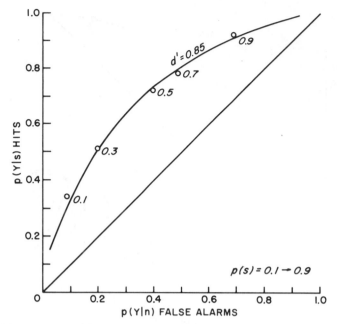

Figure 8.10. An empirical isosensitivity curve obtained by varying the probability of signal occurrence. Each point is based on 600 trials from a single subject. The diagonal line corresponds to $d'=0$; the solid curve represents an empirical $d'=0.85$. (Data from Green and Swets, 1966, Table 4-1)

accomplished by manipulating the rewards and costs associated with each of the four possible outcomes on a trial (hit, false alarm, miss, correct rejection). From Fig. 8.11 it is apparent that the subject's inclination to answer "yes, signal" was significantly influenced by the type of payoff matrix (the details of which are not shown here). As in the previous figure, the solid curve represents the theoretical isosensitivity function for $d'=0.85$ (held constant throughout).

As the difference between the means of the signal and noise distributions increases, d' follows suit. This is reflected as a shift of the isosensitivity curve toward the upper left corner of the graph $(0,1)$, as shown in Fig. 8.12. With larger d', both the hit and false alarm rates improve (the first goes up, the second, down). The 45° diagonal represents the situation where hits and false alarms are equally likely, and hence $d'=0$. Therefore, the greater the distance of the isosensitivity curve from the diagonal, the larger the estimated d', and the greater the assumed perceptual sensitivity of the subject.

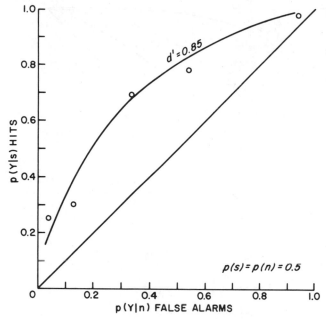

Figure 8.11. An empirical isosensitivity curve obtained by varying the entries in the payoff matrix (Fig. 8.1). Each point is based on 600 trials from a single subject. The probability of signal occurrence was fixed at .5. The diagonal line corresponds to $d'=0$; the solid curve is for $d'=0.85$. (Data from Green and Swets, 1966, Table 4-1)

This is illustrated in Fig. 8.12 for three different values of d' whose underlying distributions are shown at the right in the figure.

Calculation of Average d'

Ideally, each point on the isosensitivity curve should predict a constant d' over all changes in stimulus probabilities and the payoff matrix. In most cases this ideal is not realized exactly, so an average d' is calculated for a number of conditions. One way to determine this average is by interpreting a graph (double Gaussian, another term for normal) of the hit rate $[z_s(c)]$ versus the false alarm rate $[z_n(c)]$, both in standard score units. In other words, the probabilities in Figs. 8.9 and 8.10 are converted to z scores. The two scores (based on the empirical results) can be plotted for a number of cutoffs and a linear function fit to the data by visual inspection or by a least

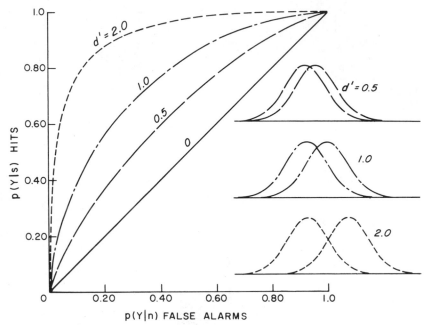

Figure 8.12. Hypothetical isosensitivity curves for different separation of noise and signal+noise distributions (shown on the right). $d'=0$ when the two distributions are identical.

squares technique. (This is equivalent to fitting a line to the original probabilities plotted on "double probability" paper.) An empirical estimate of d' is the y intercept of this straight line (where $z_n(c)=0$). More generally, d' is the vertical distance between the isosensitivity line when $d'=0$ and the isosensitivity line when some perceptual discrimination is exhibited.

The relation between $z_s(c)$ and $z_n(c)$ is linear because both z scores change by the same amount as the cutoff moves a distance along the evidence axis. Hence, the two are linearly related with a fixed separation distance d'. By rearranging Eq. 8.7 we get

$$z_s(c)=z_n(c)-d' \qquad (8.9)$$

The hypothetical data from Fig. 8.12 are replotted in Fig. 8.13, where the isosensitivity curves are parallel straight lines with vertical intercepts equal to d'. Note that the location of positive and negative values is reversed on the graph from their common arrangement. This is necessary as long as we wish to plot hits on the vertical axis and false alarms on the horizontal axis in accordance with the layout of the isosensitivity functions (Fig. 8.12).

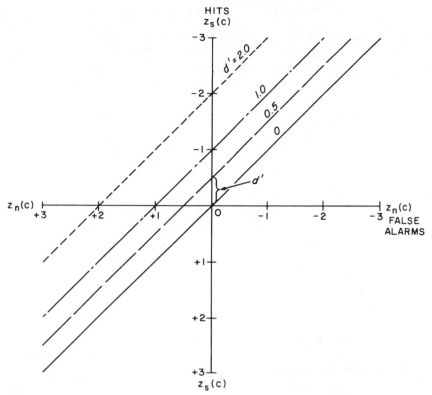

Figure 8.13   Isosensitivity functions from Fig. 8.12 plotted on z-score axes (hits against false alarms). Specific z values are calculated from $p(Y|s)$ and $p(Y|n)$ for a given location of the cutoff. The isosensitivity functions graph as straight lines of unit slope, where d' is the vertical distance separating the function from the line through (0, 0) ($d'=0$).

Unequal Variance

If the variances of the signal and noise distributions are not equal, the slope of the function relating $z_s(c)$ to $z_n(c)$ will not be 1. It can, in fact, be shown that the slope is equal to the ratio of the standard deviation of the noise to the standard deviation of the signal (σ_n/σ_s). Therefore, when the variance of the signal distribution is greater than the variance of the noise distribution, the slope of the function linking the two z scores will be less than 1.0, and when signal variance is less than noise variance the slope will be greater than 1.0. Details of this matter are peripheral to the main points of this chapter and will not be explored further. Technical elaboration can be found in Green and Swets (1966) and McNicol (1972).

The Forced-Choice Task

One common variation on the binary choice design is to have two stimulus presentations per trial, with one containing only noise and the other, signal superimposed on noise. The subject must indicate which presentation contained the signal. The signal and noise presentations are randomized over a large number of trials.

To see how these data may be analyzed, we look at one possible strategy that a subject may follow to make such a decision. Within each presentation a single value of the evidence variable is sampled. Hence, we have x_1 for the first presentation and x_2 for the second. Over many trials the x values from the signal distribution will generally be larger than the x values from the noise distribution, so the subject should choose the presentation from each trial that coincided with the larger x. It is interesting from a historical perspective to note that the probability that one event is chosen over another is the situation analyzed by Thurstone's law of comparative judgment. So, in the forced-choice task d' is simply the difference between Thurstone's scale values of noise and signal (Eq. 8.3).

Rating Scales

Forced-choice and binary tasks are extremely time-consuming if one wishes to secure a sufficient number of points (criteria) to fit an isosensitivity curve. Typically, a large number of trials will be run with one criterion, and a single pair of hit and false alarm probabilities will be found. Then the experimental setup is altered, more trials are run, and a second pair of values are determined, and so on. This procedure can be extremely tedious. Consequently, scientists with low boredom thresholds often employ a *rating-scale task*. It permits the experimenter to calculate a number of points on the isosensitivity curve from one set of experimental conditions.

In the standard situation considered thus far there are only two possible responses, yes and no. It seems likely, however, that a variety of confidence levels exist within each of these categories. Therefore, instead of being limited to a binary response, we can ask for one of the following categories (see, for example, McNicol, 1972, p. 103):

> certain, noise
> uncertain, noise
> uncertain, signal
> certain, signal

Often numbers are used in place of explicitly stated confidence categories.

RESPONSE CATEGORY

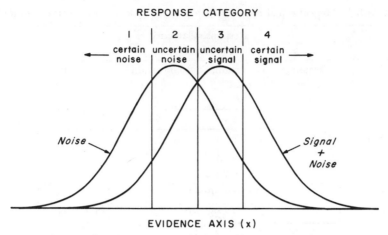

Figure 8.14. Presumed order of response categories in a rating scale task. Higher numbers imply higher confidence that a signal was presented (occurrence of higher x values).

The subject is merely asked for a confidence rating on a scale of 1 to 4, with 1 equivalent to "certain, noise" and 4 equivalent to "certain, signal." As in the usual binary task, the experimenter then informs the subject whether a signal was in fact presented on that trial. Of course, any number of rating categories can be used.

The rationale here is that each category defines a cutoff along the evidence axis and these cutoffs result in different β's. This is illustrated in Fig. 8.14 for the four response categories listed above. It is assumed that when a subject says "certain, signal," the sampled value from the evidence axis falls above a fairly high cutoff; and when he or she says "certain, noise," the sampled value is below a cutoff placed low on the evidence axis. In other words, multiple cutoffs are present on each trial and the subject merely indicates the one that exceeds the sample value by the smallest amount.

The analysis of rating-scale experiments involves some sleight-of-hand tactics since the same data are used to produce multiple points along an isosensitivity curve. Since there are N response categories, this is done by collapsing them into a binary set (yes, no) for each of $N-1$ possible cutoffs. Initially, the responses for all categories are separated into noise trials and signal trials. Next, the data are appropriately converted into hit and false alarm rates.

For the hypothetical data in Table 8.2a, all responses with the category "certain, signal" are considered "yes" and all others are considered "no." The probability of "yes" given noise [$p(Y|n)$] and the probability of "yes"

Table 8.2 Hypothetical data for rating-scale task (response frequencies)

	Certain, noise 1	Uncertain, noise 2	Uncertain, signal 3	Certain, signal 4	
	Response Category (confidence →)				
Signal	7	24	50	19	(a)
Noise	32	37	28	3	

	(1+2+3)	(4)	
Signal	(7+24+50)=81	19 hits	(b)
Noise	(32+37+28)=97	3 false alarms	

	(1+2)	(3+4)	
Signal	(7+24)=31	(50+19)=69 hits	(c)
Noise	(32+37)=69	(28+3)=31 false alarms	

	(1)	(2+3+4)	
Signal	7	(24+50+19)=93 hits	(d)
Noise	32	(37+28+3)=68 false alarms	

Total signal trials = 100
Total noise trials = 100

given signal $[p(Y|s)]$ are then calculated in the usual manner. This is done in Table 8.2b. This yields one point on the isosensitivity curve. Next, the categories "certain, signal" and "uncertain, signal" are collapsed into a single category of "yes" responses, while the other two categories are collapsed and treated as "no" responses (Table 8.2c). A second pair of hit and false alarm rates are computed, thus yielding another point on the isosensitivity curve. Finally, the three highest categories, "certain, signal," "uncertain, signal," and "uncertain, noise" are collapsed into a "yes" category, and "certain, noise" is treated as the lone contributor to the "no" category (Table 8.2d). This produces a third point on the curve. Four categories give three pairs of hit and false alarm rates; N categories yield $N-1$ points. Converting the probabilities to z scores, plotting the data, and fitting a straight line allows us to calculate d' in the manner discussed for the binary task applied over systematic variations of experimental conditions.

TSD AS A NORMATIVE MODEL

A distinction is often made in psychology between descriptive and normative models. A descriptive model is closely tied to empirical data and attempts to represent psychological processes or behavior as actually observed. A normative model is more proscriptive. It purports only to state the way subjects "ought" to behave, not the way they actually behave. The definition of "ought behavior" often coincides with that of some mathematician with strong social science interests!

For example, consider the binary choice task. The normative model we have been discussing thus far states that subjects *should* act to maximize total winnings. To do this, an ideal detector should be simulated, and a likelihood ratio computed and compared with β, which is infallibly determined by applying Eq. 8.6. A descriptive model, on the other hand, would only attempt to represent what subjects really did in this task, whether or not they followed the rules of TSD.

Usually these two types of models will be different, although they each hold a central place in science. It is seldom the case that a normative model is all wrong, and it is often helpful in guiding further research by pinpointing the exact areas where the theoretical argument runs aground. Similarly, an imperfect descriptive model often alerts us to the important variables in a situation, even if their effects are not fully understood. These areas can then be looked at more carefully, and formally, by theoreticians.

Most psychophysicists would probably admit that TSD is a normative model with a decent track record when it comes to predicting actual behavior. In this chapter, we have been emphasizing the power of the theory as a tool for understanding actual judgment processes. However, some discrepancies between theoretical predictions and the empirical data should be mentioned.

Likelihood Ratio

The TSD model assumes that decisions in the binary choice task are dependent on a cutoff relative to a likelihood ratio. When a particular x is sampled from the evidence axis, $l(x)$ is calculated, and this, or some other variable monotonically related to it, is compared with β. The same $l(x)$ should always lead to the same response—"yes" when $l(x) \geqslant \beta$; "no" when $l(x) < \beta$. Because it is not entirely obvious that subjects do in fact process information in this manner, an empirical test seems in order.

Such a test was conducted by Weissmann (1974). In his experiment, subjects were presented numbers that supposedly represented the amount of water vapor in the air. They responded with a prediction of "no rain" (no, noise) or "rain" (yes, signal). Numbers were selected randomly from a rectangular distribution, so there was an equal probability of sampling any number in the range of possible numbers (a table of random numbers is a good example of a rectangular distribution). Therefore, $l(x)$ was constant within the overlap of the two distributions, whose means were different. This should lead to a constant proportion of "rain" or "no rain" responses throughout the common interval. In fact, this did not happen. Subjects responded with different proportions of "rain" or "no rain" responses *within* the overlap. Near the lower boundary the frequency of "no rain" responses greatly exceeded the frequency of rain responses, and toward the upper boundary the opposite was true. In other words, different behavior was exhibited within different regions of the overlap even though the theoretical likelihood ratio was 1 throughout. Either subjects do not use the likelihood ratio when processing the information, or their perception of the probability distributions of the signal and noise are distorted. In any case, this result is contrary to one of the basic tenets of a strict interpretation of TSD, that is, an interpretation that does not allow for a variable cutoff.

Theoretical vs. Empirical β

It is possible to calculate the optimal β for any set of experimental conditions that specify the probability of signal $p(s)$, the probability of noise $p(n)$, and the payoff matrix. An empirical β can also be computed from the subject's response matrix. The question is, "How does the empirical value compare with the optimal one?"

Green and Swets (1966, p. 91) report that subjects perform conservatively in this regard. The empirical β is smaller than the optimal one for values greater than 1 and larger than the optimal for values less than 1. This may be due to the subjects' personal evaluation of the rewards in the payoff matrix or to biases in computing the relative proportion of signal and noise trials. These factors also compound the effects previously noted when evaluating $l(x)$. Green and Swets did report, however, that the ordinal relations among empirical β's was the same as that among optimal β's, in support of TSD.

Variable Criterion

According to TSD, the subject should decide on a cutoff for an experimental setup and stick to it throughout. The cutoff is a fixed value. But from an intuitive standpoint (speaking as a practiced subject), it seems more likely that the criterion placement would vary over trials and, in particular, would depend on the degree of success encountered by the subject on previous trials. Several investigators have suggested that, indeed, the cutoff is variable (Tanner, 1961; McNicol, 1972; Weissmann, 1974). From his experiments with numerical distributions, Weissmann concluded that although subjects enforced a cutoff rule, its location was variable over trials and depended on whether or not the decision on the preceding trial was correct or incorrect. The location of the cutoff was unaffected by correct decisions but shifted in the appropriate direction after incorrect decisions.

The existence of a sliding criterion is contrary to TSD in its strictest form. A variable cutoff would also affect sensitivity measures, since the empirical d' would be somewhat less than with a fixed cutoff (McNicol, 1972; Weissmann, 1974). In such instances, sensitivity and response bias would not be independent, a situation clearly at odds with the assumptions of TSD. This is not to say that the quantitative analysis of TSD should be abandoned. As we will see in the next chapter, alternative theories often treat data by the same quantitative models, although the psychological meaning attached to such models is different for each theory.

Predicted vs. Empirical d'

In most psychophysical studies, perceptual d''s are not predicted. This is due to an inability to describe the shape of the probability distributions for each stimulus. That is, we are unable to separately manipulate the effects on probability distributions of internal noise (for example, neuron-to-neuron transmission of messages) and of external noise (for example, variability in the stimulus generator). One method that attempts to manipulate these effects uses numbers as stimuli. Here, the variability of the stimulus generator is assumed to be set. Therefore, an objectively determined optimal d' may be compared to the perceptual d' using a TSD analysis of hit and false alarm rates. In a recent experiment, stimuli were numbers sampled from overlapping normal distributions of equal variance but different means, and presented on a computer terminal (Weissmann, Hollingsworth, and Baird, 1975). The perceptual d''s were in good agreement with the objective d'. This seems to indicate that all the information in the stimulus is used in the decision process. This could be interpreted to support the TSD model, since available information is optimally used. Additional support is presented in Kubovy, Rapoport, and Tversky (1971).

In general, then, it appears that TSD gives us a useful normative model of psychophysical judgment, even though the cognitive operations in such tasks probably are not the ones proposed by the theory!

Deviations from Normality

So far in this section we have only considered deviations from predictions of the TSD model due to underutilization of information available to the subject. In some situations we might better model these deviations using noise distributions other than the normal distribution. For example, one could ask how well the data points on the isosensitivity curve can be modeled using a logistic function,[4] $F(x) = 1/(1 + e^{-x})$, in place of the integral of the normal density function (Eq. 8.4). An even better approach may be to see what conditions the data must satisfy if any distributions can be used to model the points on the isosensitivity curve. That is, we can now distinguish between the case where the normal distribution is not adequate to model the data but some other pair of distributions could be, versus the case where no pair of distributions can ever be devised to model the shape of the points on the isosensitivity curve. Marley (1971) derives conditions that must be satisfied for any model using a pair of noise and signal distributions along an evidence axis. In addition, the distributions may or may not bear a simple relation to each other. So, the noise may be normally distributed, but the signal may be distributed in some other fashion. Here the major testable condition is that one must be able to read the points on the isosensitivity curve by starting at the point $[p(\text{HIT}) = 0, p(\text{FA}) = 0]$ and move up and to the right until one reaches the point where $[p(\text{HIT}) = 1, p(\text{FA}) = 1]$. When reading the points, one should never need to move down and to the right or up and to the left. Another way of stating this is that the probabilities of hits and false alarms are monotonic. This condition, along with some others, offers a different approach to model testing. In the view usually taken, parameters are fit to a model such as standard TSD. To determine its validity, a measure of goodness of fit such as the sum of squared deviations of observed and modeled probabilities is compared to either a statistical cutoff or rule-of-thumb criterion. In the alternative, *axiomatic* approach of Marley, one first asks if the data satisfy conditions that the model implies. Only after determining which tests are fulfilled does one proceed to scale the data. In the next chapter we will see how this approach is applied to an explanation of choice behavior in both psychophysical and nonpsychophysical situations.

REFERENCES

Coombs, C. H., Dawes, R. M., and Tversky, A. *Mathematical Psychology: An Elementary Introduction.* Englewood Cliffs, N.J.: Prentice-Hall, 1970.

Green, D. M., and Swets, J. A. *Signal Detection Theory and Psychophysics.* New York: Wiley, 1966.

[4]This function will be discussed more fully in the next chapter.

Kubovy, M., Rapoport, A., and Tversky, A. "Deterministic vs. probabilistic strategies in detection." *Perception & Psychophysics*, 1971, *9*, 427–429.

Luce, R. D. "Detection and recognition." In R. D. Luce, R. R. Bush, and E. Galanter (Eds.), *Handbook of Mathematical Psychology*, Vol. 1. New York: Wiley, 1963, pp. 103–190.

Marley, A. A. J. "Conditions for the representation of absolute judgment and pair comparison isosensitivity curves by cumulative distributions." *Journal of Mathematical Psychology*, 1971, *8*, 554–590.

McNicol, D. *A Primer of Signal Detection Theory*. London: Allen & Unwin, 1972.

Swets, J. A. "The relative operating characteristic in psychology." *Science*, 1973, *182*, 990–1000.

Tanner, W. P., Jr. "Physiological implications of psychophysical data." *Annals of the New York Academy of Sciences*, 1961, *89*, 752–765.

Tanner, W. P., Jr., and Swets, J. A. "A decision-making theory of visual detection." *Psychological Review*, 1954, *61*, 401–409.

Tanner, W. P., Jr., Swets, J. A., and Green, D. M. "Some general properties of the hearing mechanism." *University of Michigan: Electronic Defense Group, Technical Report* No. 30, 1956.

Weissmann, S. M. "Binary responses to numerical stimuli: Tests of signal detection theory and related models of psychophysical judgment." Unpublished doctoral dissertation, Dartmouth College, 1974.

Weissmann, S. M., Hollingsworth, S. R., and Baird, J. C. "Psychophysical study of numbers: III. Methodological applications." *Psychological Research*, 1975, *38*, 97–115.

CHAPTER

$$\boxed{9}$$

GENERALIZED
FECHNERIAN SCALING

In the preceding chapters we have examined several methods of data analysis. It should be stressed that each is a mathematical model for a theory of perceptual processes. As pointed out by Coombs, Dawes, and Tversky (1970), a model can be thought of as an abstract (often mathematical) system, such as the function $y = \log x$. Other models may be computer programs or organization charts. In contrast, the "real" world that the psychologist wants to study is just that: concrete, real. Theories bridge the gap between real world and model so the power and conveniences of the latter can be used as tools to help conceptualize the world. The theory is said to abstract a portion of the real world by mapping selected phenomena onto a model. For example, with a theory of an equal-interval sensation scale (W), the function $W = k \log S$ becomes Fechner's law for the scaling of perceived stimulus intensities.

The encoding of stimulus intensity based on a different theory may require a different model. By changing Fechner's approach with an assumption of increasing jnd step sizes on the sensation scale to an objective response scale, we have the model called the Stevens power function: $R = kS^n$. (The remaining cells in the fourfold way (Chapter 4) are other models.) In fact, this merely reasserts one of the major tenets of science:

Multiple models may represent the same aspects of the "real" world. On the other side of the coin, the same model may serve multiple theories. For example, in Chapter 2 it was noted that the logarithmic function was used by Fechner to study psychophysics and by Bernoulli to study the subjective utility of money.

More specifically, in psychology, there are two general types of models: (1) those providing a conceptual framework by which meaningful experiments may be conducted and (2) scaling analyses that assist the experimenter in organizing data. The close ties between scaling approaches and more general theories of behavior distinguish them from statistical tests. The latter often uncover consistencies in the data, but their application is not contingent upon the endorsement of a particular theory. For a more complete discussion of this topic, the reader is referred to Torgerson (1958) and Coombs (1964).

Scaling theory attempts to expand the scope and predictive power of models. This may be done by examining and modifying their underlying psychological assumptions. In this chapter we generalize the Fechnerian notion that stimuli may be scaled by using variability as a unit of measure. In doing so, we are also able to show how alternative approaches to the scaling of unidimensional stimuli can be viewed as special versions of the general model. We will also see how easily the basic ideas of psychophysics can be generalized to the broader realm of decision and choice, in which it is very difficult to quantify the relevant stimuli. This generalization represents a shift in emphasis away from the traditional concerns of psychophysics discussed to this point (with the exception of Chapter 7 on Thurstonian scaling). The quantitative arguments are also more advanced, although the mathematical details are not essential to the major course of the theoretical development.

SCALING METHODS

The Thurstone Model

In Chapter 3, a classical model of stimulus coding was introduced in which the stimulus is compared to a value on the subject's internal W scale. Two possible explanations were put forth to explain the variability in subject responses. Either the stimulus was always received infallibly and compared to a random internal threshold or a fallible stimulus generator was pitted against a fixed internal threshold. In addition, any random variation was assumed to be normally distributed.

There is, however, a third possibility. Both the effect of the stimulus generator and the internal threshold could be normally distributed random variables on the sensation (internal) scale. If no distinction is made between the two internal distributions, we have Thurstone's law of comparative judgment (Thurstone, 1927a, b) as introduced in Chapter 7. To review, this approach assumes that each stimulus creates an internal normal distribution available to the subject. A person asked to pick one of a pair of stimuli presumably draws two values, one from each random distribution. The stimulus with the larger value along some predetermined dimension is then chosen. The complete law of comparative judgment (LCJ) may be written as

$$u_j - u_k = z_{jk}\sqrt{\sigma_j^2 + \sigma_k^2 - 2r_{jk}\sigma_j\sigma_k} \qquad (9.1)$$

where u_j and u_k are the scale values for the jth and kth stimuli, and z_{jk} is the z score of the probability that stimulus j will be chosen over stimulus k. We also assume, as is usually done, that the distributions around all scale values have equal variance ($\sigma_j^2 = \sigma_k^2 = \sigma^2$). In addition, the mechanism for choosing the values from each pair of stimulus distributions may be biased in that the choices are correlated, so $r_{jk} \neq 0$. However, we assume that for all pairs of stimuli, $r_{jk} = r$ (a constant with $r \neq 1$). Since σ and r are constant for all pairs, the law of comparative judgment case V (denoted T-V) may be written as

$$u_j - u_k = z_{jk}\sigma^* \qquad (9.2)$$

where σ^* is a constant. Since the units of this scale are arbitrary, we may set the standard deviation, $\sigma^* = 1$, to get the more common expression for T-V:

$$u_j - u_k = z_{jk} \qquad (9.3)$$

To use this model in scaling we need only assume that all N stimuli lie on a common one-dimensional continuum. Starting with a matrix of probabilities $p(j,k)$ that stimulus j is picked over stimulus k, we next convert each $p(j,k)$ to a z score, z_{jk}. Using the procedure described in Chapter 7, we may then locate all stimuli along a continuum.

Before proceeding further, it must be noted that LCJ scales what are known as dominance data obtained by approaches such as the classical methods of constant stimuli, limits, and adjustment. In general, dominance data are collected in response to questions such as "does j have more of...than k has?" or "does j dominate k?" or even "does chicken j peck chicken k?" (see Schjelderup-Ebbe, 1935). In all cases there is at least moderate agreement as to what elements dominate what others. In contrast, with preference data one's choice order presumably depends on personal whims rather than on differences in perception of the order of the elements.

One additional important assumption is made by LCJ and all other methods to be discussed in this chapter: *All stimuli lie along a single dimension.* For this reason, the scale values can be conceptualized as a series of points on a line, representing distances from an arbitrary zero.

The Bradley-Terry-Luce Model

Thurstone's law of comparative judgment is, however, only one of several models used to scale dominance probabilities. Another frequently used method also dates back to Thurstone (1930) but is firmly situated within the realm of learning theory. Of more relevance for our purpose is its application in the statistical analysis of paired comparison data (Bradley and Terry, 1952). Somewhat later, Luce (1959) developed an axiomatic basis for this scaling technique, and Suppes and Zinnes (1963) christened it the Bradley-Terry-Luce (BTL) model. As formulated by Luce, the BTL model may be derived without reference to variable strengths of each alternative on an interval scale. Instead, each stimulus has one and only one postulated strength, but there is variability in the choice process. For this reason, the BTL model is often called a *constant utility model.*[1] In contrast, the LCJ model is sometimes called a *random utility model*, since the utilities or strengths of each alternative are assumed to vary randomly around a central scale value. (We shall see shortly why the distinction of constant and random utility models may sometimes be misleading.) Before describing Luce's formal derivation of the model, we examine two hypothetical choice situations that will elucidate the psychological assumptions.

In the first example, imagine one is trying to choose the loudest pair of loudspeakers from several stores. Suppose further that the room acoustics and speaker location are irrelevant. One approach to the problem is to exclude all except those in one store, then exclude all except those in one showroom within that store, and finally choose a pair of speakers. A second method is to exclude all speakers except those in a particular price bracket and then proceed to eventually select a single pair. We would hope that the probability that any speaker is chosen as the loudest is independent of the particular selection procedure. This assumption is the first part of *Luce's choice axiom.*[2]

---

[1]The scaling structure is now a model of decision processes, no longer solely viewed as the measurement of sensation. For this reason, much of the terminology comes from the economists who continued the line of thought begun by Bernoulli. In particular, the term *utility* comes from studies measuring the relative value of an amount of money or commodity.

[2]Luce's choice axiom should not be confused with a well-known mathematical principle, the axiom of choice (Kelley, 1955, p. 33).

In the second situation, suppose we are still selecting speakers. We compare two and find that speaker A is always chosen over speaker B. The second part of the choice axiom states that we could completely eliminate B from all further considerations without affecting any subsequent judgments. That is to say, B could be eliminated whenever there is an alternative that completely dominates it.

One possible interpretation of the axiom is that "irrelevant" alternatives can be ignored during the decision process. Part (i) covers situations where alternatives are partitioned into categories (sets). As soon as a category is picked, all alternatives in other categories are "irrelevant" to the decision process and should not affect the probability that any particular alternative is chosen. This fact should be true regardless of the categories selected to organize the alternatives. Part (ii) handles a special situation wherein an alternative is "irrelevant" due to its complete subordination to at least one other alternative.

By establishing an axiomatic basis for this choice model we obtain the machinery to determine when a set of items may be scaled. If it can be scaled, we then derive accurate predictions of choice probabilities. For example, if we want to see if the subject acts in accordance with part (ii) of Luce's choice axiom, we could take away any item that is never chosen in a particular paired comparison (for example, j is never chosen over k, $p(j,k) = 0$) and rerun the experiment with the item removed. According to the axiom, this deletion should leave the remaining probabilities among items unchanged.

Using the axiom, one can find scale values from the probability that an item is picked from a set of alternatives. The following formula can be derived for paired comparisons:

$$p(j,k) = \frac{v_j}{v_j + v_k} \tag{9.4}$$

where $p(j,k)$ is the probability that item j is preferred to item k. The scale values for alternatives j and k are v_j and v_k, respectively, and may be determined using a procedure similar to that used by the T-V model. We first note that the axiom restricts the probabilities to $p(j,k) > 0$, and so we may set all scale values so that $v_i > 0$. This allows us to divide the numerator and denominator of Eq. 9.4 by the scale values of v_j, yielding

$$p(j,k) = \frac{1}{1 + (v_k/v_j)} \tag{9.5}$$

Since both v_j and v_k are positive numbers, we can find numbers u_j and u_k

such that $v_j = e^{u_j}$ and $v_k = e^{u_k}$. This is possible because any positive number can be represented by a base (the constant e) raised to some power. Substituting these numbers into Eq. 9.5 we get

$$p(j,k) = \frac{1}{1 + (e^{u_k}/e^{u_j})} \tag{9.6}$$

$$p(j,k) = \frac{1}{1 + e^{-(u_j - u_k)}} \tag{9.7}$$

Equation 9.7 defines the *logistic* distribution, which is very similar in shape to the normal distribution. Solving for $(u_j - u_k)$:

$$1 + e^{-(u_j - u_k)} = \frac{1}{p(j,k)} \tag{9.8}$$

$$e^{-(u_j - u_k)} = \frac{1}{p(j,k)} - 1 \tag{9.9}$$

$$-(u_j - u_k) = \ln\left(\frac{1 - p(j,k)}{p(j,k)}\right) \tag{9.10}$$

$$u_j - u_k = -\ln\left(\frac{1 - p(j,k)}{p(j,k)}\right) \tag{9.11}$$

Recall that the law of comparative judgment (T-V) reduced to the formula

$$u_j - u_k = z_{jk}$$

Therefore, we can use the same procedure to produce scale values for both BTL and T-V. In T-V, the paired comparison probabilities are converted to z scores and then averaged to determine the scale values u. In BTL, the probabilities are transformed by Eq. 9.11 (also called the anti-logit since it is the inverse of the logistic function), and scale values are determined by an averaging technique.

The Dawkins Model

A third model scales dominance data starting from a very different set of theoretical assumptions. The threshold model proposed by Dawkins (1969) was originally used to scale preference of chicks for different colored stimuli.

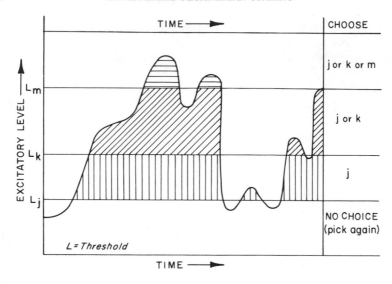

Figure 9.1. Illustration of the Dawkins model showing three hypothetical thresholds (horizontal lines) for an excitatory variable (curve). At any given moment in time (left to right) the excitatory variable exceeds some or all thresholds, as indicated by the three types of stripes. It is assumed that a subject may pick any alternative whose threshold is exceeded at a given point in time.

In this experiment preference was measured by the number of pecks for each member of a stimulus pair.

The underlying theory is as follows: An excitatory state is assumed to vary over time, and for a stimulus to be chosen the excitatory state must exceed its threshold level. In Fig. 9.1, the thresholds are represented by the horizontal lines L_j, L_k, and L_m, and the excitatory state is the fluctuating curve. If the excitatory state exceeds the threshold of only one of the pair, that stimulus is always picked (pecked). However, if the level exceeds the threshold for both, one is chosen at random. For example, if the excitatory level exceeds thresholds L_j and L_m, the probability is $\frac{1}{2}$ that L_j is chosen over L_m. To compute $p(m,j)$ (the probability that m is picked over j), the total time that the excitatory state exceeds at least one threshold, $t_{j\overline{km}} + t_{jk\overline{m}} + t_{jkm}$, is compared to the time it exceeds both, t_{jkm}. In this notation, t_{jkm} is the amount of time the level exceeds all three thresholds. This is shown on the graph by the horizontal stripes at the top. The actual time would be determined (theoretically) by projecting the two horizontally striped regions onto the time axis and then summing the result. $t_{jk\overline{m}}$ is the time the thresholds for j and k but *not* m are exceeded, as indicated by the diagonal stripes on the graph. The vertical stripes demark the time that threshold L_j is exceeded but not L_k or L_m. We now define the theoretical pair probabilities as follows:

$$p(m,j) = \frac{\frac{1}{2} t_{jkm}}{t_{\overline{j}\,km} + t_{jk\,\overline{m}} + t_{jkm}} \leqslant \frac{1}{2} \qquad (9.12a)$$

$$p(k,j) = \frac{\frac{1}{2}(t_{jk\,\overline{m}} + t_{jkm})}{t_{\overline{j}\,km} + t_{jk\overline{m}} + t_{jkm}} \leqslant \frac{1}{2} \qquad (9.12b)$$

$$p(m,k) = \frac{\frac{1}{2} t_{jkm}}{t_{jk\,\overline{m}} + t_{jkm}} \leqslant \frac{1}{2} \qquad (9.12c)$$

At this point, Dawkins developed a test of the internal consistency of the probabilities obtained in the experiment. His derivation is as follows. Taking 2 times the product of the last pair of probabilities from Eq. 9.12, we see that

$$2p(k,j)\cdot p(m,k) = 2\frac{\frac{1}{2}(t_{jk\,\overline{m}} + t_{jkm})}{t_{\overline{j}\,km} + t_{jk\,\overline{m}} + t_{jkm}} \cdot \frac{\frac{1}{2} t_{jkm}}{t_{jk\,\overline{m}} + t_{jkm}}$$

$$= \frac{\frac{1}{2} t_{jkm}}{t_{\overline{j}\,km} + t_{jk\,\overline{m}} + t_{jkm}}$$

$$2\cdot p(k,j)\cdot p(m,k) = p(m,j) \qquad (9.13)$$

This relationship was verified experimentally, but it was not until 1970 that Yellott extended the method to produce scale values. By manipulating Eq. 9.13 he was able to derive a general form:

$$p(j,k) = \int_{-\infty}^{u_j - u_k} \frac{c}{2} e^{-c|x|}\, dx \qquad \text{constant } c > 0 \qquad (9.14a)$$

This is often called the *Laplace* distribution. Evaluating the integral for the cases where $p(j,k)$ is less than or equal to $\frac{1}{2}$ and greater than $\frac{1}{2}$, we obtain

$$p(j,k) = \begin{cases} \dfrac{1}{2} e^{c(u_j - u_k)} & \text{for } p(j,k) \leqslant \dfrac{1}{2} \\[2mm] 1 - \dfrac{1}{2} e^{-c(u_j - u_k)} & \text{for } p(j,k) > \dfrac{1}{2} \end{cases} \qquad (9.14b)$$

To see how this model parallels T-V and BTL, we solve the two cases for $u_j - u_k$.

Case 1. $p(j,k) \leqslant \frac{1}{2}$

$$p(j,k) = \frac{1}{2} e^{c(u_j - u_k)}$$

$$2p(j,k) = e^{c(u_j - u_k)}$$

$$u_j - u_k = \frac{1}{c} \ln\left[2p(j,k)\right] \tag{9.15a}$$

Case 2. $p(j,k) > \frac{1}{2}$

$$p(j,k) = 1 - \frac{1}{2} e^{-c(u_j - u_k)}$$

$$\frac{1}{2} e^{-c(u_j - u_k)} = 1 - p(j,k)$$

$$e^{-c(u_j - u_k)} = 2\left[1 - p(j,k)\right]$$

$$-c(u_j - u_k) = \ln\left\{\left[1 - p(j,k)\right]\right\}$$

$$u_j - u_k = -\frac{1}{c} \ln\left\{2\left[1 - p(j,k)\right]\right\} \tag{9.15b}$$

Therefore, we have formulas comparable to Eq. 9.3 for T-V and Eq. 9.11 for BTL and may use the same averaging method to determine u.

GENERAL FECHNERIAN SCALES[3]

We have examined three choice models, all based on very different views of the decision making process. The law of comparative judgment treats the decision process as the comparison of a pair of points picked from two normal distributions. The BTL model assumes independence of intermediate steps in the decision process and the elimination of never-chosen alternatives. The Dawkins model assumes variable excitatory states over time and different thresholds for each alternative. Nevertheless, we have found that a

---

[3]The material in this section was brought to our attention by Clyde H. Coombs. Luce (1977) surveys much the same ground in discussing the applications of the choice axiom over the past 20 years.

common routine may be used to determine the scale values u. Burke and Zinnes (1965) and Yellott (1971) have also shown that the three models regenerate very similar dominance matrices from the scale values. These facts could easily lead one to believe that there is a general structure encompassing all three. These are, in fact, special cases of *General Fechnerian Scales* (GFS, sometimes called strong utility models or generalized Thurstone scales):

$$p(j,k) = F(u_j - u_k) \qquad (9.16)$$

where u_j and u_k are the scale values of j and k. F is a monotonically increasing function. If $(u_j - u_k) \geqslant (u_m - u_n)$, then $F(u_j - u_k) \geqslant F(u_m - u_n)$, where $p(j,k) = \frac{1}{2}$ when $u_j = u_k$. To see this, recall the following key equations.

T-V:

$$u_j - u_k = z_{jk}$$

BTL:

$$u_j - u_k = -\ln\left[\frac{1 - p(j,k)}{p(j,k)}\right]$$

Dawkins:

$$u_j - u_k = \ln\left[2p(j,k)\right] \qquad \text{if } p(j,k) \leqslant \frac{1}{2}$$

$$u_j - u_k = \ln\left\{2\left[1 - p(j,k)\right]\right\} \qquad \text{if } p(j,k) > \frac{1}{2}$$

(To streamline matters a little, the scale factor $1/c$ is omitted here from the Dawkins equations.)

All three models have some operation, say G, on the probability $p(j,k)$, so the general form is

$$u_j - u_k = G\left[p(j,k)\right] \qquad (9.17)$$

In all cases, $u_j - u_k$ increases with $p(j,k)$, so the function G is monotonic and therefore has an inverse operation F,

$$F\left\{G\left[p(j,k)\right]\right\} = p(j,k) \qquad (9.18)$$

This then implies

$$F(u_j - u_k) = F\{G[p(j,k)]\} = p(j,k) \qquad (9.19)$$

which is the formula for strong utility models (GFS).

A second way to verify that all three are GFS models is to treat each as a variation on Thurstone's original approach. The difference is that non-normal distributions may surround the scale values. All distributions are still assumed to be independent and identical. This means that the distributions for any two alternatives are identical but displaced by a constant. In other words, even BTL may be considered a random utility model, along with its original designation as a constant utility model.

To emphasize their similarities, the three models have been arranged in Fig. 9.2. Let us begin by reviewing LCJ. The utility strength for each alternative is assumed to vary normally on the unidimensional space. To determine the probabilities in a paired comparison task, the respondent samples one point from each distribution and picks the alternative with the higher sampled point. Over many trials it is as if the person picked from a single distribution representing the difference between the two normal distributions. The difference distribution is also normal. This process is illustrated in the top row of Fig. 9.2. Note, however, that the assumption of a normal curve is not essential to the argument. Any two random distributions will do. In Fig. 9.2 (middle row) the distributions are called extreme value distributions. Consistent with the assumptions of general Thurstone scales, the distributions are independent, identical, and centered around the scale value of the alternative. The difference between the two distributions is the logistic curve of the BTL model. Similarly, exponential distributions are combined in the Dawkins model to produce the Laplace distribution (Fig. 9.2, bottom row).

In summary, three choice models based on very dissimilar assumptions are actually special cases of GFS, or a strong utility model, or a generalized Thurstone model. We have also seen how the distinction between constant utility (BTL) and random utility (T-V) may obscure the fact that a single general model serves several theories.

There are two main ways to proceed once GFS has been identified. One might generate a whole series of models based on different distributions surrounding each scale value. This approach is probably not of general interest, and a better idea (at least, a more efficient one) is to determine the limits for scale values (the solution space) satisfying GFS. The algorithm to determine the solution space will not be discussed here. The interested reader should consult McClelland and Coombs (1975).

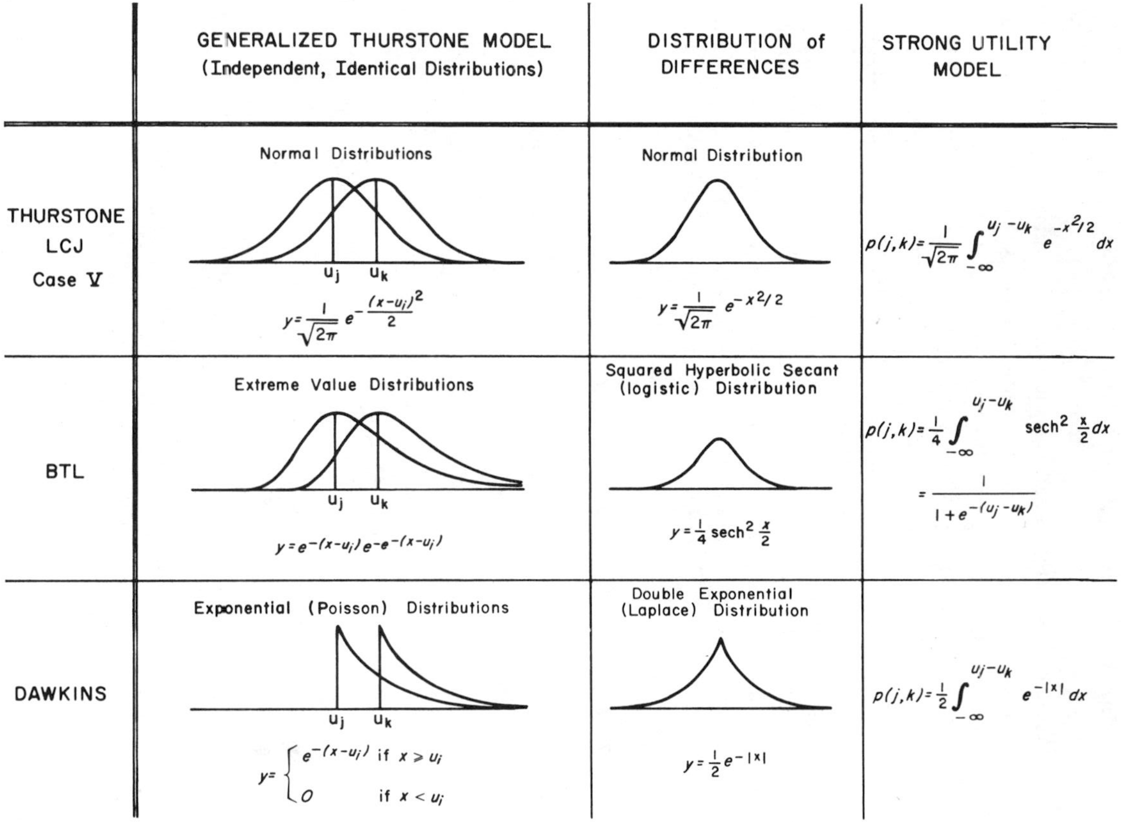

Figure 9.2. Three choice models represented as random utility models of generalized Fechnerian scales (after Yellott, 1971).

SHORTCOMINGS OF GENERAL FECHNERIAN SCALES

General Fechnerian scaling models are not without their shortcomings. In fact, they are often unable to handle some "obvious" situations and may break down completely as descriptions of complicated decision making. There is, however, a wealth of data backing the claim that GFS explains many situations extremely well and at least offers a simple method of condensing data into an understandable form. In most of the following discussion of problems encountered by GFS we will refer to the specific BTL model, but the comments apply to all scaling techniques in the family.

One of the deficiencies of GFS is illustrated by the following example. Consider a woman shopping for a new car. She examines a Chevy (C) and a Dodge (D) and has difficulty deciding which she prefers. We could say that she is indifferent, so $p(C,D)=\frac{1}{2}$. Now suppose the salesperson offers an incentive on another Chevy identical to the first but with whitewall tires added free of charge. Call this car C^*. This car is obviously preferred to the more stripped-down Chevy, so we could safely say that $p(C^*,C)=.99$. Using the BTL model, we have enough information to predict the preference probability, $p(C^*,D)$, between C^* and D. Note that the following scale values satisfy the given probabilities.

$$v_D=1; \quad v_C=1; \quad v_{C^*}=99$$

Therefore, BTL predicts the following from Eq. 9.4:

$$p(C,D)=\frac{1}{2}=\frac{v_C}{v_C+v_D}=\frac{1}{1+1}$$

$$p(C^*,C)=.99=\frac{v_{C^*}}{v_{C^*}+v_C}=\frac{99}{99+1}$$

$$p(C^*,D)=\frac{v_{C^*}}{v_{C^*}+v_D}=\frac{99}{99+1}=.99$$

This high probability seems counterintuitive, since the whitewalls are probably of only minor consequence in the decision between the Chevy and the Dodge; whereas, it is the only relevant variable when comparing two Chevy's. Items such as comfort, gas mileage, and appearance are probably much more important in the former situation. Therefore, the importance of a particular item in the comparison may be a function of the characteristics of the pair of items. This in turn places in jeopardy the entire concept of a unique scale value assigned to a stimulus. For this reason we look to develop another approach to the scaling problem.

Restle's Model

To create a model that makes predictions more in line with our intuition, we consider another way one could make decisions. In the previous example of car buying, we can assume, as does Restle (1961; Restle and Greeno, 1970), that one examines only certain *relevant* aspects of each stimulus before making a choice. We can also assume that any characteristic contained by both alternatives becomes irrelevant to the decision process, and the same is true for aspects contained in neither alternative. In a paired comparison of j and k, the scale value for alternative j depends on the scale values of all the aspects contained in j minus those contained in j and k (that is, the intersection written as $j \cap k$). In symbols, the scale value of j paired with k could be represented by $v_j - v_{j \cap k}$. In other words, the scale value of an item is not fixed but depends on which other item it is paired with. This can also be written as v_{j-k}. Similarly, the scale value for the aspects in k minus those also contained in j is v_{k-j}. These aspects in $j-k$ and $k-j$ are represented in Fig. 9.3. We next apply this new definition of scale value to BTL.

$$p(j,k) = \frac{v_{j-k}}{v_{j-k} + v_{k-j}} \qquad (9.20)$$

In Fig. 9.3 we note that the aspects in alternative j are merely those aspects in $j-k$ plus the excluded aspects in the cross-hatched intersection $(j \cap k)$. Similarly, k consists of the aspects of $k-j$ and those in the intersection. Therefore, by assuming that the scale values of aspects may be added,

$$v_j = v_{j-k} + v_{j \cap k}$$

and

$$v_k = v_{k-j} + v_{j \cap k}$$

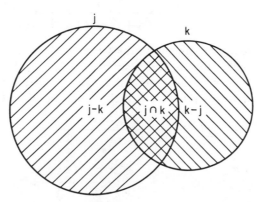

Figure 9.3. Diagram of the scale values for stimuli j and k when these alternatives are compared using the Restle (1961) choice model.

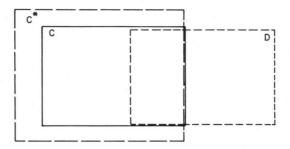

Figure 9.4.   Diagram of scale values when comparing: Dodge (D), Chevy (C), and Chevy with whitewalls ($C*$).

Substituting into Eq. 9.20, we get the more popular version of Restle's model:

$$p(j,k) = \frac{v_j - v_{j\cap k}}{v_j + v_k - 2v_{j\cap k}} \qquad (9.21)$$

Let us see how this equation handles the previous example of buying a car. Schematically, the three different cars may be represented as overlapping rectangles of attributes as shown in Fig. 9.4. We might say that each area in the figure corresponds to a scale value, with larger areas indicating larger scale values. Note that the areas representing the Chevy (C) and the Dodge (D) are roughly equal, so we can arbitrarily set $v_C = v_D = 1$. By setting $v_{C\cap D} = \frac{1}{4}$ we can compute the probability that C is chosen over D.

$$p(C,D) = \frac{v_C - v_{C\cap D}}{v_C + v_D - 2v_{C\cap D}}$$

$$= \frac{1 - \frac{1}{4}}{1 + 1 - 2\left(\frac{1}{4}\right)} = \frac{\frac{3}{4}}{\frac{3}{2}} = \frac{1}{2} \qquad (9.22)$$

Next note that the area representing the Chevy with whitewalls, $C*$, almost completely contains C (that is, C is a subset of $C*$). Another way of stating this is that $v_{C*\cap C} = v_C = 1$. Also assume that $v_{C*} = \frac{3}{2}$. Therefore, the probability that the Chevy with whitewalls is picked over the plain Chevy is

$$p(C*,C) = \frac{v_{C*} - v_{C*\cap C}}{v_{C*} + v_C - 2v_{C*\cap C}}$$

$$= \frac{\frac{3}{2} - 1}{\frac{3}{2} + 1 - 2 \cdot 1} = \frac{\frac{1}{2}}{\frac{1}{2}} = 1 \qquad (9.23)$$

That is, $C*$ is always chosen over C.

In Eqs. 9.22 and 9.23 we have shown that the model satisfies the prescribed conditions. Now let us see how it predicts the probability that C^* is picked over D. Again referring to Fig. 9.4, we see that the attributes common to C^* and D are those also common to C and D. This may be expressed as $v_{C \cap D} = v_{C^* \cap D} = \frac{1}{4}$. From this we derive the following prediction.

$$p(C^*, D) = \frac{v_{C^*} - v_{C^* \cap D}}{v_{C^*} + v_D - 2v_{C^* \cap D}}$$

$$= \frac{\frac{3}{2} - \frac{1}{4}}{\frac{3}{2} + 1 - 2 \cdot \frac{1}{4}} = \frac{\frac{5}{4}}{2} = \frac{5}{8} = .625$$

(9.24)

This seems to be a much more satisfying prediction than that made by the BTL model (that $p(C^*, D) \cong 1$), since the addition of whitewalls has only a minor effect on the decision probabilities. Namely, the two are almost the same:

$$p(C, D) = 1/2 \qquad p(C^*, D) = 5/8$$

An example of the superiority of the Restle model over the BTL model in certain situations has been demonstrated by Edgell, Geisler, and Zinnes (1973), who based their analysis on data collected by Rumelhart and Greeno (1971).

SHORTCOMINGS OF RESTLE'S MODEL

Unfortunately, this does not end the search for a model of decision processes. One of the problems that remains unsolved is that neither Restle's model nor any other predicts intransitive behavior. Basically, transitivity in choice behavior means that if j is usually preferred to k and k to m, then j is usually preferred to m. All the models discussed in this chapter assume this to be a property of the choice process, but Tversky (1969) has shown experimentally that intransitive situations exist in the real world of people making decisions. This behavior implies seemingly insurmountable theoretical problems, despite the fact that we do manage to make decisions! No model has been devised to handle such situations adequately.

Multiple Alternatives

Another area of research that invites exploration is the analysis of choices over arbitrarily large sets of options. In the family of GFS models, this means that one samples a value from each of N distributions corresponding to the N

alternatives. As in the binary case, the alternative from which the largest value was picked is the alternative chosen (largest value in the sense that it is more intense along the scale of interest).

The simplest extension of binary choice situations is the choose-one-from-three-alternatives case. But even this seemingly trivial extension causes the Dawkins model to predict behavior that seems inconsistent with all GFS models! To see why this is so, define $p(m; j,k)$ as the probability that alternative m is chosen over alternatives j and k. Then, the model predicts

$$p(m;j,k) = \frac{\frac{1}{3} t_{jkm}}{t_{\overline{j\,km}} + t_{jk\,\overline{m}} + t_{jkm}} \qquad (9.25)$$

since the potential exceeds threshold L_m for only time t_{jkm}. The intervals during which it exceeds this threshold are the only times alternative m may be picked, and it will be selected only one-third of these times. But we have already shown that

$$p(m,j) = \frac{\frac{1}{2} t_{jkm}}{t_{\overline{j\,km}} + t_{jk\,\overline{m}} + t_{jkm}} \qquad (9.26)$$

so

$$p(m;j,k) = \frac{2}{3} p(m,j)$$

The relation holds regardless of threshold L_k's location, provided it is between L_j and L_m. Expressed in terms of the GFS model, this says that the relation holds for all scale values u_k as long as $u_j > u_k > u_m$. This suggests that in moving from two alternatives to three alternatives, k takes away a constant percentage of the choices from alternative m, regardless of its relative strength or weakness. That is, no matter how close k is to m, it exerts the same effect when the excitatory level exceeds all three thresholds. This seems unreasonable.

By contrast, the T-V and BTL models extend naturally to the multi-alternative GFS model. In fact, the BTL model was originally formulated as a choice among multiple alternatives. Yellott (1977) has suggested that in the multiple alternative situation the BTL model is more intuitively compelling than the T-V model. Suppose that when you repeatedly have a choice between a cup of coffee and a cup of tea, you take the cup of coffee 2 out of 3 times. If instead of being asked to choose between a cup of coffee and a cup of tea, you are asked to pick a beverage from among four cups, two containing coffee and two containing tea, intuitively, the probability of selecting a cup of coffee should remain unchanged from the one-cup-of-each situation. Yellott proves that if the generalized Thurstone model satisfies this condition it must have extreme value distributions for the independent, identical distributions around the scale value for each item. From Fig. 9.2 we see that this means the BTL model is the only generalized Thurstone model that leaves the probabilities unchanged (coffee over tea) as the size of the set is expanded (two cups each of coffee and tea). In our example, $p(\text{coffee}) = 2/3 = v_C/(v_C + v_T)$, which is equivalent to $v_C = 2$ and $v_T = 1$.

Next, using a theorem proved by Holman and Marley (see Luce and Suppes, 1965, p. 338 or Yellott, 1977) that the extreme value distribution in the generalized Thurstone model is equivalent in all respects to the BTL model, the probability of choosing a cup of coffee from two cups of coffee and two cups of tea is

$$p(\text{coffee}) = \frac{v_C + v_C}{v_C + v_C + v_T + v_T} = \frac{4}{6} = \frac{2}{3}$$

Unfortunately, no such neat formulation exists for the Case V Thurstone model. A computer simulation for this model, using 10,000 trials on the same 2/3 probability, yielded a probability of .70 that one chooses coffee when there are two cups of coffee and two cups of tea.

Prior to Yellott's work, Tversky (1972) generalized the Restle model to multiple alternatives. He conjectured that decision processes proceed in stages as groups of alternatives are eliminated, where each alternative is characterized by a list of attributes or aspects. When alternatives are being compared, aspects contained in all of them are irrelevant in the decision process. Similarly, aspects contained by none of the alternatives are also irrelevant. Subsequently, alternatives are eliminated by the following procedure (according to the theory). An aspect is randomly chosen from the set of all aspects (for example, the number of bedrooms when home buying). All alternatives with that attribute are kept as possible options, and all alternatives without the aspect are eliminated from further consideration. This process is repeated until a single alternative remains. Appropriately enough, Tversky refers to this as the "elimination by aspects" model (EBA). Despite the differences in psychological theories, it can be shown that BTL and the Restle model are special cases of the EBA model.

First, consider the situation where each alternative is identified with one aspect and no aspect is shared by a pair of alternatives. We can give the aspects weights $v_a, v_b, \ldots$, so that

$$p(a, \{a, b, c, \ldots\}) = \frac{v_a}{v_a + v_b + v_c + \ldots} \tag{9.27}$$

But since aspect a is identified with alternative A,

$$p(A,\{A,B,C,\dots\}) = \frac{v_a}{v_a + v_b + v_c + \dots} \qquad (9.28)$$

As promised, this is the multiple-alternative version of the BTL model.

Second, restrict the EBA model to the binary case. Characterize the alternatives by the following list of aspects:

$$A: \quad a_1, a_2, \dots, a_j, c_1, c_2, \dots, c_l$$
$$B: \quad b_1, b_2, \dots, b_k, c_1, c_2, \dots, c_l$$

The only shared aspects are $c_1, \dots, c_l$. Each aspect has a weight proportional to the probability that it is chosen. Therefore the probability that an aspect unique to A is chosen may be written

$$\frac{\displaystyle\sum_{i=1}^{j} v_{a_i}}{\displaystyle\sum_{i=1}^{j} v_{a_i} + \sum_{i=1}^{k} v_{b_i} + \sum_{i=1}^{l} v_{c_i}} \qquad (9.29)$$

Since the shared aspects are irrelevant to the decision process,

$$p(A,B) = \frac{\displaystyle\sum_{i=1}^{j} v_{a_i}}{\displaystyle\sum_{i=1}^{j} v_{a_i} + \sum_{i=1}^{k} v_{b_i}} \qquad (9.30)$$

Using the notation in Eq. 9.20, we can make the following substitutions

$$v_{A-B} = \sum_{i=1}^{j} v_{a_i}, \qquad v_{B-A} = \sum_{i=1}^{k} v_{b_i}$$

to get the final form of the probability

$$p(A,B) = \frac{v_{A-B}}{v_{A-B} + v_{B-A}}$$

This, however, is the Restle model.

Therefore, the EBA model is the generalized form of both the Restle and BTL models when one is considering multiple alternatives. The demonstration of this relation is a remarkable tribute to the power of careful theoretical argument.

DOMINANCE SCALING IN A BROADER PSYCHOLOGICAL CONTEXT

Despite certain limitations, the GFS, Restle, and Tversky models are of interest both as scaling tools for dominance data and as conceptual frameworks of the choice process. As a scaling tool, a large mass of data may be condensed into a single number for each alternative. From the scale values one obtains a general idea of the similarity of different alternatives and makes predictions about preferences.

As a conceptual framework, the GFS model has its roots in Fechner's ideas of stimulus and threshold variability. These notions have had wide applicability. Even Hull (1943), the learning theorist, used this model of choice in his general behavior theory: The organism does (chooses) the activity that is currently dominant in the hierarchy of potential activities. Later, models developed by Luce and Dawkins were shown to be specific cases of the GFS model (the same assumptions of random variations around scale values on an internal unidimensional continuum). To overcome shortcomings of GFS, Restle and Tversky developed approaches that generalize the decision process to a multidimensional space of overlapping aspects of each alternative. This concept of objects in a multidimensional psychological space is very interesting indeed and will be explored in the next chapter. The main thing to remember here is the progression from specific models (Fechner) attached to specific scaling tasks, to general models (Restle, Tversky) that cover the more extensive field of decision making. This is truly a significant advance.

REFERENCES

Bradley, R. A., and Terry, M. E. "Rank analysis of incomplete block designs: I. The method of paired comparison." *Biometrika*, 1952, *39*, 324–345.

Burke, C. J., and Zinnes, J. L. "A paired comparison of pair comparisons." *Journal of Mathematical Psychology*, 1965, *2*, 53–76.

Coombs, C. H. *A Theory of Data*. New York: Wiley, 1964.

Coombs, C. H., Dawes, R. M., and Tversky, A. *Mathematical Psychology: An Elementary Introduction* Englewood Cliffs, N.J.: Prentice-Hall, 1970.

Dawkins, R. "A threshold model of choice behavior." *Animal Behavior*, 1969, *17*, 120–133.

Edgell, S. E., Geisler, W. S., III, and Zinnes, J. L. "A note on a paper by Rumelhart and Greeno." *Journal of Mathematical Psychology*, 1973, *10*, 86–90.

Hull, C. L. *Principles of Behavior*. New York: Appleton-Century, 1943.

Kelley, J. L. *General Topology*. New York: Van Nostrand, 1955.

Luce, R. D. *Individual Choice Behavior*. New York: Wiley, 1959.

Luce, R. D. "The choice axiom after twenty years." *Journal of Mathematical Psychology*, 1977, *15*, 215–233.

Luce, R. D., Suppes, P. "Preference, utility, and subjective probability." In R. D. Luce, R. R. Bush, and E. Galanter (Eds.), *Handbook of Mathematical Psychology*, Vol. III. New York: Wiley, 1965.

McClelland, G. H., and Coombs, C. H. "Ordmet: A general algorithm for constructing all numerical solutions to ordered metric data." *Psychometrika*, 1975, *50*, 269–290.

Restle, F. *The Psychology of Judgment and Choice: A Theoretical Essay*. New York: Wiley, 1961.

Restle, F., and Greeno, J. G. *Introduction to Mathematical Psychology*. Reading, Mass.: Addison-Wesley, 1970.

Rumelhart, D. L., and Greeno, J. G. "Similarity between stimuli: an experimental test of the Luce and Restle choice models." *Journal of Mathematical Psychology*, 1971, *8*, 370–380.

Schjelderup-Ebbe, T. "Social behavior of birds." In E. A. Murchison (Ed.), *Social Psychology*, Worcester: Clark University, Vol. 2, 1935, pp. 947–972.

Suppes, P., and Zinnes, J. L. "Basic measurement theory." In R. D. Luce, R. R. Bush, and E. Galanter (Eds.), *Handbook of Mathematical Psychology*. Vol. I. New York: Wiley, 1963.

Thurstone, L. L. "Psychophysical analysis." *American Journal of Psychology*, 1927a, *38*, 368–389.

Thurstone, L. L. "A law of comparative judgment." *Psychological Review*, 1927b, *34*, 373–286.

Thurstone, L. L. "The learning function." *Journal of General Psychology*, 1930, *3*, 469–493.

Torgerson, W. S. *Theory and Methods of Scaling*. New York: Wiley, 1958.

Tversky, A "Intransitivity of preferences." *Psychological Review*, 1969, *76*, 31–48.

Tversky, A. "Elimination by aspects: a theory of choice." *Psychological Review*, 1972a, *79*, 281–299.

Tversky, A. "Choice by elimination." *Journal of Mathematical Psychology*, 1972b, *9*, 341–367.

Yellott, J. I. "The relationship between Thurstone's, Luce's and Dawkins' models for paired comparisons." Paper given at the Annual Meeting of Mathematical Psychology, Miami, Florida, September, 1970.

Yellott, J. I. "Generalized Thurstone representations for three choice theories: uniqueness theorems." Paper given at the Annual Meeting of Mathematical Psychology, Princeton, New Jersey, 1971.

Yellott, J. I. "The relationship between Luce's choice axiom, Thurstone's theory of comparative judgment, and the double exponential distribution." *Journal of Mathematical Psychology*, 1977, *15*, 109–144.

CHAPTER

10

MULTIDIMENSIONAL
SCALING

Throughout most of its history, experimental psychology has concentrated on the scaling of stimuli along a single dimension. This assumption is basic to Stevens's method of magnitude estimation and Fechner's classical methods (for example, constant stimuli), as well as general Fechnerian scales. However, the concept of a multidimensional psychological space is probably as old as experimental psychology. Wilhelm Wundt (1874), one of psychology's founders, characterized sensations as elements in a "mental chemistry." Later his concepts were expanded by those in the introspection school, such as Titchener, who stated in 1924 that each stimulus is analyzed along five dimensions: quality, intensity, extensity, protensity, and attensity. More recently, there has been renewed interest in multidimensional scales, or rather in the placement of stimuli in a multidimensional space. Part of the motivation for this revival is the implausibility of psychological mechanisms that must be invoked for evaluating stimuli on a single sensation scale. In addition, many unidimensional models are simply unable to adequately scale the data (see Chapter 9).

Certainly, another compelling reason to examine multidimensional spaces is their intuitive appeal. When examining an object, one is usually aware that it has several attributes that may be changed independently. For example, a table may be classified according to length, width, number of legs, and so forth. Since an attribute may be varied more or less independently of others, each may be viewed as a dimension in some "table space," with any particular table represented as a point in that space. But there is still the question of the appropriate model. There are two types of models: one where items are vectors (arrows), and one in which items are points in everyday Euclidean space. The subsidiary considerations of what objects are to be placed in such a space, and what sorts of interrelations among items are to be observed, are entirely up to the experimenter and so are not discussed here. We will consider only the type of space and how one places items in it.

One model represents stimuli as points in a Euclidean space. That is, stimuli are points on a line, plane, or some higher dimensional space. This spatial notion has intuitive appeal since it is the same one used to describe the "real" world. By assuming that a set of stimuli are placed somewhere in Euclidean space, we mean that (1) the space has dimensions—up-down, north-south, east-west, etc.; (2) each stimulus may be located by coordinates (for example, 10 meters north and 5 meters west of zero); and (3) the distance between two points is computed by the Euclidean formula

$$d_{jk} = \sqrt{(x_{j1} - x_{k1})^2 + (x_{j2} - x_{k2})^2}$$

where x_{j1} is the first coordinate of stimulus j, and x_{j2} is the second. The Euclidean formula satisfies a set of properties that define a *metric*. Momentarily we will examine these properties and some of the functions that satisfy these requirements.

A second form of representation is the *vector* model, which represents stimuli by lines extending from a common origin. The distance or difference between two stimuli represented by a pair of vectors is a function of the length of each vector and the angle between them. Therefore, two stimuli are very close together only if both vectors are the same length and point in about the same direction. In mathematical terms, the distance between two points in this space is computed by

$$d_{jk} = x_{j1}x_{k1} + x_{j2}x_{k2}$$

This is equivalent to

$$d_{jk} = \sqrt{x_{j1}^2 + x_{j2}^2} \ \sqrt{x_{k1}^2 + x_{k2}^2} \ \cos\theta_{jk}$$

where θ_{jk} is the angle between the two vectors extending from the origin to the points x_j and x_k. This model is usually associated with the method known as factor analysis and with Ekman's work (Ekman, 1963; Ekman et al., 1964) on scaling of multiple attributes (such as color and odor). Here we will not explore this model as thoroughly as the Euclidean model even though the computational procedures of multidimensional scaling could have been adapted as well to the vector as to the Euclidean model.

Assume now we have a constellation of N points in a Euclidean psychological space. Each of the $N(N-1)/2$ pairs of points has an interpoint distance d that could be manifested in a variety of experimental tasks. For instance, the latent proximity (smallness of the interpoint distance) of two stimuli could be manifested in experiments where these stimuli are found to be easily confused in recognition tasks, to be similar in taste, to contain the same kinds of components, and so on. The interpretation would be derived from outside the methodological area. Unfortunately, most psychological data do not come to us as locations of points in space. Instead, we are given a matrix of all interpoint proximities among stimuli and must create a constellation of points. In other words, the matrix of d values is given and the stimulus points must be determined. How should this be done? This is the question tackled by multidimensional scaling. The solution can best be appreciated as the end result of a historical line of creative work.

HISTORICAL ANTECEDENTS

Most of the original scaling models and techniques were developed in the search for basic components of personality and from the field of intelligence testing. Beginning with Charles Spearman's 1904 article "General Intelligence: Objectively Determined and Measured," attempts have been made to quantify the factors underlying intelligence. The analysis of "general intelligence" into several fundamental factors evolved into Spearman's two-factor theory, which is the forerunner of modern factor analysis.

Factor Analysis

Factor analysis was originally seen as a way to segregate the major factors (dimensions) of general intelligence from properties unique to a particular intelligence measure. Even though the method never completely fulfilled this desire, it has proven useful in the study of group behavior, intelligence testing, construction of composite variables for sociological analysis, and so on. In the basic model, scale values of stimuli are modeled as the weighted sum of latent factors. Rather than approaching this problem directly, factor analysis decomposes a correlation matrix (all possible interstimulus correlations) using a vector representation. Unfortunately, interval scale data are required for computing correlations, and the logic of the factor analysis model cannot be extended to meaningfully process similarities and relative distance measures. In addition, linearity is assumed to hold in a metric space, such as Euclidean. This means that stimuli may only be rotated, uniformly moved, or spread in space. Individual stimuli are therefore locked into a configuration that does not allow relocation to improve the solution. Another common objection to factor analysis is the large number of dimensions sometimes required to "fit" the data. Structures in more than three dimensions create difficulties in visualization and graphing, to say nothing of the problems of interpreting a large number of factors (dimensions).

Fixed Dimensions

There are several ways to overcome the problems of factor analysis. For example, Attneave (1950) analyzed similarity data by prespecifying the interpretation of dimensions. In one experiment, subjects were presented rectangles that varied along two dimensions, area and tilt, as shown in Fig. 10.1. The subject rated the similarity of rectangles i and j, without being supplied with further judgment criteria.

To analyze these data, a model is required to predict how subjects judge similarity. Because the rectangles are located in a stimulus space, we can specify the dimensions, coordinates, and metric of this model in terms of that space. In other words, since the dimensions (physical tilt and area) had been decided upon, stimuli could be located by their coordinates in the space. From examining the similarity judgments in the same terms, Attneave concluded that the psychological dimensions were in an additive space, later referred to as the *city block* metric. (This metric is also called the Manhattan metric—one walks a total of ten blocks to get from 33rd Street and 7th Avenue to 42nd Street and 8th Avenue—9 blocks north and 1 block west.) That is, the judged similarity or, more correctly, dissimilarity (d) of two rectangles could be predicted by adding the physical dissimilarity along the area dimension (a) to the physical dissimilarity along the tilt dimension (t). If i and j are two rectangles, x_{ia} and x_{ja} are the projections (coordinates) of the points representing the rectangles on the area dimension, and x_{it} and x_{jt} are projections onto the tilt dimension. The following formula can now be used to predict the judged dissimilarity d_{ij}.

$$d_{ij} = |x_{ia} - x_{ja}| + |x_{it} - x_{jt}| \tag{10.1}$$

To summarize, the objects (rectangles) are points in a theoretical model

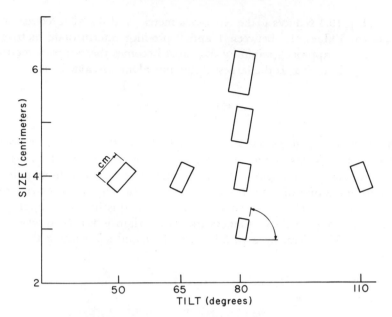

Figure 10.1. Stimulus rectangles arranged by size and tilt, as employed by Attneave (1950). Perceived dissimilarity among the stimuli can be described by a city block metric.

called psychological space. The reported dissimilarities are equated with the distances between points in this space. This measure can be generalized to the city block metric, usually written in the form

$$d_{ij} = \sum_{k=1}^{N} |x_{ik} - x_{jk}| \tag{10.2}$$

For this particular example, the number of dimensions is $N=2$. This formula contrasts with the Euclidean metric, mentioned previously, that is assumed in most physical measurements:

$$d_{ij} = \left[\sum_{k=1}^{N} |x_{ik} - x_{jk}|^2 \right]^{1/2} \tag{10.3}$$

But both distance formulas are part of the same structure and may in fact be generalized to the Minkowski r metric.

$$d_{ij} = \left[\sum_{k=1}^{N} |x_{ik} - x_{jk}|^r \right]^{1/r}, \qquad 1 \leqslant r \leqslant \infty \tag{10.4}$$

If $r=1$, Eq. 10.4 reduces to the city block metric, and if $r=2$ it reduces to the Euclidean. Values of r between 1 and 2 produce intermediate metrics. In addition, as r approaches infinity, Eq. 10.4 becomes the *supremum* metric in which the distance d_{ij} is the largest difference along any one axis:

$$d_{ij} = \max_{k=1}^{N} |x_{ik} - x_{jk}| \tag{10.5}$$

A graphical way to represent the various Minkowski metrics is to show the locations of all points that are a unit distance from a fixed point. In Fig. 10.2 the fixed point is the origin of the diagram, 0. Consider first those points on the solid line a unit distance from the origin by the city block metric ($r=1$). To see this, we look at two points A and B on this line. The appropriate formula to compute their distances from the origin is Eq. 10.4, where $r=1$ and $N=2$. Therefore, by expanding Eq. 10.4 and substituting the coordinates:

$$d_{0,A} = |0-0| + |1-0| = 1$$

$$d_{0,B} = |\tfrac{1}{4}-0| + |\tfrac{3}{4}-0| = 1$$

The remaining lines in Fig. 10.2 represent equidistance contours for other Minkowski metrics.

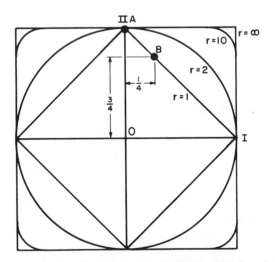

Figure 10.2.   Equidistance contours from the origin 0 for various Minkowski metrics. $r=1$ represents all points that are the same distance from the origin using the city block metric. $r=2$ shows the equidistant points for the Euclidean metric.

Other functions to determine the distance between A and B, $d(A,B)$, can be used in place of the Minkowski metric provided they satisfy the following conditions, which define a metric:

1. $d(A,A)=0$ Point A is zero distance from itself.

2. $d(A,B)>0$; $A\neq B$ The distance between two distinct points is positive.

3. $d(A,B)=d(B,A)$ Distance does not depend on the order of the points.

4. $d(A,B)+d(B,C)\geqslant d(A,C)$ The triangle inequality must hold. The shortest distance between two points is the length of the line connecting those points.

With the notable exception of Attneave's analysis, most of the groundwork on multidimensional scaling was restricted to Euclidean space. Only recently have the implications of other spaces been explored.

Traditional Multidimensional Scaling

Another way to approach the problem of scaling similarities was introduced by Torgerson (1952, 1958). In his "traditional" method, the probabilities that stimulus A is judged more similar to stimulus B than to stimulus C are converted to z scores and averaged to produce a similarity score $h_{A,B}$ for all pairs of stimuli A and B (remember Thurstone?). The values of h are, however, interval scale data with no fixed or "natural" zero point. To represent stimuli in a space, the similarities must be converted to distances by adding a constant to fix zero. The solution to the "additive constant" problem is not taken lightly, because some constants will produce a space with minimum dimensionality, while others will produce nonmetric spaces (containing distance functions that violate the four conditions of a metric stated above). Finally, using a formula developed by Young and House-holder (1938), coordinates may be computed from the distance values.

This mapping of similarities into a space is still inadequate for many problems, since the requirements of the model are quite severe. First, a Euclidean psychological space is required, which, as was shown by Attneave, may not be the case. Second, computed similarities are assumed to be interval scale data. Third, the formula developed by Young and House-holder assumes errorless distance measures, an unreasonable restriction.

Unfolding

A third type of scaling, the unfolding approach, was developed by Coombs (1964). Instead of giving similarities, the subject rank orders stimuli according to preference. In addition, the subject is assumed to prefer a particular quantity along a continuum. For instance, most coffee drinkers prefer a certain number of teaspoons of sugar. Any cup with more or less than this amount is less desirable. These preferences over many subjects may then be "unfolded" to reveal both the locations of the stimuli and the "ideal" point of each subject in one or more dimensions. In one dimension, unfolding may be visualized as a subject placing stimuli along the length of a string. When rank ordering, he picks the string up at his ideal point and reads down toward both ends of the string to determine the preference ordering. Sample data from two subjects are shown in Fig. 10.3, where it is apparent that stimuli on opposite sides of the ideal point (C and F) may be very close in preference ordering. Unfolding is an attempt to straighten the string to place stimuli and subjects along a common dimension. Note how this scaling model for preference data differs from that for dominance data. For preference data, all subjects are assumed to view a common dimension but from different perspectives on the dimension. By contrast, dominance data could be seen as judgments from a point of view removed from the stimulus continuum. For this reason, only the stimuli are positioned on the continuum.

With a rough measure like preference ordering, however, the results of many subjects must be combined to obtain a solution consisting of the order of the stimuli and some information on the relative distances between stimuli. The extension of unfolding to multidimensional stimuli is attractive because all steps from data collection to the final solution are *nonmetric* in the sense that an interval scale is not required.

One major drawback in the original formulation of multidimensional unfolding is the need for complete data. That is, subjects' ideal points must be distributed throughout the space, with each point representing a unique preference ordering. This is an unreasonable expectation in many experimental situations, since the number of subjects needed increases exponentially with the number of stimuli and dimensions. For example, to secure complete data with 30 stimuli in five dimensions, one needs 1,122,776,355 subject scales, *each one unique*. To obtain this many unique scales, and assuming there will be shared scales, the required subject population would probably have to be greater than the number of people who ever lived! Solutions have been proposed to compensate for incomplete data, but these involve *metric* assumptions to constrain the results (Schönemann, 1970). For these and other reasons, then, it is desirable to employ the more general method of multidimensional scaling.

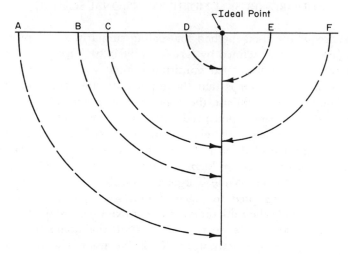

SUBJECT NUMBER I STIMULUS PREFERENCE ORDERING: DEFCBA

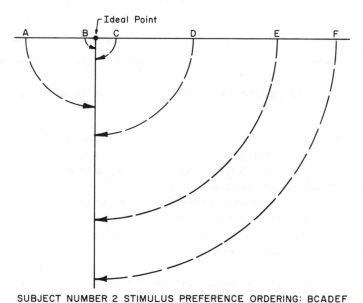

SUBJECT NUMBER 2 STIMULUS PREFERENCE ORDERING: BCADEF

Figure 10.3. The unfolding model for generation of preference orderings on a unidimensional space. Two different orderings are generated depending on the subject's ideal point.

SHEPARD-KRUSKAL MULTIDIMENSIONAL SCALING

The most frequently used method for scaling similarities was proposed by Shepard (1962a,b) and refined by Kruskal (1964a,b). This procedure is the basis for what is usually called multidimensional scaling. One of the big advantages of this method is that the input data are only assumed to be ordinal. Therefore, we will use the general term *proximity*, which includes similarities, dissimilarities, perceived distances, correlations, and so forth. Shepard (1962a,b) starts with relative proximity measures and develops a spatial representation of the stimuli in a minimum number of dimensions. Although this is the same problem tackled by Torgerson (1952), the approach is very different. While Torgerson rescaled the proximities to distances and then attempted to place stimuli into space, Shepard uses a *nonmetric* process (only the rank orders of the proximities are used to scale the locations of the stimuli in a metric space). With this nonmetric process, N stimuli may be placed perfectly in an $N-2$ dimensional space in all but a limited number of degenerate situations, where $N-1$ dimensions are required (Lingoes, 1971). For example, four stimuli can be put in a plane regardless of the ranks of their proximities. But to secure a more comprehensible representation of the stimulus constellation, the interpoint distances in the $N-2$ dimensional space are changed so that

1.   The stimuli can be adequately represented in a (sub)space of *minimum dimensionality*.
2.   The ranked distances are in the same order as the ranked proximities (*monotonicity*).

In everything that follows, it is important to realize that only the distances in the model's configuration are changed and not the original proximity data. In addition, we consider only the ranks of the proximities in attempting to match the ranks of the distances.

The first goal (minimum dimensionality) requires "flattening" of the configuration by shrinking the smaller distances and stretching the larger ones. This is referred to as "increasing the variance" of the interpoint distances. Even though this operation tends to obscure some of the underlying structure by flattening curves and to act contrary to the search for monotonicity, it is needed to eventually get the points into a comprehensible spatial form.

The second goal (monotonicity) is accomplished by stretching the distances that are too short and shrinking those that are too long. In other words, we are looking for a monotonic function to relate proximities (empirical data) and distances (theoretical data) so that the nearest proximity is mapped into the smallest distance, the second nearest into the second smallest distance, and so on. There are $N(N-1)/2$ distances separating N stimuli; stated another way, each stimulus has $N-1$ distance measures, one to each of the others. To attain monotonicity, the points representing the stimuli act as if they were connected by springs; each one moves in the direction of points that are too far away in terms of ranked proximity and away from those too close. The process is repeated over several iterations and without further constraints (such as minimum dimensionality) would eventually fit the empirical data exactly in an $N-2$ dimensional space.

Therefore, from an arbitrary configuration in $N-2$ space, each of the points is subject to the operations used to obtain monotonicity and minimum dimensionality. This iterative procedure is repeated until a sufficiently good "fit" is obtained. (Later we shall see how this concept may be quantified.) Then the configuration is rotated with respect to the axes, and the dimensions best able to describe the interpoint distances are retained for the final representation. For instance, suppose nine points are operated on until a sufficiently good "fit" is obtained, and these points may be adequately located in a two-dimensional plane within the seven-dimensional space $(N-2)$. To observe this, the configuration must be rotated so that the plane is described by the first two dimensions. The other five dimensions may now be ignored and the points plotted in two-dimensional space.

In contrast to previous approaches, such as factor analysis, Shepard's method leads to interpretable solutions in few dimensions and without the assumption of metric data (for example, correlations as required by factor analysis): Indeed, *the method's popularity is due mainly to the fact that a wide variety of proximity measures can be treated.*

An example of this flexibility is provided in a study by Wolford and Hollingsworth (1974), who were interested in the types of confusions made when subjects attempt to identify letters of the alphabet briefly viewed (15 to 25 msec). On each trial, five consonants were presented and subjects attempted to recall them. A confusion matrix was constructed for the group data showing the frequency with which each stimulus letter was mistakenly called something else. A subset of this matrix is presented in Table 10.1. Only the lower left or upper right triangle of the matrix is required to apply the scaling methods. The diagonal contains asterisks to indicate that a letter cannot logically be confused with itself.

The entries in the matrix were first converted to dissimilarity measures by changing the sign of each.[1] The large negative numbers now represent

---

[1]This operation is done only for technical reasons. Many computer programs have the option to input similarity or dissimilarity measures. At the time of the analysis, our program did not contain this option.

Table 10.1   Confusion matrix
(subset of data from Wolford and Hollingsworth, 1974)

	C	D	G	H	M	N	Q	W
C	*							
D	5	*						
G	12	2	*					
H	2	4	3	*				
M	2	3	2	19	*			
N	2	4	1	18	16	*		
Q	9	20	9	1	2	8	*	
W	1	5	2	5	18	13	4	*

highly confusable, similar letters; numbers nearer to zero represent dissimilar letters. The matrix was then supplied as data to a multidimensional
scaling program and a configuration obtained in two dimensions, as shown
in Fig. 10.4. The results suggest that visual confusions dominated. Those
letters with straight line features (H, M, N, and W) are located together in
one part of the space, whereas letters with curved features (D, Q, C, and G)

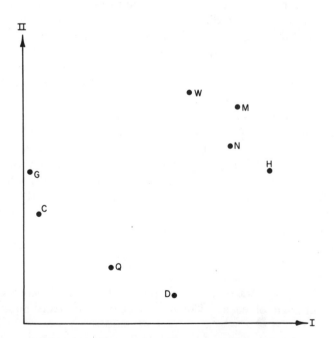

Figure 10.4.   A representation of the Wolford and Hollingsworth (1974) letter confusion
data in two dimensions produced by Shepard-Kruskal multidimensional scaling. Items
located close together imply high confusability.

are grouped closer together in another part of the space. In some cases, such as M & N and C & G, confusions could be either auditory or visual, but the overall picture favors the hypothesis that visual confusions dominate. The claim here is that placing stimuli in the two-dimensional space aids in the psychological interpretation of results that might otherwise remain in the confusing state of a confusion matrix.

Measures of Fit

The major weakness in Shepard's formulation of multidimensional scaling is the lack of a mathematically explicit definition of the solution. In other words, how does one determine the goodness of fit? Kruskal (1964a) starts from Shepard's concept of monotonicity and develops a *stress* measure for this purpose.

One possible approach to the definition of the goodness of fit is to follow the original intent of nonmetric multidimensional scaling. Since the goal there is to match the rank orders of the input proximities with that of the derived distances, one might start by comparing the two orders in a graph. This plot is called a Shepard diagram and is illustrated in Fig. 10.5. For any point in the Shepard diagram, the x coordinate represents the distance between two points in the final configuration and the y coordinate represents the rank of the original proximity of the same two stimuli. Ideally, the Shepard diagram for the final configuration should permit one to start with the smallest interpoint proximity at the lower left-hand corner and join all the points in the diagram by moving up and to the right. One should never move to the left. This is one interpretation of monotonicity. Mathematically this notion is expressed as follows:

$$\text{If } \delta_{ij} < \delta_{kl}, \quad \text{then } d_{ij} < d_{kl}$$

where δ_y is the ranked proximity between objects i and j and d_{ij} is the computed distance between points i and j (the open circles in the diagram). In many cases, however, the ranked interpoint distances will not be in the same order as the ranked proximities. This is illustrated by points V and W in Fig. 10.5.

To match an intuitive notion of goodness of fit, the configuration of points giving rise to the Shepard diagram in Fig. 10.5 should have a nonzero (not perfect) "fit." How is it to be computed? Since we wish to make no further assumptions about the ordinal scaled input data, the actual proximities should not be included in the calculations. The calculations should therefore be done solely on the distances d_{ij}. If we denote locations of points (along the

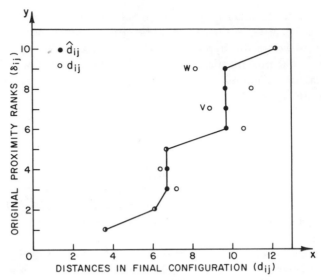

Figure 10.5. A Shepard diagram of the original proximity measures (y axis) versus the corresponding distances in the final configuration (x axis). The points V and W violate the rule of monotonicity, since the larger the original proximity, the larger should be the corresponding scaled interpoint distances. The open circles represent distances in the present configuration. The filled circles represent comparable points on the monotonic line.

x and y axes) in the Shepard diagram by (d_{ij}, δ_{ij}), we should compute the squared deviations from the monotonic line $(\hat{d}_{ij}, \delta_{ij})$, where $\hat{d}_{ij}$ is the distance when monotonicity is satisfied (the filled circles in the diagram). These values are also read from the x axis. The squared deviations $(d_{ij} - \hat{d}_{ij})^2$ are combined for all pairs of points to produce a measure called *raw stress*:

$$\text{raw stress} = S^* = \sum_{i=1}^{N} \sum_{j=i+1}^{N} \left(d_{ij} - \hat{d}_{ij} \right)^2 \tag{10.6}$$

A scaling factor T_1^* is introduced so stretching or shrinking of the overall configuration will not affect the stress

$$T_1^* = \sum_{i=1}^{N} \sum_{j=i+1}^{N} d_{ij}^2 \tag{10.7}$$

Therefore, let us call S_1:

$$\text{stress} = S_1 = \sqrt{\frac{S^*}{T_1^*}} \tag{10.8}$$

Kruskal and Carroll (1969) also proposed a second scaling factor,

$$T_2^* = \sum_{i=1}^{N} \sum_{j=i+1}^{N} \left(d_{ij} - \bar{d}_{ij} \right)^2 \tag{10.9}$$

where $\bar{d}_{ij}$ is the average of all interpoint distances. Consequently, S_2 is an alternative stress measure.

$$S_2 = \sqrt{\frac{S^*}{T_2^*}} \tag{10.10}$$

A criterion for goodness of fit is now established. To improve the fit, decrease the stress. A value of zero means a perfect fit with no violations of monotonicity.

To complete our discussion of stress, we need only determine how to compute the $\hat{d}_{ij}$ values. For now we will only examine the somewhat tedious Kruskal (1964a,b) algorithm. To compute the $\hat{d}_{ij}$'s, first set $\hat{d}_{ij} = d_{ij}$ and list the $\hat{d}_{ij}$ values in ascending order according to the size of the corresponding δ_{ij}. (This is the only time in the algorithm that we will use the original dissimilarities.) Ideally, this ordering of the $\hat{d}$'s should be in an increasing order to satisfy the monotonicity requirement. The poorer the fit, the greater the deviations (higher stress). To obtain the lowest possible stress, given the original d values and the monotonicity requirement, we use an averaging technique as follows: First, define a list of blocks each containing only a single element, $\hat{d}_{ij}$. This is the value of the block. Next, compare the values of the first and second blocks in the list. If the second block is smaller, merge the first and second blocks into a new two-element block. The value of this merged block, and the $\hat{d}$ values within the block, are set to the mean value of the $\hat{d}$'s in the two components. Repeat this comparison and merger procedure for all pairs of blocks in both ascending and descending order. That is, combine blocks into new ones to ensure that any given block is preceded by a smaller-valued block and followed by a larger-valued one. Once this has been achieved, each d_{ij} has a corresponding $\hat{d}_{ij}$ that satisfies the monotonicity requirement.

To illustrate this procedure we treat a hypothetical example of five points located in a two-dimensional space. First, the coordinates of the points (see below) are substituted into Eq. 10.3 to secure the Euclidean distances (d_{ij}'s). Second, these values are ordered by ranks of the appropriate δ_{ij}'s. For our example, the specific numbers are as follows:

Points	Coordinates	Entries are Euclidean interpoint distances (d)					Entries are ranked proximities (δ) 1 = most proximal				
		1	2	3	4	5	1	2	3	4	5
1	(0,8)	1	12.17	6.40	6.71	7.21		10	4	5	3
2	(12,6)	2		10.63	6.08	8.94			6	2	7
3	(4,13)	3			8.25	11.00				9	8
4	(6,5)	4				3.61					1
5	(4,2)	5									

Next, we successively block and average the distances to insure monotonicity. This is demonstrated below, where the left (first) column gives the
original proximities (δ_{ij}'s), the second column gives the configuration distances (d_{ij}'s), and the seventh column gives the final monotone values ($\hat{d}_{ij}$'s).
The entries in a column reveal details of the successive steps in the blocking
procedure, the results of which are shown in the Shepard diagram of Fig.
10.5. The stress can now be calculated by appropriate substitution in Eqs.
10.6, 10.7, and 10.8. By this means we find that $S^* = 5.57$, $T_1^* = 718$, and
stress $= S_1 = .088$.

δ values blocks ranked by proximity	d values original distances	combine (3)+(4)	combine (3,4)+(5)	combine (6)+(7)	combine (8)+(9)	$\hat{d}$ values combine (6,7)+(8,9)
1	3.61	3.61	3.61	3.61	3.61	3.61
2	6.08	6.08	6.08	6.08	6.08	6.08
3	7.21	6.81	6.77	6.77	6.77	6.77
4	6.40	6.81	6.77	6.77	6.77	6.77
5	6.71	6.71	6.77	6.77	6.77	6.77
6	10.63	10.63	10.63	9.79	9.79	9.71
7	8.94	8.94	8.94	9.79	9.79	9.71
8	11.00	11.00	11.00	11.00	9.62	9.71
9	8.25	8.25	8.25	8.25	9.62	9.71
10	12.17	12.17	12.17	12.17	12.17	12.17

Note that in this procedure the ratio scale properties of the d_{ij}'s are used,
but the original dissimilarities were used only to order the d_{ij}'s. This
approach tells us how well we are doing. However, the goal of multidimensional scaling is to minimize stress. Now we turn to a method by which this
can be achieved.

The Iterative Process

Since we start with an arbitrary configuration, we must usually move it to decrease the stress. One way to do this is to randomly change the configuration until no further improvement (decrease) in stress is obtained. This process is very time consuming. A far better approach, and the one most often used, is called the *method of steepest descent* or the *method of gradients*.[2] Here we compute the direction in which *each point should move*. (Moving a point is equivalent to changing each of its coordinates along each of the dimensions.) Using this strategy, the stress is decreased bit by bit by stepping the configuration in the direction specified by the negative gradient (G) of stress S.

To describe how this works, let us first write the locations of all points in space in matrix form:

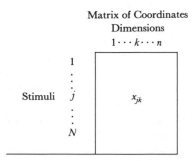

where x_{jk} is the kth coordinate of the jth point. To step the configuration, we would like to add or subtract values from each of the current coordinates of the points to get a new configuration. This may be drawn as:

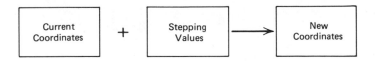

To compute the matrix of stepping values, we start with the derivative of the stress with respect to the first coordinate of the first point, x_{11}, assuming all other point coordinates are fixed. This is denoted by $\partial S / \partial x_{11}$. Before entering this value in the stepping matrix we multiply by -1 (since we want to get a smallest stress configuration) and then multiply by some constant fudge factor, α, which determines the step size. We place this value, $-\alpha(\partial S / \partial x_{11})$, in the first column, first row of the stepping matrix so it will

[2]For a more technical discussion of the method of steepest descent, see Jacoby, Kowalik, and Pizzo (1972, Ch. 5).

be added to the coordinate x_{11} when computing the new configuration. To find the value added to the second coordinate of the first point, x_{12}, we multiply $\partial S/\partial x_{12}$, the partial derivative of the stress with respect to x_{12}, by $-\alpha$ and place this value in the first row, second column position of the stepping matrix. The matrix is filled in this way. The stepping matrix is also called the negative gradient.

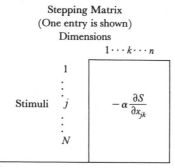

Stepping Matrix
(One entry is shown)

A new configuration of points is now formed by adding each element of the stepping matrix to the corresponding coordinates of a point in the current configuration. This is done simultaneously for all points. Therefore, the iterative process is as follows: (1) obtain an original configuration of points in a space, (2) compute the gradient G of the original stress, (3) step the configuration by adding the appropriate number from G to the coordinates of each point, (4) compute the gradient for the configuration, etc. When all values in the stepping matrix become zero, the configuration is in a local minimum and we have a solution. In a moment we will see that this minimum need not produce the lowest possible stress.

Since the method of steepest descent is a general method for finding the minimum value of a function, we may illustrate the procedure on an arbitrary equation in an unknown x.

$$S = x^4 - \tfrac{32}{3}x^3 + 38x^2 - 48x + 25 \qquad (10.11)$$

The graph of the equation appears in Fig. 10.6. This is analogous to minimizing the stress of a configuration with one point on one dimension. (For example, assume all the other points are fixed.) Assume that the starting configuration is at $x=0$, so S is initially at point A in Fig. 10.6. To decrease the value of S, we would like to increase x by adding a positive number. This is exactly what the method of gradients does. To see this, compute the gradient of Eq. 10.11.

$$G(S) = -\frac{dS}{dx} = -(4x^3 - 32x^2 + 76x - 48) \qquad (10.12)$$

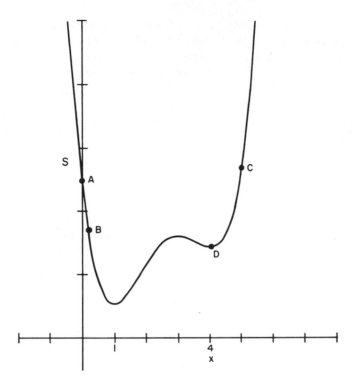

Figure 10.6. A hypothetical application of the method of gradients in the search for the minimum at $x=1$. The idea is to start with an arbitrary value for x and slowly move toward the minimum. At $x=4$ (point D) there is a local minimum that should be avoided.

and substitute the current value of x (that is, set $x=0$):

$$G(S) = \frac{-dS(0)}{dx} = -\left(4(0)^3 - 32(0)^2 + 76(0) - 48\right) = 48 \quad (10.13)$$

To get the new configuration (new value for x), multiply a predetermined fudge factor ($\alpha = .004$) by $G(S_x)$ and add the result to the previous value for x (i.e., 0). By computing this new value we have stepped the configuration of x in a positive direction (along the x axis) and obtained a lower stress at point B in Fig. 10.6. The process is then repeated. After many iterations, the value of the stress will approach a local minimum and may even reach it, in which case the gradient $G(S)=0$.

Note, however, that there are two local minima in this example (at $x=1$ and $x=4$). The chances are very great that S will take on a value at some nonoptimal minimum. For example, if the initial configuration were at $x=5$

with stress C, the local minimum at $x = 4$ with stress D would probably be reached by the iterative process. From Fig. 10.6 it can be seen that D is not the lowest stress, but there is no way to step the configuration toward the area of lower stress using the method of gradients (α times the gradient $G(4)$ equals zero, which, when added to $x = 4$, leaves x unchanged). The best way to avoid this problem is to run the multidimensional scaling starting from several initial (random) configurations of the points. By comparing the stress values for several solutions, it is easy to determine the best fit. Some guidelines for evaluating the minimum stress so obtained are given in Table 10.2.

Table 10.2   Stress measures

S_1 (Eq. 10.8)	S_2 (Eq. 10.10)	Evaluation
20. %	40%	poor
10. %	20%	fair
5. %	10%	good
2.5%	5%	excellent
0. %	0%	perfect

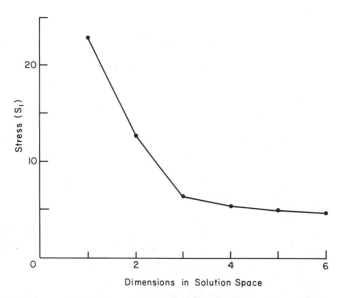

Figure 10.7.   Stress obtained by arranging items (hypothetical) in varying numbers of dimensions. The elbow of the curve at three dimensions indicates that such a space would adequately fit the data.

The relevance of a stress value depends on broader theoretical and practical considerations. If one has an *a priori theory* (based on other empirical considerations), the stress level should be interpreted within the confines of that theory. For example, if the theory explicitly states that results should fall into two dimensions, such a stricture might be followed even though the stress was relatively high. On the other hand, low stress need not imply easy interpretation if no further information is available about the stimuli under study. In exploratory research, stress is sometimes plotted against the number of dimensions to gain some idea of an appropriate configuration. In Fig. 10.7, for example, a data matrix was analyzed by varying the number of dimensions in a Euclidean space ($r = 2$). The elbow in the curve indicates a point of diminishing returns as number of dimensions increases. In this example, we would choose the configuration represented in three dimensions, provided that this fact is consistent with our knowledge of the stimuli. These practical guidelines should then be supplemented with additional experimental or theoretical work to firm up and modify the interpretation.

A more technical description of multidimensional scaling may be found in Kruskal (1964b).

ALTERNATIVE METHODS

Since Kruskal's work in 1964, several parallel methods of nonmetric scaling have appeared. Each has its own distinct way of approaching the problem with modifications in the assumptions of monotonicity, the stress function, and so on. But all have the common goal of monotonically relating the empirical proximities to the computed interpoint distances of the theoretical configuration.

Scaling over Individuals

Often, experiments are conducted in which several subjects generate interstimulus proximities. To analyze these data, one could average proximities over subjects and scale the resultant matrix using Shepard-Kruskal multidimensional scaling. There are, however, other possibilities such as the methods proposed by Carroll (see Carroll and Wish, 1974) and McGee (1966, 1968).

The model for Carroll's technique, INDSCAL, assumes there is a psychological space shared by all individuals but that each individual stresses different aspects of the stimuli while making judgments. For instance, suppose a group of psychophysicists are dining in a restaurant, and the dessert tray is brought out. One person may choose a dessert by its perceived sweetness, while another individual might emphasize color, and a third, texture. To represent this difference in emphasis among people, INDSCAL produces two configurations, a stimulus constellation and a subject space. The stimulus constellation is equivalent to the output from data averaged over subjects in Shepard-Kruskal multidimensional scaling. The subject space indicates the emphasis each person places on aspects of the stimulus space by plotting a multiplication (weighting) factor for each dimension. By using the value of a multiplication factor as coordinates, each subject may be represented as a point in the space, revealing the relative emphasis on the different dimensions. It is as if the subject had generated the proximities of a point by locating it in the common psychological space, multiplying each of its coordinates by a personal dimension weight, and then computing its proximity to all other points.

INDSCAL, despite its power and flexibility, is a metric approach to the problem. A method that is more in the spirit of nonmetric scaling is McGee's nonmetric "elastic" multidimensional scaling, EMD (McGee, 1966, 1968), which uses a modified version of Kruskal's stress function. CEMD ("common" elastic multidimensional scaling), an extension of EMD, has options to use different monotonic transformations for each subject but produce one set of final coordinates, or to use a common monotonic transformation for all subjects but produce separate spatial representations (coordinates) for each.

Guttman-Lingoes Smallest Space Analysis

Guttman (1968) and Lingoes (1972) have developed a series of programs to produce spatial representations from nonmetric data. The SSA (smallest space analysis) series grew from Guttman's (1968) work independent of Kruskal. The first program in the series, MINISSA, uses a two-step process to move from one configuration to the next (as opposed to the single step used by Kruskal's program M-D-SCAL). The primary difference between this algorithm and that of M-D-SCAL lies in the function to be minimized. Recall that Kruskal's algorithm minimizes the stress:

$$S_1 = \left[\frac{\displaystyle\sum_{i=1}^{N} \sum_{j=i+1}^{N} \left(d_{ij} - \hat{d}_{ij}\right)^2}{\displaystyle\sum_{i=1}^{N} \sum_{j=i+1}^{N} d_{ij}^2} \right]^{1/2}$$

The values for $\hat{d}_{ij}$ are determined by a procedure by which d_{ij} must equal $\hat{d}_{ij}$

for all points i and j in order to satisfy the requirement of monotonicity (stress equals zero). Guttman (1968) defines $\hat{d}_{ij}$ (d_{ij}^* in his notation) such that if objects i and j are most similar (δ_{ij} is rank 1), and d_{kl} is the smallest computed distance in the current configuration, then d_{ij}^* is set to the value of d_{kl}. This is then carried out for the second ranked similarity and computed distance. If the rank-ordered similarity matches the order of a distance—for example, the tenth most similar pair also has the tenth smallest computed distance—the value of $d_{ij} - d_{ij}^* = 0$. Therefore, as in M-D-SCAL, if monotonicity is satisfied, the stress value is zero.

TORSCA-9 (Young)

Another program, TORSCA-9, developed by Young (1968) uses a combined "semimetric" and nonmetric approach. The initial proximities are scaled as distances using the semimetric approach of traditional multidimensional scaling (Torgerson, 1952). TORSCA-9 next computes Kruskal's d_{ij} and then reapplies Torgerson's semimetric procedures to the newly computed pseudo distances. This process, termed an "alternating least squares" algorithm (called *alternate* due to the two approaches used, and *least squares* since the traditional multidimensional scaling algorithm produces a least squares fit of the distances to the configuration), is continued until a stopping criterion has been reached.

Comparison of Algorithms

Despite the differences among approaches to multidimensional scaling, all algorithms currently in vogue have several things in common. All are iterative, thereby making it very difficult to objectively compare and evaluate their relative strengths and weaknesses. All attempt to minimize a value closely related to the residual sum of squares:

$$S^* = \sum_{i=1}^{N} \sum_{j=i+1}^{N} \left(d_{ij} - \hat{d}_{ij}\right)^2 \tag{10.14}$$

where d_{ij} is the computed distance between stimuli in the current configuration and $\hat{d}_{ij}$ is the pseudo distance matching a criterion such as monotonicity. To minimize S^*, the method of steepest descent is used to step the configuration. In his evaluation of several algorithms, Spence (1972) concludes that the differences between solutions using M-D-SCAL, SSA1, or TORSCA-9 are so small as to be of little importance. He does conjecture that some algorithms are better at avoiding nonoptimal local minima.

THEORY AND INTERPRETATION

Scalable Data

Controversy over what properties can be scaled dates back to Fechner. He assumed that jnd's could be summed to produce a scale but that direct estimates of stimulus magnitude were not reliable. Thurstone (1927) laid down guidelines suggesting that Fechner's law be applied only to data from a measurable physical dimension that corresponds to a single psychological dimension. Obviously, less stringent guidelines apply to multidimensional scaling, but some restrictions can still be noted. (1) The data must be reliable (the criteria of proximity or preference must remain constant for individual subjects and across subjects), and there must be a sufficient number of data points to constrain the solution. (2) Successful application requires some knowledge of or theory about the underlying structure of the stimulus attributes. (3) Of course, certain configurations may be uninterpretable or trivial, in which case the results are of dubious value.

Assuming the data satisfy these basic conditions, interpretation requires understanding two parameters: number of dimensions and type of metric. Both are necessary interrelated components, since a correct choice of parameters may facilitate creation of a space that is both low in stress and easily interpretable. However, they are distinct parameters involving different assumptions about the goals of multidimensional scaling and the underlying structure of the data.

Dimensionality

The number of dimensions is in some sense the crucial criterion. The goal of multidimensional scaling is to take nonmetric data and spatially represent it by a small number of parameters. Dimensionality, and in particular the orientation of the axes with respect to the stimulus locations, can offer great assistance in interpreting the underlying structure. Axes are often assumed to represent a continuum, such as size, luminance, or sound. Stimuli ordered only according to this axis will show small stimuli at one end of the scale and large stimuli at the opposite end. Care should be taken in interpreting the dimensions; otherwise the search for meaning may become a Rorschach test and will not uncover any useful structure. In this regard it is sometimes best merely to assume that some dimensions are garbage and therefore uninterpretable (Torgerson, 1965). As always, the best guide to interpreting the locations and axes is to develop a good *a priori* theory of the underlying structure. The scaling solution is then used to locate the stimuli more precisely within this structure. An example of this application is provided by one of our studies on the planning of ideal towns, where subjects manipulated items (representations of buildings) in two dimensions (Baird, Degerman, Paris, and Noma, 1972). The relative distances between items were averaged across subjects, and the distance matrix (a genuine one in this case) was treated by multidimensional scaling to locate the items as a composite map in a Euclidean space. Since subjects were planning in two dimensions, and since most small towns (appropriate here) are built in two dimensions, the solution was naturally limited to a two-dimensional map. The scaling solution was merely used to specifically locate items in this plane, thus revealing subject preferences for building locations. Some further examples of the use of multidimensional scaling in the perception laboratory (with more established theories under test) are given by Indow (1974) and Marks (1974).

The Metric

The nature of the metric is a more subtle question. The metric constraints on multidimensional scaling have not been adequately explored. As noted previously, there are many possible distance functions. The Minkowski metric is the only one currently in use, but even the assumptions needed to apply this metric are not fully understood. This may be due to our inability to determine the appropriate exponential constant (r) for the stimuli being scaled. As mentioned before, Attneave (1950) showed that at least some stimuli require a city block metric to be successfully placed in a multidimensional space.

Later, Shepard (1964) concluded that some sets of attributes are analyzable whereas others are not. A pair of attributes such as size and tilt are analyzable when the dissimilarity of two stimuli is judged by the sum of the dissimilarities along both continua (the difference in size plus the difference in angle of tilt). This is equivalent to the city block metric. Some pairs of attributes (called integral), however, are not analyzable and are therefore handled as if they were unitary. An example of such a pair is hue and saturation of colors. Such a compound stimulus cannot readily be seen in terms of the separate contribution of its two components. Therefore a metric should be used that gives the same interpoint distance between two fixed points regardless of the orientation of the axes. For this reason, nonanalyzable stimuli should be plotted using the Euclidean metric, $r=2$. Unfortunately, Shepard also shows that the exponent r for pairs of attributes varies according to the subject's attention and may vary within an experimental session or across subjects. Even though Micko and Fischer (1970) argue that aggregate data will still produce a metric space under these circumstances, the problem of picking a suitable exponent remains.

Multidimensional Scaling as a Psychophysical Model

Unlike statistics or other measures of sample behavior, multidimensional scaling must be considered more than an analytic tool. It is in part a model of some internal psychological space (Beals, Krantz, and Tversky, 1968). We are attempting to minimize some criterion based on our conception of this internal space. The assumption of some form of metric is justifiable, but incorrect evaluation of this metric may cause us to scale noise instead of the actual data. The use of the stress values to evaluate goodness of fit does not help matters, since we have no alternative way of evaluating how appropriately the structure is represented or even if a configuration of higher stress may be more interpretable. In addition, as in all models, some form of data reduction and an accompanying loss of information occurs. On the other side of the ledger, the visual representation of stimuli often helps in finding an underlying structure in the data. Therefore, despite its drawbacks, multidimensional scaling is a definite improvement over previous methods.

Recent Developments

Some recent work has suggested two possible ways to improve multidimensional scaling. One is an interactive program that does not require a complete data matrix. The second uses metrics that are more flexible than the Minkowski r metric.

In traditional multidimensional scaling, N stimuli are located in some spatial pattern using $N(N-1)/2$ similarities, one for every possible pair of stimuli. Young and Cliff (1972) describe an interactive scaling program where the subject at a computer terminal inputs similarities only for the pairs needed to determine dimensionality and location of points. Redundant data are not requested. Unfortunately, the program assumes that judgments reflect underlying interpoint distances on a ratio scale—hence, the current method is not truly nonmetric. Eventually, we expect that nonmetric interactive methods will be devised, allowing experimenters to scale many more points because of the smaller number of required similarities.

Another area that has gone relatively unexplored is the use of metrics other than the Minkowski. Alternative metrics would allow greater flexibility in proposing assumptions about the underlying structure. For example, Micko and Fischer (1970) have examined ways in which different areas of the space could have different metrics. This decreases the importance of axis orientation in determining interpoint distances, an important advance over current techniques. Further discussion of recent advances can be found in the two-volume work edited by Shepard, Romney, and Nerlove (1972) and Romney, Shepard, and Nerlove (1972).

SUMMARY AND STRICTURES

In closing, let us summarize the steps followed in employing nonmetric multidimensional scaling. The standard method of operation is to produce a configuration with the Euclidean metric ($r=2$) in two dimensions. Next, repeat the process with fewer and greater numbers of dimensions. When stress values are plotted against the number of dimensions, as in Fig. 10.7, the elbow of the curve helps to indicate the appropriate number of dimensions; additional dimensions do not significantly reduce the stress.

If the dimensions are interpretable and match an *a priori* theory of the structure of psychological space, one may proceed to fine-tune the metric constant r. To fine-tune, run the scaling program with several values for $r \geqslant 1$. Pick the value of r that produces the lowest stress. If the dimensions are uninterpretable, replot the stimuli in varying dimensions with $r=1$ (city block metric) and see if the dimensions make sense. If they still do not make sense, then maybe the data are not suitable for scaling.

If one knows either the dimensionality or the metric—for example, as in the case of judgments of interbuilding distances on a campus (two-dimensional Euclidean space)—one goes directly to the relevant parameters. The foregoing approach could be followed in using any of the MDS programs currently available.

REFERENCES

Attneave, F. "Dimensions of similarity." *American Journal of Psychology*, 1950, *63*, 516–556.

Baird, J. C., Degerman, R., Paris, R., and Noma, E. "Student planning of town configuration." *Environment and Behavior*, 1972, *4*, 159–188.

Beals, R., Krantz, D. H., and Tversky, A. "Foundations of multidimensional scaling." *Psychological Review*, 1968, *75*, 127–142.

Carroll, J. D., and Wish, M. "Models and methods for three-way multidimensional scaling." In *Contemporary Developments in Mathematical Psychology*, Vol. II: *Measurement, Psychophysics and Neural Information Processing*, D. H. Krantz, R. C. Atkinson, R. D. Luce, and P. Suppes (Eds.), San Francisco: Freeman, 1974, pp. 57–105.

Coombs, C. H. *A Theory of Data.* New York: Wiley, 1964.

Ekman, G. "A direct method for multidimensional ratio scaling." *Psychometrika*, 1963, *28*, 33–41.

Ekman, G., Engen, T., Künnapas, T., and Lindman, R. "A quantitative principle of qualitative similarity." *Journal of Experimental Psychology*, 1964, *68*, 530–536.

Guttman, L. "A general nonmetric technique for finding the smallest coordinate space for a configuration of points." *Psychometrika*, 1968, *33*, 469–506.

Indow, T. "Applications of multidimensional scaling in perception." In *Handbook of Perception: II. Psychophysical Judgment and Measurement.* E. C. Carterette and M. P. Friedman (Eds.), New York: Academic, 1974.

Jacoby, S. L. S., Kowalik, J. S., and Pizzo, J. T. *Iterative Methods for Nonlinear Optimization Problems.* Englewood Cliffs, N.J.: Prentice-Hall, 1972.

Kruskal, J. B. "Multidimensional scaling by optimizing goodness of fit to a nonmetric hypothesis." *Psychometrika*, 1964a, *29*, 1–27.

Kruskal, J. B. "Nonmetric multidimensional scaling: A numerical method." *Psychometrika*, 1964b, *29*, 115–129.

Kruskal, J. B., and Carroll, J. D. "Geometrical models and badness-of-fit functions." *International Symposium on Multivariate Analysis*, Vol. II. New York: Academic, 1969, pp. 639–671.

Lingoes, J. C. "Some boundary conditions for a monotone analysis of symmetric matrices." *Psychometrika*, 1971, *36*, 195–203.

Lingoes, J. C. "A general survey of the Guttman-Lingoes nonmetric program series." In R. N. Shepard, A. K. Romney, and S. B. Nerlove (Eds.), *Multidimensional Scaling: Theory and Applications in the Behavioral Sciences*, Vol. 1. New York: Seminar Press, 1972, pp. 49–68.

Marks, L. E. *Sensory Processes: The New Psychophysics.* New York: Academic, 1974.

McGee, V. E. "The multidimensional analysis of 'elastic' distances." *The British Journal of Mathematical and Statistical Psychology*, 1966, *19*, 181–196.

McGee, V. E. "Multidimensional scaling of N sets of similarity measures: A nonmetric individual differences approach." *Multivariate Behavioral Research*, 1968, *3*, 233–248.

Micko, H. C., and Fischer, W. "The metric of multidimensional psychological spaces as a function of the differential attention to subjective attributes." *Journal of Mathematical Psychology*, 1970, *11*, 118–143.

Romney, A. K., Shepard, R. N., and Nerlove, S. B. (Eds.), *Multidimensional Scaling: Theory and Applications in the Behavioral Sciences*, Vol. 2. New York: Seminar Press, 1972.

Schönemann, P. H. "On metric multidimensional unfolding." *Psychometrika*, 1970, *35*, 349–366.

Shepard, R. N. "The analysis of proximities: Multidimensional scaling with an unknown distance function I." *Psychometrika*, 1962a, *27*, 125–140.

Shepard, R. N. "The analysis of proximities: Multidimensional scaling with an unknown distance function II." *Psychometrika*, 1962b, *27*, 219–246.

Shepard, R. N. "Attention and the metric structure of the stimulus space." *Journal of Mathematical Psychology*, 1964, *1*, 54–87.

Shepard, R. N., Romney, A. K., and Nerlove, S. B. (Eds.), *Multidimensional Scaling: Theory and Applications in the Behavioral Sciences*, Vol. 1. New York: Seminar Press, 1972.

Spearman, C. "'General Intelligence': Objectively determined and measured." *American Journal of Psychology*, 1904, *15*, 201–293.

Spence, I. "A Monte Carlo evaluation of three nonmetric multidimensional scaling algorithms." *Psychometrika*, 1972, *37*, 461–486.

Thurstone, L. L. "Three psychophysical laws." *Psychological Review*, 1927, *34*, 424–432.

Titchener, E. B. "The term 'attensity'." *American Journal of Psychology*, 1924, *35*, 156.

Torgerson, W. S. "Multidimensional scaling: I. Theory and method." *Psychometrika*, 1952, *17*, 401–419.

Torgerson, W. S. *Theory and Methods of Scaling*. New York: Wiley, 1958.

Torgerson, W. S. "Multidimensional scaling of similarity." *Psychometrika*, 1965, *30*, 379–393.

Wolford, G. L ., and Hollingsworth, S. "Evidence that short-term memory is not the limiting factor in the tachistoscopic full-report procedure." *Memory and Cognition*, 1974, *2*, 796–800.

Wundt, W. *Grundzüge der Physiologischen Psychologie*. Leipzig: 1874 (5th ed., 1903).

Young, F. W. "Torsca-9, a Fortran IV program for nonmetric multidimensional scaling." *Behavioral Science*, 1968, *13*, 343–344.

Young, F. W., and Cliff, N. "Interactive scaling with individual subjects." *Psychometrika*, 1972, *37*, 385–415.

Young, G., and Householder, A. S. "Discussion of a set of points in terms of their mutual distances." *Psychometrika*, 1938, *3*, 19–22.

CHAPTER

$$\boxed{11}$$

CLUSTER ANALYSIS

Grouping objects and experiences into categories is one of the most important activities of all living organisms. The lowly earthworm, dividing its world into classes of edible and inedible objects, has this in common with the leader of a country making decisions on the basis of similarities and differences between current and previous crises. Grouping similar experiences allows us to compare new experiences with generalizations of previous ones. If we deem that a previous situation or set of situations is similar to the current one, we should find it easier to react appropriately. This type of classification may be effective, but it is not necessarily systematic.

The systematic grouping of items according to common properties dates back to Aristotle, whose ideas led others to define what was thought to be the *essence* of a class of plants or animals (Cain, 1958). Historically, this position emphasized the initial creation of a logical framework into which the observed phenomena of nature could be placed. In contrast to this "structural" view, Sneath and Sokal (1973) propose that organizing structures be closely tied to, and in fact derived from, empirical observations of items or their properties. Once a structure is created in this fashion, new items may more readily be classified. Furthermore, because the basis for the original classification is empirical, the approach is considered "objective" or "operational" in the sense intended by Bridgman (1927). Because of this presumed objectivity, the set of items being clustered are traditionally referred to as operational taxonomic units (OTU's). Examples of OTU's might be individuals, cities, or letters of the alphabet, which possess attributes such as IQ, population, or number of horizontal lines.

In certain subfields of biology (especially evolutionary theory), controversy still rages concerning the relative merits of the "structural" and "operational" philosophies (see, for example, Pratt, 1972; Sokol and Camin, 1965). In psychology, however, this battle was never fought, because the widespread use of clustering techniques is comparatively recent, and most of the heated controversy about the value of empirical data dissipated years ago.

Operationally defining both the data collection and the methods of clustering has become standard fare in experimental psychology. The data collection procedures are varied and include techniques for obtaining similarity ratings or other measures that can be converted to such ratings. Since many such methods were covered in previous chapters, we will concentrate here on the essence of the clustering techniques.

If we are to cluster directly from the data, certain ground rules must be established. When we classify items, we are more or less attempting to group similar items together and to separate dissimilar ones. This is often impossible, but it nevertheless offers a criterion that the clustering method can try to optimize. In addition, it would seem reasonable to require that an item belong to one and only one cluster in the classification scheme. That is, no two clusters can have an item in common (they may not "overlap"), nor may an item be only partially contained in a cluster. For this reason, clusters in this context may be called partitions. Beyond these requirements (which may be relaxed, as we shall see later), there are few fast rules. Even the definition of similarity or dissimilarity is very flexible.

For this reason, a wide variety of methods and criteria have been developed. However, each clustering method combines two components: a criterion used to determine if similar objects are being clustered and dissimilar items are being segregated, and a procedure by which different clustering configurations are tested and an optimal one picked. It should be noted that even though particular criteria and procedures are paired in the examples in this chapter, any criterion may be paired with any procedure with only slight modifications in each. Initially we will deal only with the criterion without regard for the method of assigning items to clusters.

CLUSTERING CRITERIA

A multitude of criteria are used by clustering programs. Each makes certain assumptions and tradeoffs when testing whether a new item is to be added or deleted from a cluster, since there is always the central question of how

much the particular item will add or subtract from the intracluster homo-
geneity. The item will probably be similar to some items in the cluster but
dissimilar to others. The criterion attempts to balance the opposite effects of
similar and dissimilar items and produce a number indicating the ap-
propriateness of the new clustering. When all possibilities are compared, a
decision can be made as to the optimal clustering. Because there is no best
tradeoff in all cases, a single criterion cannot be endorsed under all circumstances and for all forms of input data, so we will present only a sampling of
the various measures. In addition, the picture is complicated by the variety
of data input to the clustering algorithms. Again, no form of data or method
of analysis seems clearly superior, so we will mention only some of the more
prevalent ones. In particular, we will look at stimulus ratings, distances,
correlations, and proximities.

Stimulus Ratings

Suppose in the first instance we wish to cluster judgments [perhaps similarity
of stimuli varying in intensity, as in Künnapas and Künnapas (1973)]. To
cluster stimuli receiving similar response magnitudes (assuming they are
interval scale data), one possible criterion is to minimize the sum of the
intracluster variances (ICV). Ward (1963) called this the error sum of
squares:

$$\text{ICV}_i = \sum_{j=1}^{N_i} \left(x_{ij} - \bar{x}_i \right)^2 \qquad (11.1a)$$

$$\text{ICV}_{\text{Total}} = \text{ICV}_1 + \text{ICV}_2 + \cdots + \text{ICV}_N \qquad (11.1b)$$

where N_i is the number of items in the ith cluster, and $\bar{x}_i$ is the mean
response in the ith cluster. In this case, x_{ij} is simply the response associated
with the jth item within the ith cluster. It is not the similarity of two stimuli.

Distances

Some interstimulus data, such as distance measures, are treated as ratio scale
data. If this is true, then it is possible to minimize the within-clusters sum of
squares using the method proposed by Edwards and Cavalli-Sforza (1965).
They show that this criterion is equivalent to minimizing the average

squared distances within a cluster:

$$S\,DIST_i^2 = \frac{1}{N_i} \sum_{j=1}^{N_i} \sum_{k=j+1}^{N_i} d_{jk}^2 \tag{11.2a}$$

$$S\,DIST_{total}^2 = S\,DIST_1^2 + S\,DIST_2^2 + \cdots + S\,DIST_N^2 \tag{11.2b}$$

where d_{jk}^2 is the squared distance between two items j and k in the same cluster, and the ith cluster contains N_i stimuli.

Correlations

If the data are interstimulus correlations (rho squared $=\rho_{ij}^2$), a measure similar to that employed by Fortier and Solomon (1966) may be appropriate. Their criterion is called C^* and is defined as follows. If i and j are in the same cluster, define D_{ij} as

$$D_{ij} = \left(\rho_{ij}^2 - .5\right) \tag{11.3}$$

For stimuli k and m not in the same cluster, we arbitrarily define $D_{km} = 0$. This is equivalent to assuming that the correlation is 0.5 between any two items not in the same cluster. The clustering procedure then tries to maximize

$$C^* = \sum_{i=1}^{N} \sum_{j=i+1}^{N} D_{ij} \tag{11.4}$$

Proximities

In many situations, proximity data are not correlations or distances but only the rank orders of the dissimilarity measures. In other words, the measures are assumed to be ordinal data. For example, in the planning of an ideal town, the preferred distances between facilities are proximities. In this case the data are often handled in a nonmetric way, using only the ranks of the interstimulus proximities. Here the distance between clusters is determined by the proximity of only two stimuli, one in each cluster. Typically these two stimuli are either the closest or the farthest apart in their original proximities [closest = minimum method = single-linkage method; farthest = maximum method = complete-linkage method; Johnson, (1967)]. Later in the chapter we will see that intermediate criteria are also possible. This leads us to the clustering procedures that attempt to satisfy various criteria.

CLUSTERING PROCEDURES

Random Method

At first glance it would seem that grouping similar stimuli is an extremely simple task; merely compute the criterion for all possible configurations and pick the one with the highest or lowest (as the case may be) value. Unfortunately, this approach is impractical in all except the smallest of populations, since the number of possible partitions explodes as the number of stimuli increases. For example, 25 stimuli may be partitioned 4,638,590,332,229,999,353 distinct ways. The large-number game may be avoided by using random samples of configurations. A method proposed by Fortier and Solomon (1966) accomplishes this in two steps.

First, it is possible to group N stimuli into M distinct clusters, where M is a number varying from 1 to N. By computing C^* measures (Eq. 11.3) for many, many randomly selected configurations, distributions of C^*'s are obtained for each value of M. By comparing the distributions across M values, an optimal number of clusters, called M', is determined. Next, configurations of M' clusters are extensively sampled (for the second time) to choose a "best" configuration (maximum C^*). This procedure rapidly becomes unwieldy or produces unrepresentative solutions as the number of stimuli increases.

In contradistinction to the random method, most clustering methods are deterministic in building a configuration. These are usually labeled *hierarchical* or *nonhierarchical*.

Nonhierarchical Methods

Nonhierarchical procedures attempt to optimize a criterion by following some or all of the rules suggested by Lance and Williams (1967a).

1. Create an initial configuration of clusters. (This problem has its analog in multidimensional scaling.)
2. Allocate new stimuli to existing clusters or fuse existing clusters.
3. Determine the final number of clusters (also, those containing a single stimulus).
4. Reallocate any stimuli that may have been misclassified.

A procedure using step 1 and a combination of Steps 2, 3, and 4 is presented by Friedman and Rubin (1967). From an arbitrary initial config-

uration composed of an arbitrary number of clusters, stimuli are systematically moved from one cluster to another in an attempt to maximize a
criterion. If no move improves matters, the stimulus remains in its current
group. When the process is repeated several times for all stimuli, a configuration is attained where the criterion cannot be improved. The configuration is then in a local maximum. Other procedures are then invoked to jump
the configuration toward a more optimal value. (This is very similar to the
local minimum problem in multidimensional scaling.)

This typifies the general approach to nonhierarchical clustering. Unfortunately, it is extremely time-consuming and nonexhaustive (not all possible
solutions are examined). In some ways it is comparable to multidimensional
scaling without the method of steepest descent (Chapter 10), since the best
fit is found by random motion of the stimuli in the configuration.

Hierarchical Clustering

Another attack on the problem is exemplified by algorithms for hierarchical
clustering, a type of technique preferred by many psychologists. In contrast
to the nonhierarchical methods, there is no reshuffling of stimuli, so once a
stimulus is assigned to a cluster it remains. This, however, means that
"mistakes" (such as separation of similar items into different clusters) are
never rectified at a later stage in the process of grouping. This disadvantage
is counterbalanced by the speed with which the algorithm produces an
acceptable clustering. Many configurations can be created using different
criteria with the hope that one can avoid these "mistakes." There are two
primary techniques used for this: *divisive* and *agglomerative*.

In both methods, a tree structure, often called a *dendrogram*, represents the
clustering order, where the tips (leaves) of the branches represent stimuli and
nodes indicate points of clustering among branches. The divisive method
starts at the trunk of the tree, by assuming that all stimuli are initially in the
same cluster. Successive divisions of the main trunk into branches eventually
lead to the situation where each stimulus is a separate cluster. The
agglomerative method moves in the opposite direction. It starts with single-
item clusters at the tips of the branches and successively joins clusters until
the main trunk is reached.

One main difference between hierarchical and nonhierarchical methods is
that no claim is made in the former that stimuli at any level beyond the
initial step will minimize the within-group scatter criterion. Instead, at each
clustering level, only the clusters that can be formed by joining (or splitting)
others are examined. Even though the optimal new configuration is picked

from this set, it may not be the optimal one for all configurations with the same number of clusters.

A typical divisive hierarchical process is described by Edwards and Cavalli-Sforza (1965). To illustrate this method we work on the distance matrix in Table 11.1. The cell entries there represent average distances between facilities in an ideal town (as created by 12th grade students). Facilities were written on cardboard squares and were moved within a 5×5 matrix to represent the ideal arrangement from the subjects' standpoint. Interfacility distances (Euclidean) averaged across the plans of 15 students are given in the table for a subset of the items actually employed in the experiment.

Initially the sums of intracluster similarities for all possible divisions into two groups are compared. We can apply the criteria from Eq. 11.2 since we assume the proximities represent distances. The best initial split divides the eight items into a home-apartment-school-hospital cluster and a police department-fire department-factory-shopping center cluster. The dissimilarity measure is decreased from 28.7 for all eight items to 19.9 (11.0 for the home cluster plus 8.9 from the municipal cluster). All other possible splits result in a smaller decrease. The sequential division into two partitions continues for each branch until the number of branches equals the number of stimuli. Figure 11.1 traces these splits. The major drawback of this method is by now familiar: Too many splits must be tested (there are $2^{N-1} - 1$ ways of dividing N stimuli into two clusters). This is still an improvement over random sampling! Only in the worst possible splits (for example, 25 stimuli split into clusters of 24 and 1 and then into 23, 1, 1, etc.) does the number of splits to be tested approach the maximum of $2^N - N$, a mere 33,554,407 comparisons for 25 stimuli. As we shall see shortly, there are

Table 11.1   Distance matrix for facilities in an ideal town. Entries are based on the average data of fifteen 12th graders. Units are based on a 5×5 matrix

	School	Hospital	Home	Apartment	Factory	Police Dept.	Fire Dept.	Shopping Center
School	*							
Hospital	2.24	*						
Home	2.32	2.86	*					
Apartment	2.70	2.86	3.14	*				
Factory	3.68	3.32	4.28	3.43	*			
Police Dept.	2.21	2.61	3.39	2.82	2.83	*		
Fire Dept.	2.62	2.59	3.32	2.64	2.48	1.82	*	
Shopping Center	2.88	2.91	3.18	2.48	2.47	2.44	2.43	*

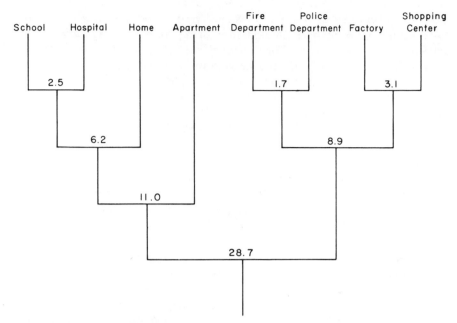

Figure 11.1. Example of a dendrogram produced by a divisive hierarchical clustering of intracity facilities. The numbers are the average within-cluster distance before the cluster was split (average data of fifteen 12th graders).

more efficient clustering methods in terms of the number of configurations to be evaluated for N stimuli. But the divisive method optimizes the first splits of the entire set. These are probably the most crucial partitions when interpreting the clustering structure, so they should be evaluated with the most care.

For larger numbers of items, agglomeration is preferred to division. In terms of the rules suggested by Lance and Williams (1967a), this method uses only steps 1 and 2 mentioned previously. That is, each stimulus is initially considered a cluster, and the two most similar (those best satisfying the criterion) are combined. This procedure is repeated until all items are in a single group. No mechanism exists to terminate the process before all stimuli are clustered, and no attempt is made to reclassify a stimulus once it has been assigned.

Two major types of agglomeration are in current use. They differ only in the grouping criterion and therefore are really the same method. This last point, however, is not commonly observed, so the methods are described separately.

Ward (1963) combines groups to minimize the intracluster variance, ICV

(Eq. 11.1). Initially there are N clusters, one for each stimulus. There are $N(N-1)/2$ pairs to be evaluated in moving from a configuration of N clusters to one of size $N-1$. The pair of clusters having the smallest increase in the ICV are joined, and the procedure is repeated N times, until all stimuli are absorbed into a single group.

To cluster items from a matrix of interstimulus proximities, one can apply the method described by Lance and Williams (1966, 1967b) and Johnson (1967). The procedure is identical to that of Ward, but the grouping criteria are different. The distance between single-stimulus clusters is obviously the proximity of the individual stimuli. The problem is to obtain a distance between two multistimulus clusters. One of the most common solutions, called the minimum (connectedness) method, defines the distance between two clusters as the smallest intercluster distance between any pair of stimuli (the most proximal pair).

To show how this works, we operate upon data from the letter-confusion experiment reported by Wolford and Hollingsworth (1974) and discussed in Chapter 10. The groupings of items is a function of their confusability when subjects attempt to recall letters seen during very brief flashes. The greater the confusability of two letters, the greater the number of times one was mistaken for the other. By converting confusion frequencies into negative values, we secure measures of *dissimilarity*. Larger values (closer to zero) mean more dissimilarity. The resulting matrix is presented in Table 11.2, which is the basis for the dendrogram in Fig. 11.2.

The algorithm proceeds by searching for the smallest value in the matrix. In Table 11.3 (the same data as in Table 11.2) the most proximal pair is (D, Q). The distance d to cluster (D, Q) from any other cluster (x) is defined as $d((x),(D,Q))$, and is computed by

$$d((x),(D, Q)) = \min\big[\, d(x,D), d(x, Q)\,\big] \tag{11.5}$$

Table 11.2   Confusability of letters in the Wolford and Hollingsworth study (1974). Larger values (closer to zero) mean more dissimilarity

	C	D	G	H	M	N	Q	W
C	*							
D	−5	*						
G	−12	−2	*					
H	−2	−4	−3	*				
M	−2	−3	−2	−19	*			
N	−2	−4	−1	−18	−16	*		
Q	−9	−20	−9	−1	−2	−8	*	
W	−1	−5	−2	−5	−18	−13	−4	*

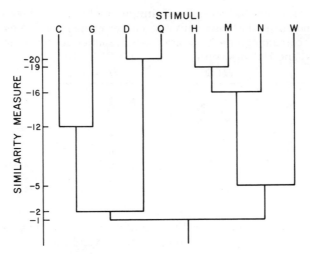

Figure 11.2. Example of a hierarchical tree structure (dendrogram). An agglomerative hierarchical clustering method was applied to the Wolford and Hollingsworth (1974) letter confusion data.

Alternatively, numbers may be substituted for the elements to obtain

$$d((x),(2,7)) = \min\left[d(x,2),d(x,7)\right]$$

where 2 and 7 refer to the second (D) and seventh (Q) letter in Table 11.2. Generally, then, a cluster is indicated by placing parentheses around all its elements. The use of a numerical index is convenient in cases where elements are not readily defined in abbreviated form. The right-hand side of the equation indicates we evaluate the two possible distances, $d(x,2)$ and $d(x,7)$, and select the smallest. The matrix is reorganized and the smallest proximity is again picked. This process is illustrated for the set of stimuli in Table 11.3. At the -21 level (Fig. 11.2) there are eight clusters, each containing one stimulus. At the next level, -20, there are seven clusters; one now contains stimuli (D,Q) and the other six contain a single stimulus. This level is illustrated in Table 11.3, where the minimum distance of each letter to either D or Q is listed. (The choice can be made by examining data in Table 11.2.) There are five clusters at the -16 level (Fig. 11.2), and so on.

A second method, called the maximum (diameter) method, employs the same procedure but replaces Eq. 11.5 with

$$d((x),(y,z)) = \max\left[d(x,y),d(x,z)\right] \tag{11.6}$$

That is, the maximum distance between stimuli in the two clusters is the

Table 11.3 Illustration of minimum method of hierarchical (agglomerative) clustering with one cluster containing two elements and six containing one. Data are from the letter confusion study of Wolford and Hollingsworth (1974).

	C	(D,Q)	G	H	M	N	W
C	*						
(D,Q)	-9	*					
G	-12	-2	*				
H	-2	-1	-3	*			
M	-2	-2	-2	-19	*		
N	-2	-4	-1	-18	-16	*	
W	-1	-4	-2	-5	-18	-13	*

criterion. When the data are well nested and clear distinctions exist between clusters, the minimum and maximum methods yield the same result.

Several other techniques have been proposed in recent years. Lance and Williams (1967b) mention several possibilities, including the centroid, where the distance between clusters is the distance between their centers of gravity. In other words, each cluster is assumed to be a single point located at its center. Another alternative is to generalize the minimum and maximum methods so that a distance between a cluster (x) and the combined clusters (y,z) is computed as follows:

$$d((x),(y,z)) = \alpha_y d(x,y) + \alpha_z d(x,z) + \beta d(y,z) + \delta |d(x,y) - d(x,z)| \quad (11.7)$$

where $\alpha_y, \alpha_z, \beta$, and δ are parameters determined by the nature of the method. If $\alpha_y = \alpha_z = \frac{1}{2}$, $\beta = 0$, and $\delta = -\frac{1}{2}$, Eq. 11.7 becomes Eq. 11.5, so we have the minimum method. If $\alpha_y = \alpha_z = \frac{1}{2}$, $\beta = 0$, and $\delta = +\frac{1}{2}$, we have the maximum method (Eq. 11.6). Lance and Williams also suggest a "flexible strategy" with the constraint that

$$(\alpha_y + \alpha_z + \beta) \geqslant 1 \qquad (11.8)$$

The centroid and the "flexible strategy" approaches are not as easy to interpret as the minimum and maximum and therefore are not as widely applied. When clustering any set of items, one should probably begin by deciding if there is any *a priori* (theoretical) reason for using a particular set of parameter values. At present, few theories are capable of making such detailed refinements. If there are no obvious values, both the minimum and maximum methods should be tried, with the most interpretable solution preferred. One may always try intermediate parameters to improve interpretability.

GOODNESS OF FIT

One way to test the usefulness of the clustering is by a goodness-of-fit formula called the *cophenetic correlation* (see Sokal and Rohlf, 1962; Farris, 1969). This can be seen as analogous to Kruskal's stress function for multidimensional scaling (Chapter 10). It gives us a criterion by which we can pick the "best" solution. The cophenetic value for any pair of stimuli is the level at which the members of the pair were first clustered. So, from Fig. 11.2, we note that the cophenetic value for the pair (M, W) is -5. By computing the values for each stimulus pair we create a matrix similar to the original data matrix. The correlation using the corresponding cell values of the two matrices is the cophenetic correlation. A correlation of 1 means a perfect match, and correlations near zero mean that the hierarchical scheme was not very successful in representing the structure of the stimuli. We try not to consider the possibility of correlations near -1.

RECENT VARIATIONS

The primary advantage of agglomerative hierarchical clustering over all random and nonhierarchical methods lies in speed of execution. For example, only $\sum_{j=1}^{25} j(j-1)/2 = 2925$ comparisons are needed to form a hierarchy for 25 stimuli. This is to be contrasted with a maximum of 33,554,407 comparisons for the divisive procedure and with 4,638,590,332,229,999,353 possibilities for an exhaustive search through all cluster configurations. One major drawback of hierarchical clustering is that no objective stopping criterion is specified. Therefore, a subjective criterion is used such as, "What items do I feel should cluster together?" or "Can we put a meaningful label on this cluster?" In place of this reading of the tea leaves, methods have been proposed to combine the speed of hierarchical clustering with the stopping criterion of nonhierarchical methods. We next discuss two such schemes. One proposed by Page (1974) is called *minimal spanning tree*; the other, proposed by Jarvis and Patrick (1973), is called *shared neighbors*.

Minimal Spanning Tree

Page (1974) offers a method that first constructs what is known as a minimal spanning tree and then breaks the tree into clusters by eliminating branches.

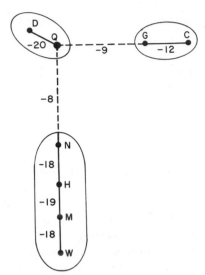

Figure 11.3. One possible representation of a minimal-spanning-tree clustering applied to the data from Wolford and Hollingsworth (1974). Note that two branches of length -8 and -9 were deleted (dotted lines) in the branch elimination phase.

Such a tree grows by successively joining the nearest remaining stimuli to the partially formed tree until all stimuli are included. This procedure is illustrated in Fig. 11.3 for the letter confusion data in Table 11.2 (recall that large negative values imply high similarity). The shortest interstimulus proximity is between D and Q so a branch is drawn connecting the two; D and Q become the first nodes. The proximities from the remaining stimuli to the nearest stimulus in the developing tree are then examined. The smallest proximity is picked and a branch is grown to include the stimulus. (The second branch in Fig. 11.3 adds G to the tree.) Branches are added until all stimuli are included. The sequential growth of this particular tree is D, Q, G, C, N, H, M, W.

The minimal spanning tree is next broken into clusters by eliminating branches that are too long. Even though there are many possible criteria for pruning, Zahn (1971) suggests two: (1) Prune if the length is greater than a constant f times the average length of nearby branches, and (2) prune if the length is more than a constant S times the standard deviation of the lengths of all nearby branches (f and S are determined by the user). As in hierarchical clustering, this approach is fast enough to permit grouping of very large numbers of stimuli. For example, with 25 stimuli, only 2925 interstimulus proximities need be checked and only 24 branches are examined in the branch-elimination phase.

Shared Neighbors

The shared-near-neighbors approach of Jarvis and Patrick (1973) is based on the notion that similar stimuli should share many near neighbors. A near neighbor of a stimulus could be defined as any one of the five most proximal stimuli (to that stimulus) as determined from the original proximity matrix. In more concrete terms, a list of near neighbors is compiled for each stimulus. Then those stimuli are clustered that are near neighbors of each other and whose near-neighbor lists have more than a prespecified number of stimuli in common. By varying the criteria for determining neighbors and the required number of common near neighbors, different clustering patterns may be realized.

Overlapping and Fuzzy Clusters

As mentioned previously, some of the ground rules for clustering could be relaxed—in particular, the one requiring that clusters should partition the data such that an item is completely contained in one and only one cluster. Relaxing this rule can take one of two forms. One approach (Shepard and Arabie, 1975) permits an item to be contained in several overlapping clusters. Even though the increase in the number of clusters and their overlapping nature may make interpretation more difficult, in other situations this approach may reveal important aspects of the data structure. For instance, a clustering of the perceived similarity of furniture using overlapping clusters might show that 'couch' clusters with both 'easy chair' and 'bed.' Note, however, that it would make less sense to cluster 'easy chair' and 'bed,' so they would not be in the same cluster.

A second approach clusters items into what are called *fuzzy sets* (Zadeh, 1965; Yeh and Bang, 1975). This is akin to the notion that in some clusters, certain items could be considered more central or representative than others (for example, a leader as a spokesman for a group opinion). Using this argument, it seems clear that these special items should be given higher rates of belongingness to the cluster. So, instead of assigning 1 and 0 to items contained in and excluded from a cluster, respectively, we use all the numbers between 0 and 1. The closer the value is to 1, the surer we are that the item is contained in the cluster. To date, very little has been done with this approach. Eventually, however, the models of overlapping and fuzzy clusters will probably be combined.

Other considerations in applying cluster analysis include the preprocessing of data, limitations on clustering techniques, and the interpretation of clustered output. The final section of this chapter examines these topics.

PREPROCESSING THE DATA

In many applications of cluster analysis the original data are not similarities or proximity measures. Instead, they are attribute ratings for a set of items, called operational taxonomic units (OTU's). Data sets of this sort are usually organized in a matrix of OTU's by attributes, the analysis of which may result in the clustering of either. To facilitate discussion from here on, assume that we are dealing with OTU's, although, with slight modifications, all comments are also relevant to attribute clustering.

The first requirement is to secure a measure of proximity between all pairs of OTU's. This means that attribute values must be compared to produce a proximity measure (see Anderberg, 1973, pp. 114–187). Because many details of these methods are beyond the scope of this book, the present discussion is restricted to the more common operations on binary and interval scale data.

Binary Data

In the simplest situation, an OTU has or does not have an attribute. Appropriately enough, this binary classification is designated by 1 (presence) or 0 (absence). Consequently, there are four possible outcomes when two OTU's for a single attribute are compared: both or neither OTU is characterized by the attribute; only the first or the second OTU has the attribute. For several attributes upon which two OTU's are compared, the number of occurrences of the four outcomes is represented in Table 11.4 by the letters a, d, b, and c, respectively.

Table 11.4   2×2 contingency table containing counts of shared and contrasting attributes

OTU A	OTU B		Totals
	1	0	
1	a	b	$a+b$
0	c	d	$c+d$
Totals	$a+c$	$b+d$	$n=a+b+c+d$

One commonly used measure of overall similarity is "simple matching." Using the cell entries from Table 11.4, this measure is

$$SM = \frac{a+d}{a+b+c+d} \qquad (11.9)$$

that is, the percentage of attributes present or absent in both OTU's. To illustrate this approach, we turn to an example in human pattern perception —the recognition of letters of the alphabet. In Selfridge's (1959) Pandemonium model, as modified by Lindsay and Norman (1972), a letter is characterized by its separate types of feature (such as horizontal and oblique lines, right angles). Therefore, the perceived similarity of two letters depends on the extent to which their features coincide. A list of features (together with their frequency) for a subset of the alphabet is given in Table 11.5 (The entries in the table apply only to the type font shown.) For simple matching the only consideration is the presence or absence of features. For example, to compute the dissimilarity of the letters C and D, we first tally the numbers from the first two rows of Table 11.5 in the form shown in Table 11.6. (All positive numbers are recoded as ones.) The simple matching measure then is evaluated:

$$\frac{a+d}{a+b+c+d} = \frac{1+3}{1+0+3+3} = \frac{4}{7} = .571$$

If we wish to convert to a dissimilarity measure, this value is subtracted from one: 1-.571 = .429. Reapplying simple matching to all pairs of letters, a matrix of dissimilarities is generated (Table 11.7), and clustering then proceeds through analysis of the cell entries. Figure 11.4 illustrates sample results based on the minimum method of agglomerative hierarchical clustering, to which we will return in a moment.

Table 11.5 Matrix of OTU's versus attributes for each OTU

Letter	Vertical lines	Horizontal lines	Oblique lines	Right angles	Acute angles	Continuous curves	Discontinuous curves
C							1
D	1	2		2			1
G	1	1		1			1
H	2	1		4			
M	2		2		3		
N	2		1		2		
Q			1		2	1	
W			4		3		

Table 11.6 Tally of agreements and disagreements for attributes of letters C and D

		D		
		Presence	Absence	Total
C	Presence	1	0	1
	Absence	3	3	6
	Total	4	3	7

Table 11.7 Dissimilarities generated by the simple matching measure applied to the data in Table 11.5

	C	D	G	H	M	N	Q	W
C	*							
D	.429	*						
G	.429	0.0	*					
H	.571	.143	.143	*				
M	.571	.714	.714	.571	*			
N	.571	.714	.714	.571	0.0	*		
Q	.571	1.0	1.0	.857	.286	.286	*	
W	.429	.857	.857	.714	.143	.143	.143	*

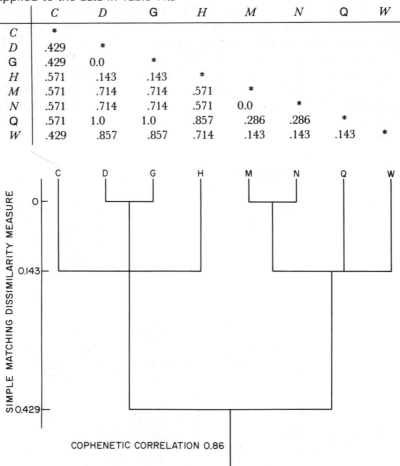

Figure 11.4. Dendrogram for letter clusters using the minimum (single-linkage) method applied to dissimilarities generated by the simple matching measure.

222

Interval Scale Data

There are a multitude of measures to create a dissimilarity matrix from interval scale attributes. Two of the more common are distance and correlation measures. The distance measures are usually variations on the family of Minkowski metrics, the most commonly employed being the city block:

$$d_{ij} = \sum_{k=1}^{N} |x_{ik} - x_{jk}| \qquad (11.10)$$

and the Euclidean:

$$d_{ij} = \left(\sum_{k=1}^{N} |x_{ik} - x_{jk}|^2 \right)^{1/2} \qquad (11.11)$$

As noted in Chapter 10, distance measures have a strong intuitive appeal because they are very much akin to our real-world perception of physical space. So, if the OTU's are plotted in a two-dimensional attribute space, pairs of OTU's that are "near" each other should be assigned small distances, thus increasing the likelihood of their being clustered. Take, for instance, the hypothetical set of points in Fig. 11.5. We can be pretty confident that the three groups of points will be designated as three separate clusters.

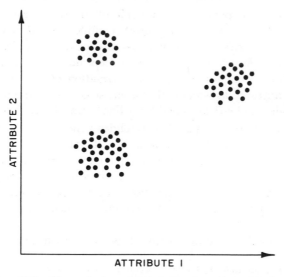

Figure 11.5.   Three clusters of points in a two-dimensional space.

It would be convenient if these intuitive notions of clusters in a plane could be extended to more than three dimensions, but we cannot easily visualize these higher spaces. We therefore rely on the formal equations to help us "see," even though there is one major drawback with this approach: The overall distance measure is useful only when the measures along each dimension are compatible. For instance, if the height and width of printed letters are being assessed, we are best advised to measure both dimensions in the same units. If height were assessed in centimeters and width in meters, differences in height would be overrepresented in computing inter-OTU distance. Moreover, this difficulty is compounded when we compare measures such as a person's IQ and height. That is, a difference of 25 IQ units may or may not be comparable to 25 centimeters. For more details on how this problem is handled, see Anderberg (1973).

A second interval-scale measure is the correlation coefficient:

$$
r_{ij} = \frac{\sum\limits_{k=1}^{N} (x_{ik} - \bar{x}_{i\cdot})(x_{jk} - \bar{x}_{j\cdot})}{\sqrt{\left(\sum\limits_{k=1}^{N} (x_{ik} - \bar{x}_{i\cdot})^2\right)\left(\sum\limits_{k=1}^{N} (x_{jk} - \bar{x}_{j\cdot})^2\right)}}
\tag{11.12}
$$

where r_{ij} is a measure of similarity ranging from -1 to 1. It is converted to a dissimilarity in the usual manner $(1 - r_{ij})$. In contrast to the distance metrics, the correlation is independent of the unit of measure for each attribute. Unfortunately, we are faced with another difficulty. Although identical OTU's do have a correlation of 1, it is possible for two non identical OTU's also to have a correlation of 1. For instance, consider the attributes of height and width: Two rectangles will have a correlation of 1 even when one is twice as tall and twice as wide as the other, since the characteristics of the second rectangle can be determined by a linear transformation of the first.[1] Suppose now we wished to apply the Euclidean metric to the letters whose features are given in Table 11.5. Imagine, if you dare, the letters in a seven-dimensional space (one dimension for each attribute). The distance between OTU's is computed by Eq. 11.11, where x_{ik} is the value of the kth attribute for the ith OTU. At this stage one is free to apply any of the clustering techniques discussed in this chapter to secure a grouping of the letters.

A parallel example could be presented for the correlation coefficient (Eq.

[1]To demonstrate this, substitute $ax_{ik} + b$ for all occurrences of x_{ik} in Eq. 11.12, where a and b are constants.

11.12). For the letter data in Table 11.5, the Euclidean and correlation measures yield almost the same dendrogram as simple matching (Fig. 11.4) and hence will be omitted here.

LIMITATIONS OF CLUSTERING METHODS

Cluster analysis, like multidimensional scaling, is a model that cannot be falsified. If a cluster is identified, that cluster exists by definition; there is no way to independently verify it. Ultimately, then, the importance of clustering techniques and their results rests upon their heuristic value. For this reason, we cannot say that one technique is always better than another. Such judgment depends on the type of data processed and the accompanying psychological model.

In many situations it is assumed that data are measured on an ordinal scale (Chapter 1). Johnson (1967) notes that both the minimum (single-linkage) and maximum (complete-linkage) methods produce clusterings that are invariant for all monotonic transformations of the data—thus satisfying ordinal scale requirements. In contrast, the clusters obtained using methods such as the centroid or intracluster variance (Ward, 1963) may be drastically changed by monotonic transformations.

INTERPRETATION OF CLUSTERS

Although it would be impossible, as well as fruitless, to exhaustively list the rules for interpreting clusters, several general suggestions can be proposed.

1. There is no absolute best way to cluster, since each method emphasizes certain properties at the expense of others. There is, therefore, a great deal of information contained in conflicts among cluster structures obtained by different methods. Such conflicts may suggest a variety of interpretations of the data; or it may be that clusters with special characteristics are under- or overrepresented. On the other hand, recurring clusters should be given more weight in the evaluation of the supporting psychological theory.

2. Assuming one has a substantive theory (as we strongly recommend), its predictions should always be compared with the resulting clusters. Without such a theory the clusters are not falsifiable (since they are true by definition), although they may suggest a testable theory.

3. Data points that fall outside the major clusters (outliers) should not be automatically discounted, since they might be the only representative of an

undersampled family of OTU's. In short, one should attempt to rationally explain all outliers before discarding them as noise.

4.   A more extreme comparison of models involves the superimposition of clusters on a spatial configuration produced by multidimensional scaling. This is shown in Fig. 11.6 for the letter confusion data given in Table 11.2. The clusters successively enclose stimuli located in a two-dimensional space.

This approach gives an indication of the common characteristics extracted from the data by different analytical techniques, since it is generally agreed that multidimensional scaling gives a broad overview of the distances among stimuli, whereas cluster analysis is more fine-grained and indicates local relations better. The latter situation holds because the joining of clusters depends on individual stimulus pairs, which become less representative of the entire clusters as the hierarchical process continues toward a single grouping. As in comparisons across clustering methods, aspects that are emphasized by more than one method should be considered more stable and therefore of greater importance for theory development.

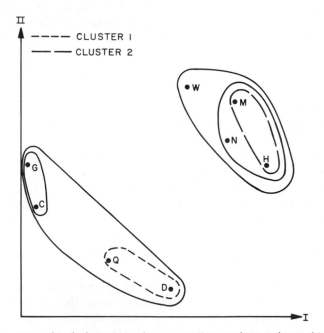

Figure 11.6.   Hierarchical clustering scheme superimposed over the multidimensional scaling solution (Chapter 10, Fig. 10.4). Data are from Wolford and Hollingsworth (1974). These are the same data used in Fig. 11.2. The dotted contour encloses the first two letters clustered; the dashed contour encloses the second two.

A THEORETICAL APPLICATION

Using the data in Table 11.5, the simple matching measure was computed for all letter pairs to generate dissimilarity measures (Table 11.7). Since the Pandemonium model predicts that letters with similar features should be confused, we would like to compare the structure of these dissimilarities with the confusion data (Table 11.2) collected by Wolford and Hollingsworth (1974). Comparing the dendrograms in Figs. 11.2 and 11.4, there is fair agreement except that Q and *H* are clustered with different letters. This deficiency is also reflected in the cophenetic rank correlation of 0.253 obtained from the predicted dissimilarities from the two clusterings.

The agreement between the Wolford and Hollingsworth data and the Pandemonium model can also be evaluated by comparing their respective multidimensional scaling outputs. To do this, Shepard-Kruskal multidimensional scaling was applied to the data set in Table 11.5 (simple matching) and the constellation of points was rotated and centered to optimally fit the output in Fig. 11.6. (For a discussion of the method of best fit, see Lingoes and Schönemann, 1974.) The arrows in Fig. 11.7 point from the prediction

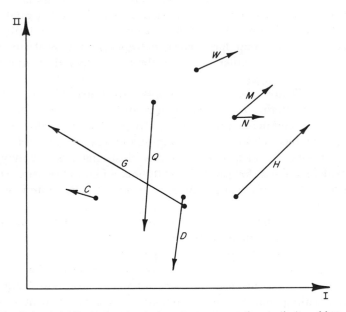

Figure 11.7. Two multidimensional solutions to represent the similarity of letters: proximities based on confusion data (Wolford and Hollingsworth, 1974), and proximities based on application of the Pandemonium model (Selfridge, 1959). Arrows point from Pandemonium model predictions to scaled confusion data.

of the Pandemonium model to the relevant locations of items used in the letter-confusion experiment. The results again highlight the strengths and weaknesses of our rather naive application of the Pandemonium model (for a more sophisticated theory of letter recognition see Wolford, 1975). The general agreement is evident, even though the letters H and Q are misplaced and the letters D and G should be spread out more. Further exploration of such modeling approaches is left for the entertainment of the interested reader.

CLUSTER ANALYSIS AS A PSYCHOLOGICAL MODEL

Cluster algorithms may suggest how people organize their environment into meaningful categories. One approach has been to model the clustering process as a grouping of attributes characterizing similar stimuli. That is, the items raft, sled, train, car, truck, and wheelbarrow could be clustered in the category of vehicles. Most of these could also be clustered as items characterized by the attributes "has wheels," "moves people," "has a steering mechanism," and so on. This conceptualization of the clusters can be used either to model the classification procedures used in everyday life or to formally describe the mechanisms invoked by specific cluster analysis techniques. Rosch (1975) models everyday classification by postulating natural categories and shows that for a given category prototypical stimuli share more attributes with all other stimuli in the cluster than do nonprototypical stimuli.

Tversky (1977) uses these same concepts—attributes, stimuli, and clusters —to identify clustering algorithms with set-theoretical operations on attribute sets. This permits construction of a psychological analog to methods such as hierarchical clustering, overlapping clusters, or fuzzy sets. Combining both approaches, identifying everyday clustering schemes may eventually provide guidelines for psychologically meaningful clustering techniques and methods for preprocessing item-by-attribute data into interitem similarity measures.

Even as a purely heuristic device, however, clustering methods make less stringent assumptions than multidimensional scaling techniques and are therefore more generally applicable. In particular, they do not require that the final stimulus configuration be interpretable in terms of an underlying dimensionality. With this in mind, Degerman (1972) proposed that multidimensional scaling and clustering methods be combined within the same model. This interesting extension of standard thinking will, it is to be hoped, generate some new ideas about psychological processes.

REFERENCES

Anderberg, M. R. *Cluster Analysis for Applications*. New York: Academic, 1973.

Bridgman, P. *The Logic of Modern Physics*. New York: Macmillan, 1927.

Cain, A. J. "Logic and memory in Linnaeus's system of taxonomy." *Proceedings of the Linnaeus Society of London, 169th Session*, 1958, 144–163.

Degerman, R. "The geometric representation of some simple structures." In R. N. Shepard, A. K. Romney, and S. B. Nerlove, (Eds.), *Multidimensional Scaling: Theory and Applications in the Behavioral Sciences*, Vol. 1. New York: Seminar Press, 1972, pp. 194–211.

Edwards, A. W. F., and Cavalli-Sforza, L. L. "A method for cluster analysis." *Biometrics*, 1965, *21*, 362–375.

Farris, J. S. "On the cophenetic correlation coefficient." *Systematic Zoology*, 1969, *18*, 279–285.

Fortier, J. J., and Solomon, H. "Clustering procedures." In R. P. Krishnajah (Ed.), *International Symposium on Multivariate Analysis, Dayton, Ohio, 1966*. New York: Academic, 1966.

Friedman, H. P., and Rubin, J. "On some invariant criteria for grouping data." *Journal of the American Statistical Association*, 1967, 1159–1178.

Jarvis, R. A., and Patrick, E. A. "Clustering using a similarity measure based on shared near neighbors." *IEEE Transactions on Computers*, 1973, *C-22*, 1025–1034.

Johnson, S. C. "Hierarchical clustering schemes." *Psychometrika*, 1967, *32*, 241–254.

Künnapas, T., and Künnapas, U. "On the relation between similarity and ratio estimates." *Psychologische Forschung*, 1973, *36*, 257–265.

Lance, G. N., and Williams, W. T. "Computer programs for hierarchical polythetic classification (similarities analysis)." *Computer Journal*, 1966, *9*, 60–64.

Lance, G. N., and Williams, W. T. "A general theory of classificatory sorting strategies. I. Hierarchical systems." *Computer Journal*, 1967a, *9*, 373–380.

Lance, G. N., and Williams, W. T. "A general theory of classificatory sorting strategies. II. Clustering systems." *Computer Journal*, 1967b, *10*, 271–277.

Lindsay, P. H., and Norman, D. A. *Human Information Processing*. New York: Academic, 1972, p. 120.

Lingoes, J. C., and Schönemann, P. H. "Alternative measures of fit for the Schönemann-Carroll matrix fitting algorithm." *Psychometrika*, 1974, *39*, 423–427.

Page, R. L. "Algorithm 479: A minimal spanning tree clustering method [Z]." *Communications of the ACM*, 1974, *17*, 321–323.

Pratt, V. "Numerical taxonomy—a critique." *Journal of Theoretical Biology*, 1972, *36*, 581–592.

Rosch, E. "Cognitive reference points." *Cognitive Psychology*, 1975, *7*, 532–547.

Selfridge, O. "Pandemonium: A paradigm for learning." In *Symposium on the Mechanization of Thought Processes*. London: H.M. Stationery Office, 1959.

Shepard, R. N., and Arabie, P. "Additive cluster analysis of similarity data." Paper presented at U.S.-Japan Seminar, Theory, Methods and Applications of Multidimensional Scaling and Related Techniques, San Diego: 1975.

Sneath, P. H. A., and Sokal, R. R. *Numerical Taxonomy*. San Francisco: W. H. Freeman, 1973.

Sokal, R. R., and Camin, J. H "The two taxonomies: Areas of agreement and conflict." *Systematic Zoology*, 1965, *14*, 176–195.

Sokal, R. R., and Rohlf, F. J. "The comparison of dendrograms by objective methods." *Taxon*, 1962, *2*, 33–40.

Tversky, A. "Features of similarity." *Psychological Review*, 1977, *84*, 327–352.

Ward, J. H. "Hierarchical grouping to optimize an objective function." *Journal of the American Statistical Association*, 1963, *58*, 236–244.

Wolford, G. "Perturbation model for letter identification." *Psychological Review*, 1975, *82*, 184–199.

Wolford, G., and Hollingsworth, S. "Evidence that short-term memory is not the limiting factor in the tachistoscopic full-report procedure." *Memory and Cognition*, 1974, *2*, 796–800.

Yeh, R. T., and Bang, S. Y. "Fuzzy relations, fuzzy graphs, and their applications to cluster analysis." In L. A. Zadeh, K. S. Fu, K. Tanaka, and M. Shimura (Eds.), *Fuzzy Sets and their Applications to Cognitive and Decision Processes*, New York: Academic, 1975.

Zadeh, L. A. "Fuzzy sets." *Information and Control*, 1965, *8*, 338–353.

Zahn, C. T. "Graph-theoretical methods for detecting and describing Gestalt clusters." *IEEE Transactions on Computers*, 1971, *C-20*, 68–86.

CHAPTER

$$\boxed{12}$$

INFORMATION THEORY

The indices of perceptual sensitivity treated thus far assume that human beings are measuring instruments yielding scale values at the ratio (magnitude estimation), interval, or ordinal (multidimensional scaling) level. In the last chapter, however, we found that clustering techniques relax this requirement and only provide for the grouping of stimuli into categories. In the present chapter we explore another approach that is based on weak measurement assumptions.

Information theory has its roots in electrical engineering and statistics. Especially important was the mathematical treatment put forth in 1948 by Claude Shannon of Bell Telephone Laboratories. Others laid much of the groundwork in statistics and telegraphy before 1940 (for review, see Luce, 1960; Garner, 1962; or Kullback, 1968), but *The Mathematical Theory of Communication* (Shannon and Weaver, 1964) had the greatest impact on the new field and was the impetus for numerous psychophysical investigations. Throughout the 1950's, psychologists conducted hundreds of experiments within the framework of information theory. Research was reviewed and its implications made clear by Miller (1956) in a now famous paper entitled "The Magical Number Seven, Plus or Minus Two: Some Limits on Capacity for Processing Information." (We will find out what that's all about later.) A more complete overview was given by Attneave (1959) and Garner (1962), and mathematical details were thoroughly discussed by Luce (1960),

231

and more recently by Coombs, Dawes, and Tversky (1970). In this chapter we will emphasize the spirit of this approach without delving too deeply into technical matters.

TWO COMMUNICATION MODELS

The Engineering Model

The fundamentals of this model can be seen by examining the communication system in Fig. 12.1 (adapted from Carlson, 1968, p. 4). The stimulus *source* produces a *message* (for example, lights, sounds, words), which usually must be converted into electrical signals by a *transducer*. A transmitter then carries the signal on to the transmission medium (*channel*) and eventually to the *receiver*. At that point the signal is transduced again to produce an acceptable output—for example, human speech.

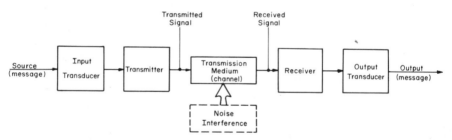

Figure 12.1.　Schematic diagram of the engineering model of information flow.

The trouble spot in this system is usually the channel, because it is subject to noise, interference, and distortion, thus disrupting the faithful transmission of information. As Luce (1960) points out, noise can be thought of as information from an unwanted source, so that whether something is classified as a noise or signal depends upon where one's interest is focused. One individual's noise can be another's signal! In an electrical system, noise will usually be in the form of random electrical signals. The engineer studies the flow of information through such a system and devises strategies for optimum coding of the signal to increase the amount of information accurately transmitted under "noisy" conditions.

The Psychophysical Model

A diagram of one possible psychophysical model is given in Fig. 12.2. Here a person is the communication system; the peripheral receptors are transducers of environmental stimuli, sensory neurons are the channels, neurons mediating cognitive processes receive the signal, and effectors eventually produce a response. Unwanted or unspecified physiological noise in this system will result in degradation of performance, just as in any communication system. Since different stimulus attributes will be processed over different sensory channels, their relative efficiency can be compared by the use of a suitable index. One of the most widely used indices is the *channel capacity* of the system: a limit on the amount of information that can be transmitted per unit time. To complete the analogy between the engineering and psychophysical models, mathematics must be introduced. We turn now to this matter.

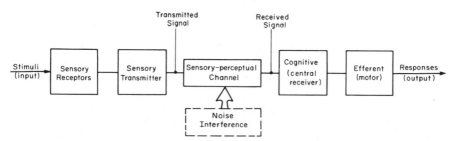

Figure 12.2.   Schematic diagram of the psychophysical model of information flow.

INFORMATION MEASURES

So far in our discussion, the word "information" has been loosely used according to its everyday meaning. The term also has a technical meaning: *that which is transmitted from the source to the user* (Carlson, 1968, p. 321). This definition suggests that the source contains *potential* information, not sent to the user, and that the amount of information gained depends on the alternatives available at the source.

To be more concrete, imagine a person in a dormitory room contemplating a walk to the library to pick up some books. A friend arrives on the scene and offers information in one of three messages:

1.   The library is still standing.
2.   The stacks are closed.
3.   The library was destroyed by a fire.

The amount of information conveyed by each message is quite different. The first tells us nothing very startling, since the probability is just about 1 that the building will be intact in a peace-loving society. Initially the person receiving the message had no uncertainty about that! On the other hand, the second message does convey information. Depending on the time of day, whether or not classes are in session, and so on, the *a priori* uncertainty will vary concerning the accessibility of the stacks. Hence, the person is more uncertain about the actual state of nature, and the friend's message is informative. The third message carries even more information because the occurrence of a fire in the library is very unlikely. The information will also be *useful* to the person (a rise in tuition can be anticipated), but the usefulness or meaning of the message has nothing to do with the amount of information conveyed. The latter depends only on the prior uncertainty concerning the event, that is, on its initial probability. The lower the probability of an event, the more uncertain we are about it, and the more information is gained when the event actually occurs. High probability events such as touching the ground while walking in the woods, contacting cement while walking in the city, and seeing the sun at least once a year, contain less information than do low probability events. In brief, information is a function of initial event probability.

Moving onward now to a quantitative definition of information, let x and y be events from a set, occurring with probabilities $p(x)$ and $p(y)$, respectively. Then, the information I_x and I_y are defined ($\equiv$) as functions of the probabilities.

$$I_x \equiv f\left[\, p(x)\,\right] \tag{12.1}$$

$$I_y \equiv f\left[\, p(y)\,\right]$$

The idea is to find $f[\ \ ]$ in Eq. 12.1 so that it agrees with our concept of information. To do this, we follow a line of reasoning similar to one originally suggested by Howard Raiffa and documented by Luce (1960). For further discussion, see Carlson (1968) and Coombs et al. (1970). The desired function must meet several conditions.[1]

----

[1] The actual proof is beyond the scope of this work, See Luce (1960) or Ash (1965, Chapter 1) for more details.

1. If $p(x)=1$, the outcome is certain, so no information is contained in the event; $I_x=0$.

2. If event x is less likely than event y, $p(x)<p(y)$ and $I_x>I_y$ because low probability implies high information.

3. Information is additive for independent events. That is, if I_x is obtained from the occurrence of event x and I_y is obtained from event y, the total information received when both occur (if x and y are independent as is assumed hereafter) should be I_x+I_y. For example, if two friends arrive to discuss our student's trip to the library, one friend may deliver information about the library itself, the other may have something to say about the weather. The information received from the two sources should be additive.

From the rules of probability theory, the probability of the compound event, x and y (denoted by $x \cap y$), is found by multiplying the individual probabilities. Therefore, for the compound event $c=x \cap y$, $p(c)=p(x) \cdot p(y)$. Also,

$$I_c=f\left[p(x) \cdot p(y)\right]$$

As far as the student is concerned, the information obtained from the two friends is I_x+I_y, so

$$I_c=I_x+I_y=f\left[p(x)\right]+f\left[p(y)\right]$$

and

$$f\left[p(x) \cdot p(y)\right]=f\left[p(x)\right]+f\left[p(y)\right] \qquad (12.2)$$

There is only one function that satisfies Eq. 12.2 and the three other conditions listed above (assuming the function is continuous). This is a logarithmic function. To serve as a measure of information, Eq. 12.1 can now be rewritten as

$$I_x=-k\log_b p(x), \qquad k>0$$

where k is a constant and b is the base of the logarithm. If k is set to 1,

$$I_x=-\log_b p(x)=\log_b\left(\frac{1}{p(x)}\right) \qquad (12.3)$$

The minus sign poses no special difficulty because probabilities range from 0 to 1; in other words, $p(x)$ is either 0, 1, or a fraction. Since the logarithm of a number in that range is negative, the information measure is a positive number. This may also be seen when the equation is rewritten, as in the last term of Eq. 12.3. The ratio $1/p(x)$ is greater than or equal to 1, and so its logarithm is always positive.

The base b of the logarithm is arbitrary since the logarithm to one base is equivalent to the logarithm to another multiplied by a constant. In information theory, however, base two is employed, and the unit of information is the "bit," suggested by the statistician John Tukey as a contraction of "binary digit." Thus,[2]

$$I_x = -\log p(x) \text{ bits} \qquad (12.4)$$

The meaning of a "bit" is easier to grasp in terms of a particular event x from a set of N alternative events. If each alternative $x, y, z, \ldots$ has the same probability of occurrence, the probability that x occurs is $p(x) = 1/N$, so that $N = 1/p(x)$. Substituting in Eq. 12.3, we obtain

$$I_x = \log N$$

The information in a specific event x is equal to the logarithm of the number of equally likely events, N. Hence,

From a set of 1 event: $I_x = \log 1 = 0$ bits
From a set of 2 events: $I_x = \log 2 = 1$ bit
From a set of 4 events: $I_x = \log 4 = 2$ bits
From a set of 8 events: $I_x = \log 8 = 3$ bits

Intermediate (non-whole number) bits are also possible. In each case the measure of information is the power to which the base must be raised to equal the number of alternatives. So $2^0 = 1$, $2^1 = 2$, $2^2 = 4$, and $2^{4.64} = 25$.

Another way to attack this problem is to view the exponent as the number of decisions necessary to specify an event among N alternatives.[3] For example, say a government agency secretly places an M&M candy in one of 4 cells in a 2×2 matrix. We have to determine which cell by asking a minimum number of binary questions (in response to any inquiry we receive merely a "yes" or "no"). Using an optimal strategy, half the remaining alternatives should be eliminated with each succeeding question. For instance, we might first ask whether the candy is in the left half of the matrix. An answer reduces the number of alternatives (our uncertainty as well) by one-half, since either a "yes" or "no" answer restricts the prize to one of two cells. The second question might be whether the candy is in the

---

[2]All future logarithms in this chapter will be base two. The log of a number may be looked up in a table of base two logarithms or converted from a table of base ten logarithms by multiplying the logarithm by 3.32.

[3]For a related treatment of the topics in this and the succeeding section, see Edwards (1969).

upper half of the matrix, the answer to which reduces our uncertainty to zero. It would take two binary questions to locate the candy from among four alternatives. This agrees nicely with the definition of information, since

$$I_x = \log 4 = 2 \text{ bits}$$

Average Uncertainty

The terms information and uncertainty are often interchangeable, since the amount of information gained depends on the amount of uncertainty reduced. From here on we will talk mainly about uncertainty, because it is more frequently found in the psychological literature!

Under many circumstances the probabilities are not the same for all events and an average measure of uncertainty is required. This average is, in fact, the keystone to the measure of transmitted information and therefore the capacity of a channel. At first glance, the type of average seems a little strange, so we will take special care in describing it.

Suppose we wish to compute an average for a set of numbers. The usual procedure is to add up all the values and divide by the number of cases. For example, the average of 1, 1, 2, 2, 2, 3, 3, 3, 3, 4 is 2.4. A second way, perhaps less familiar, is shown in the left half of Table 12.1. There are four events with values 1, 2, 3, 4 and each occurs in our ensemble (set) with the frequencies shown. The total number of cases is 10. The average is found by multiplying each event value V by its frequency of occurrence F, adding up the results, and dividing by 10. The answer is still 2.4.

A slight variation on this approach brings us closer to the procedure used to find average uncertainty. This variation is presented in the right half of Table 12.1. The four events are the same, but instead of frequencies we have probabilities obtained by dividing the frequency of each event by the total number of cases (10). In the third column the probabilities are multiplied by

Table 12.1 Two simple methods for finding an average

Event Value (V)	Frequency (F)	$V \cdot F$	Event Value (V)	Probability $p(x)$	$V \cdot p(x)$
1	2	2	1	2/10	2/10
2	3	6	2	3/10	6/10
3	4	12	3	4/10	12/10
4	1	4	4	1/10	4/10
	10	24/10 = 2.4			24/10 = 2.4

their respective event values and summed to give the average value of 2.4. This example points out the use of probabilities in calculating a *weighted average*. Note that summing the weighted scores yields the average directly; there is no need to divide the sum by the number of cases as in the two other methods. Average uncertainty is computed by analogous reasoning, since a *weighted* sum is obtained from a set of probabilities over the ensemble of events.

The event value is now an uncertainty defined as $-\log p(x_i)$, whose probability is $p(x_i)$. Therefore, to secure an average over N alternatives, multiply each individual uncertainty by its probability and add up the results.

$$U(x) = -\sum_{i=1}^{N} p(x_i)\log p(x_i) \qquad (12.5)$$

This average uncertainty depends entirely on the number of events and their probabilities. It turns out that the maximum uncertainty is attained when the probabilities are the same for each alternative. That is, if there are four equally likely alternatives, the probability of each is $\frac{1}{4}$. Hence, the average uncertainty of the set is

$$+\left(-\frac{1}{4}\log\frac{1}{4}\right)$$

$$+\left(-\frac{1}{4}\log\frac{1}{4}\right)$$

$$+\left(-\frac{1}{4}\log\frac{1}{4}\right)$$

$$+\left(-\frac{1}{4}\log\frac{1}{4}\right)$$

which reduces to

$$-U(x) = -\log\tfrac{1}{4} = -(\log 1 - \log 4) = \log 4$$

$$= 2 \text{ bits per alternative}$$

It is interesting to note that the measure of information for a single event x from the 4 equally probable alternatives is also 2, since

$$I_x = \log 4 = 2$$

This matches our intuitions about average value, since any event x is representative of the ensemble. This implies that the information measure for any event x should equal the average uncertainty, and indeed this is true, since $I_x = U(x) = 2$ bits. If probabilities are unequal among events, the average will be different from the equal-probability case. It will in fact always be less. That is, all other distributions of probabilities lead to lower average uncertainties. In the extreme case, where the probability of a single event is 1 and for all other outcomes it is 0, the average uncertainty is also 0, since there is no uncertainty about an event that always occurs.

One final remark before we move on to calculation of transmitted information. The information measure computed by Eq. 12.5 is, after all, a statistic, no different from your garden variety mean or standard deviation. Therefore, few psychological assumptions are needed concerning the nature of the phenomenon being described. However, it also serves as the mathematical model for a theory of information processing (Fig. 12.2). Therefore, we view the information measure as a statistic with a somewhat wider latitude of application.

Information Transmission

In psychophysics we are interested in the relative ability of different sensory channels to transmit information. We are therefore working toward an index of perceptual sensitivity for the amount of information transmitted between the signal (stimulus) ensemble and the receiver (response) ensemble. The greater the amount transmitted by a channel, the greater its presumed sensitivity.[4]

The calculation of information transmitted involves the application of Eq. 12.5 in several contexts, which can best be understood by an analogous case that does not rely upon detailed equations. Once this analog is understood, the details should fall into place more easily.

AN ANALOG FROM TRINOCULAR PERCEPTION

Here we offer a model to elucidate the procedures and rationale for calculating transmitted information. The reader, however, should neither

---

[4]In electrical engineering applications, a time element is usually included, so one refers to the transmission of so many bits per second. In the psychophysical applications emphasized here the rate aspect is ignored. It is assumed that the subject has sufficient time to process the stimuli, and hence amount of information per stimulus is the only measure of interest.

interpret what follows as bearing any more than a superficial relationship to what is known about binocular vision nor overextend this visual analog of information transmitted.

To further discourage unwarranted comparisons and unnecessary confusion, imagine we are among the first earthlings on Jupiter (our first trip since Chapter 8), and that we encounter some character with three eyes (trinocular vision). Two of the three eyes have circular fields of view, separated laterally but not too far apart. The left and right eye fields can then be represented as two overlapping circles, as shown in Fig. 12.3 (left). The third eye is *cyclopean* with a field of view containing all the elements of the left and right fields, as shown in the right-hand diagram in Fig. 12.3. It can now be seen that the elements in the total display fall within one of three subregions, x, i, and y. The elements in x are unique to the left eye (F_l), the elements in y are unique to the right eye (F_r), and those in i are present within the

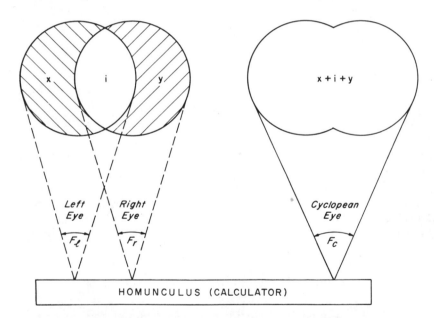

Figure 12.3. Model to represent analysis in terms of information theory. The left and right eyes have unique elements in their visual fields (F_l and F_r) as well as an overlapping region (i). The cyclopean eye (right diagram) contains all the elements from the fields of the left and right eyes (F_c). The homunculus operates on inputs from all three fields to obtain an estimate of the intersection i, which is analogous to amount of information transmitted.

intersection. The view of the cyclopean eye (F_c) contains elements from all of these regions.[5]

In a way, it may be said that the three visual regions can be weighted and manipulated by the rules of arithmetic. That is, if F is a visual field, then

$$F_l = x + i \qquad \text{(left eye)}$$

$$F_r = y + i \qquad \text{(right eye)}$$

$$F_c = x + y + i \qquad \text{(cyclopean eye)}$$

Eventually we will see that information transmitted is equated with the intersection of the left and right fields (i in Fig. 12.3). Because of mathematical constraints, this intersection cannot be found directly and must be obtained by manipulation of F_l, F_r, and F_c. To carry out the processing of elements in the three fields, a "homunculus" is fabricated and located somewhere in the far reaches of the Jovian brain (see Fig. 12.3). Its job is to find the size of the intersection i. Unfortunately, the homunculus cannot do this directly but must gain a result by adding and subtracting elements from the individual fields of the left, right, and cyclopean eyes. According to Earth logic there are three ways to do this.

1. In the first method the homunculus sums the elements in the left and right fields and subtracts the elements in the cyclopean field. Thus,

$$F_l + F_r - F_c = i$$

or

$$(x + i) + (y + i) - (x + y + i) = i$$

The second and third methods are more direct.

2. The homunculus takes all the elements in the left field and subtracts those that do not overlap with the elements in the right. The latter operation

---

[5]All this may sound like duck soup for set theory. However, in the following discussion the standard set theory notation will not be used. Instead, we employ what we feel is a more intuitive approach, in closer agreement with the uncertainty measures introduced later. In the set theory notation introduced in Chapter 9, F_l and F_r are two sets whose union is $F_l \cup F_r = F_c$ and whose intersection is $F_l \cap F_r = i$. If $\bar{F}_l$ are elements not in F_l and $\bar{F}_r$ are elements not in F_r, the conditionals to be mentioned in a moment are $F_l \cap \bar{F}_r = x$ and $\bar{F}_l \cap F_r = y$. For more details on notation, see Kemeny, Snell, and Thompson (1966).

can be written in the conditional form

$$F_l | F_r = x$$

so

$$F_l - (F_l | F_r) = i$$

or

$$(x + i) - x = i$$

3. Similarly, the homunculus can take the elements in the right field and subtract those that do not occur in the left. This conditional is equal to y:

$$F_r | F_l = y$$

and therefore

$$F_r - (F_r | F_l) = i$$

or

$$(y + i) - y = i$$

Each of the three methods yields the same result, the intersection i. Returning now to earthbound problems, these approaches are analogous to those used to find the amount of information transmitted by a channel. The larger the intersection, the greater the amount transmitted.

Application of these procedures requires that one specify the content associated with the two overlapping circles in Fig. 12.3. So let's do that. Say one visual field represents a stimulus ensemble, the other a response ensemble—by an ensemble we simply mean a collection or *set* of discrete items. The intersection is then the amount of information transmitted by the subject when asked to attach the correct response label to each of the stimuli; that is, the degree of overlap (intersection) or correlation between stimuli and responses. The exact form of this overlap can be understood by examining the equations that define the measure at a general level. In particular, the discussion will center upon how one analyzes results from the psychophysical method known as *absolute judgment* or *absolute identification*. Before we get to the analysis, though, the basic format of this experimental method must be described.

METHOD OF ABSOLUTE IDENTIFICATION

Suppose we were to construct a stimulus ensemble of four lines, each of a different length. In the method of absolute identification the lines are then presented in a random order on many occasions and a subject must identify each by a response label. The labels might be the integers 1 through 4 or the letters A through D, or any other set of four distinctive names, not necessarily arranged in any natural order (for example, "red," "one," "house," and "Alice" would be acceptable). Since the experimenter designates the "correct" match between individual stimuli and responses, the subject is told the correct label after each judgment.

Hypothetical results from a study employing 64 trials (16 with each stimulus) are given in the form of a stimulus-response matrix in Table 12.2. Actually, this number of trials is inadequate for such an experiment but is more manageable for purposes of exposition. All information theory calculations are based on such a matrix. First, however, we define some terms by referring to Fig. 12.4. The diagram is a modified version of the trinocular vision example given in Fig. 12.3, where the following mapping is assumed between the two:

$F_r \rightarrow U(S)$ (uncertainty of the stimulus set)
$F_l \rightarrow U(R)$ (uncertainty of the response set)
$F_c \rightarrow U(S,R)$ (uncertainty of the union of stimuli and responses)
$y \rightarrow U(S|R)$ (uncertainty of the stimulus set conditional upon the response set)
$x \rightarrow U(R|S)$ (uncertainty of the response set conditional upon the stimulus set)
$i \rightarrow I_t$ (information transmitted between the stimulus and response sets)

Returning to the data matrix (Table 12.2), each of the relevant terms can be computed with variations on the formula for average uncertainty (Eq. 12.5).

Uncertainty of the Stimulus Set[6]

The average uncertainty of the stimulus set is

$$U(S) = -\sum_{i=1}^{N} p(s_i)\log p(s_i) \qquad (12.6)$$

where $p(s_i)$ is the probability of the ith stimulus in a set of N. Referring to the data matrix, the relative frequency (equated with probability) is found

[6]The numerical calculations in the next few pages can be skimmed without losing the main thread of the argument.

Table 12.2   Stimulus-response matrix for method of absolute identification. Entries are response frequencies.

		Stimuli (lines)				
		1	2	3	4	Total
	1	10	5	0	2	17
Responses	2	3	9	0	2	14
(labels)	3	3	2	14	2	21
	4	0	0	2	10	12
	Total	16	16	16	16	64

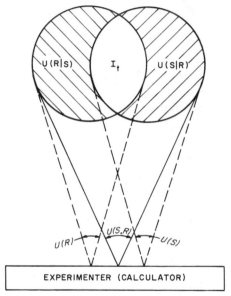

Figure 12.4.   Schematic diagram of the elements required to calculate information transmission (I_t) from conditional and joint uncertainties. The structure of the diagram follows that of the model in Fig. 12.3.

by dividing the total number of presentations (64) into each of the stimulus frequencies, given as the column totals. We have designed the experiment so the stimuli were presented an equal number of times (column totals = 16), hence, $\frac{16}{64} = \frac{1}{4}$. Substituting in Eq. 12.6,

$$U(S) = -4\left(\tfrac{1}{4}\right)\log\left(\tfrac{1}{4}\right)$$

since there are 4 stimuli of the same probability, and therefore

$$U(S) = 2 \text{ bits/stimulus}$$

Uncertainty of the Response Set

The average uncertainty of the response set is found in a similar way. The probability of each response is equated with the relative frequency obtained by dividing each row total by the grand sum (64). Substituting in Eq. 12.5,

$$U(R) = - \sum_{j=1}^{M} p(r_j) \log p(r_j) \tag{12.7}$$

$$U(R) = - \tfrac{17}{64} \log\left(\tfrac{17}{64}\right) = 0.508$$

$$- \tfrac{14}{64} \log\left(\tfrac{14}{64}\right) = 0.480$$

$$- \tfrac{21}{64} \log\left(\tfrac{21}{64}\right) = 0.528$$

$$- \tfrac{12}{64} \log\left(\tfrac{12}{64}\right) = 0.453$$

$$U(R) = 1.969$$

Joint Uncertainty

The joint uncertainty is the union of the stimulus and response sets $[U(S)]$ $\cup [U(R)]$. The elements of this set are the individual cell entries (cartesian product $S \times R$) in the data matrix (Table 12.2), where relevant probabilities are obtained by dividing each cell frequency (i,j) by the grand sum. Then the joint uncertainty is secured by summing over all the cells:

$$U(R,S) = - \sum_{i=1}^{N} \sum_{j=1}^{M} p(s_i, r_j) \log p(s_i, r_j) \tag{12.8}$$

where N is the number of stimuli and M is the number of response alternatives. For our example,

$$U(R,S) = 2\left[-\tfrac{10}{64}\log\left(\tfrac{10}{64}\right)\right] = 0.837$$

$$-\tfrac{5}{64}\log\left(\tfrac{5}{64}\right) = 0.287$$

$$5\left[-\tfrac{2}{64}\log\left(\tfrac{2}{64}\right)\right] = 0.781$$

$$2\left[-\tfrac{3}{64}\log\left(\tfrac{3}{64}\right)\right] = 0.414$$

$$-\tfrac{9}{64}\log\left(\tfrac{9}{64}\right) = 0.398$$

$$-\tfrac{14}{64}\log\left(\tfrac{14}{64}\right) = 0.480$$

$$U(R,S) = 3.197$$

Uncertainty of Responses Conditional on Stimuli

The uncertainties for the stimulus and response sets are calculated independently, since it is not necessary to know one to find the other. To find the overlap I_t between the two, however, we must bring them together in the form of conditional uncertainties.

Assume that a single stimulus is presented on many trials. There will be a distribution of responses associated with this stimulus, as represented by a single column in the data matrix (Table 12.2). The probability of each response conditional on presentation of a single stimulus $(r_j|s_i)$ is found by dividing the appropriate cell entry by the column total. Then the average conditional uncertainty for this single stimulus, s_i, over M responses is

$$U(R|s_i) = -\sum_{j=1}^{M} p(r_j|s_i)\log p(r_j|s_i) \qquad (12.9)$$

This formula must be applied for each column (stimulus), weighted by the appropriate probability $p(s_i)$, and summed. The average uncertainty of the response set conditional on the stimulus set then becomes

$$U(R|S) = -\sum_{i=1}^{N} p(s_i)\sum_{j=1}^{M} p(r_j|s_i)\log p(r_j|s_i) \qquad (12.10)$$

The term $U(R|S)$ is sometimes referred to as *response equivocation* because it is a measure of the response variability (uncertainty) remaining after the stimulus is specified. For our data matrix,

$$U(R|s_1) = -\left[\tfrac{10}{16}\log\left(\tfrac{10}{16}\right) + \tfrac{3}{16}\log\left(\tfrac{3}{16}\right) + \tfrac{3}{16}\log\left(\tfrac{3}{16}\right)\right] = 1.329$$

$$U(R|s_2) = -\left[\tfrac{5}{16}\log\left(\tfrac{5}{16}\right) + \tfrac{9}{16}\log\left(\tfrac{9}{16}\right) + \tfrac{2}{16}\log\left(\tfrac{2}{16}\right)\right] = 1.366$$

$$U(R|s_3) = -\left[\tfrac{14}{16}\log\left(\tfrac{14}{16}\right) + \tfrac{2}{16}\log\left(\tfrac{2}{16}\right)\right] = 0.544$$

$$U(R|s_4) = -\left[\tfrac{2}{16}\log\left(\tfrac{2}{16}\right) + \tfrac{2}{16}\log\left(\tfrac{2}{16}\right) + \tfrac{2}{16}\log\left(\tfrac{2}{16}\right) + \tfrac{10}{16}\log\left(\tfrac{10}{16}\right)\right] = 1.549$$

Weighting each column by the stimulus probability $(\tfrac{1}{4})$ and summing, we get

$$U(R|S) = \tfrac{1}{4}(1.329) + \tfrac{1}{4}(1.366) + \tfrac{1}{4}(0.544) + \tfrac{1}{4}(1.549) = 1.197$$

Uncertainty of Stimuli Conditional on Responses

Similarly, the average uncertainty of the stimulus set conditional on the response set can be determined by summing the weighted uncertainties for each row of the matrix. That is,

$$U(S|R) = -\sum_{j=1}^{M} p(r_j) \sum_{i=1}^{N} p(s_i|r_j)\log p(s_i|r_j) \qquad (12.11)$$

When Eq. 12.11 is evaluated with the data in Table 12.2, $U(S|R) = 1.229$. The term $U(S|R)$ is sometimes called *stimulus ambiguity*. It is a measure of the uncertainty remaining in the stimulus set once the response has been specified.

Information Transmitted

As mentioned previously for the visual analog, the operation of the homunculus leads to three equivalent methods for calculating information transmitted. At this point it may prove helpful to reexamine Fig. 12.4.

$$I_t = U(S) + U(R) - U(R,S)$$
$$I_t = U(R) - U(R|S)$$
$$I_t = U(S) - U(S|R)$$

Substituting the appropriate values from our example

$$
\left.\begin{array}{l}
I_t = 2 + 1.968 - 3.197 = 0.771 \\
I_t = 1.968 - 1.197 = 0.771 \\
I_t = 2 - 1.229 = 0.771
\end{array}\right\} \qquad (12.12)
$$

Each approach gives the same answer—a reassuring way to end this section! The information transmitted depends on the amount of stimulus and response uncertainty, but once these are specified, the critical determinant is the uniqueness of the mapping between individual stimuli and responses. Recall that maximum uncertainty occurs when all events have the same probability. In the case of an $S \times R$ data matrix, this means that all cells contain the same frequency, and therefore zero information is transmitted. The highest transmission occurs when each stimulus is always identified by the proper response. These two extremes are demonstrated for the line length example in Table 12.3.

Table 12.3   Two stimulus-response matrices for the absolute identification of line lengths (hypothetical data)

| | | Stimuli (lines) | | | | |
		1	2	3	4	Totals
	1	4	4	4	4	16
Responses	2	4	4	4	4	16
(labels)	3	4	4	4	4	16
	4	4	4	4	4	16
	Total	16	16	16	16	64

Minimum information transmitted $I_t = 0$

| | | Stimuli (lines) | | | | |
		1	2	3	4	Totals
	1	16	0	0	0	16
Responses	2	0	16	0	0	16
(labels)	3	0	0	16	0	16
	4	0	0	0	16	16
	Totals	16	16	16	16	64

Maximum information transmitted $I_t = 2$ bits

In the top matrix in Table 12.3, the subject could have been making arbitrary, evenly distributed responses regardless of the stimulus presented. It is as if the subject is blind, so there is no information transmitted ($I_t = 0$). The calculated value matches these intuitions.

By contrast, the matrix at the bottom of Table 12.3 is from a subject who uniquely and consistently labels each stimulus. All the lines are correctly identified, so we would assume all stimulus information is transmitted as response information. Perfect transmission, in this case, means $I_t = 2$. Again, the calculations verify this fact.

Unidimensional Stimuli

Two stimuli whose intensities are well separated along the continuum of interest (sound, light, length, or whatever) are usually identified without error in an absolute identification task. Transmission is perfect. As the number of stimuli (uncertainty) increases, however, a point is eventually

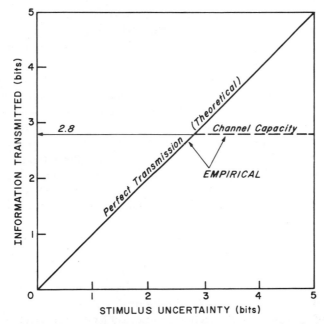

Figure 12.5. Hypothetical relation between information transmitted and stimulus uncertainty for the method of absolute identification. Channel capacity is indicated by the horizontal dashed line, breaking off from the line of perfect transmission at 2.8 bits.

reached where confusions occur in the labeling process, even if the intensities are clearly different (let us say, 5 jnd's apart). Therefore the amount transmitted is reduced—it is less than the potential information in the stimulus ensemble. Thereafter, increases in stimulus uncertainty produce no further increases in transmitted information, and we then claim that the *channel capacity* of the system has been reached.

Figure 12.5 is an idealized picture of how the empirical data (dashed line) supports the notion of channel capacity. The information transmitted (I_t) for different stimulus uncertainties $U(S)$ would be secured in separate experiments and plotted against each other. Perfect transmission coincides with the diagonal line, whereas the empirical data (dashed line) level off at about 2.8 bits. This value is called the channel capacity of the system (defined as an experimental subject, sensory channel, information processor, black box, or whatever).

Two Empirical Examples

Among the early applications of information theory to psychophysics was a study by Hake and Garner (1951) on the absolute identification (by sight) of pointer positions along a line, and a series of experiments by Pollack (1952) on the identification of sound frequencies.

Hake and Garner employed four different numbers of possible pointer positions: 5, 10, 20, and 50; thus the stimulus uncertainty was 2.32, 3.32, 4.32, and 5.64, respectively. Each series was presented 200 times, and subjects were run under two instructional conditions: (1) The responses were a set of integers, supplied by the experimenter, and were to represent the relative position of the pointer. (2) The subject was allowed to use any of the integers from 0 to 100. Under both instructions the information transmitted varied systematically with stimulus uncertainty until a limit was reached at approximately 3.2 bits. These results are shown in Fig. 12.6 for the "limited" response condition.

In the Pollack (1952) experiment, a series of from 2 to 15 tones were presented, spanning a frequency range from 100 to 8000 cycles per second. Hence, the stimulus uncertainty ranged from 1 to 3.9 bits. The response set consisted of the integers 1 through N, where N was the total number of tones, and the natural order of the frequencies was preserved in the order of the response integers. After each response, subjects were given the correct value before moving on to the next stimulus. A variety of experimental conditions were employed in which Pollack varied the specific tones in the

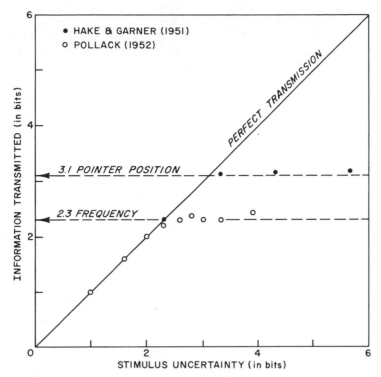

Figure 12.6. Information transmitted as a function of stimulus uncertainty for visual marker position and auditory tones. The solid diagonal line indicates perfect transmission. The horizontal dashed lines indicate the channel capacities.

series, their range over the frequency continuum, and the number of judgments per stimulus. Although these conditions did not lead to identical results, they were similar enough to invite the conclusion that channel capacity was a real phenomenon in perception and was not easily altered through the introduction of relatively strong contextual changes. Once again, the information transmitted increased linearly with increases in stimulus uncertainty and leveled off at a relatively small value, approximately 2.3 bits; the channel capacity for tones was considerably lower than for position of a point (although the smaller number of trials used by Pollack may have biased his results somewhat). A sample of these results is also shown in Fig. 12.6.

An impressive array of further experiments has been reported (mostly in the 1950s) in which the method of absolute identification (judgment) was used to determine channel capacities for a variety of unidimensional continua (Miller, 1956; Luce, 1960; Garner, 1962). The results of some of these studies are summarized in Table 12.4. The data presented there were reviewed previously (Baird, 1970a), so specific references to the original studies are not given (when there were two values for the same continuum, the higher was taken for the table). The channel capacities range from 1.5 bits for odor intensity to 3.9 bits for position of a point on a line. The average is 2.3 bits. Assuming equally likely alternatives, this implies that the number of stimuli that can be perfectly discriminated in this type of task is

$$2^{2.3} \approx 5$$

It was data such as these that prompted Miller (1956) to conclude that the channel capacity for unidimensional continua is 7 ± 2 alternatives. This conclusion assumes that the variability among the values in Table 12.4 is due to random error, either unrelated to the continuum under investigation or at least unimportant to Miller's suggestion of a constant channel capacity. From a psychophysical standpoint, this seems to be a dubious conclusion. It is much more likely, from all we know about other indices of sensitivity, that the values in Table 12.4 reflect, at least in part, differences in the ability of the sensory channels to process intensity information. The greater the channel capacity, the greater the perceptual sensitivity. This argument has been developed elsewhere (Baird, 1970a) and receives support from recent work in which channel capacities were determined for several types of stimulus continua in the same study (Baird, Romer, and Stein, 1970; Landau, et al., 1974).

Table 12.4   Representative channel capacities for different continua

Continuum	Channel capacity
Position of a point (visual)	3.9
Length of lines (visual)	3.0
Squares (visual)	2.8
Brightness (munsell squares)	2.3
Loudness (1000 Hz)	2.1
Electrical (skin)	1.7
Taste (salt, sucrose)	1.7
Vibration (skin)	1.6
Odor	1.5

Relations with Other Sensitivity Indices

The relation between channel capacities in Table 12.4 and Weber fractions for the same continua has been pointed out previously (Baird, 1970a). With the exception of electric shock, there is a general negative relationship between the two indices of sensitivity. The greater the channel capacity, the smaller the Weber fraction. This is as it should be if different psychophysical methods reveal the same underlying sensory processes.

To understand why this is so, consider first a single stimulus located arbitrarily along an intensity continuum. Following the lead of both Fechner and Thurstone, let us assume that the effects of repeated presentations of this stimulus are normally distributed along a psychological scale. At this point if we were to perform some experiments using the classical methods (Chapter 3) it would be possible to measure the just-noticeable-difference (jnd), which would, of course, be a direct function of the stimulus variance. The larger the variance, the larger the jnd and the resulting Weber fraction.

If now a second stimulus is introduced, its discriminability from the first must depend upon how far it is displaced along the scale. If the d' of signal detection (Chapter 8) is used as an index of discriminability, its magnitude will clearly depend on the variances of the two stimuli as well as the distance between their means. With the same separation between means, d' shrinks as variance increases.

Let us assume now that a fixed stimulus range is decided upon and N stimuli are equally distributed within that range. The discriminability of the stimuli one from the other depends on the resulting d' between pairs of stimuli. The smaller d' is (due to relatively higher variance), the more confusion there will be among stimuli, and therefore the larger the average uncertainty of responses conditional upon presentation of stimuli $[U(R|S)]$. Accordingly, if subjects were required to uniquely identify each stimulus, the information transmitted would depend on the size of the conditional uncertainty, since

$$I_t = U(R) - U(R|S)$$

This completes the cycle: The jnd of classical psychophysics can be defined as the standard deviation of the distribution underlying the conditional uncertainty. Small variance is associated with high information transmitted —assuming a fixed number of N stimuli are spread over the same stimulus range.

Exact quantitative predictions of the relationship between the jnd (Weber fraction, actually) and channel capacity would have to take into account several additional factors: Weber's law, end effects (the smallest and largest stimuli in a series are more readily identified), and the physical spacing between stimuli. A thorough study of these theoretical problems apparently has not been done (though see Durlach and Braida, 1969; and Weber, Green, and Luce, 1977). Some related work on the effects of stimulus range is discussed below.

Another index of sensitivity, which might be expected to show a meaningful link with channel capacity, is the exponent of the power function obtained by ratio methods (Chapter 5). We would expect a positive relationship between exponents and channel capacity, and in general this is true (Baird, 1970b). (Once again, however, electric shock is an outlier.) High exponents imply high channel capacities, although the relationship is not a strong one.

We would not expect a smooth, tidy function between these various sensitivity indices, since the data are taken from studies conducted in different laboratories, and procedural variations across studies will tend to blur the exact form of the connections among indices (Chapter 6). In addition, even under the most favorable conditions, differences in psychophysical methods, leading to alternative subject strategies, may prevent us from finding a perfectly consistent relationship between indices.

Information Transmission and Stimulus Range

The amount of information transmitted depends on the separation among stimuli, because error-free behavior is impossible if stimulus distributions overlap (along the psychological scale). The notion of a fixed channel capacity also implies the following: For a sufficiently large number of stimuli, say 10, as the separation of stimuli along the physical continuum is increased, a point will be reached beyond which no further increment in transmitted information occurs. When the stimuli are packed together, there is considerable overlap of the distributions, identification errors are frequent, and transmission is low. As interstimulus separation increases, transmission increases. However, this increase eventually levels off at a channel capacity less than the maximum possible (given 10 intensities). The natural question then becomes: "Why does the function level off so soon?"

Empirical evidence bearing on this question is available from several sources. Both Braida and Durlach (1972) and Luce, Green, and Weber (1976) have shown that increasing stimulus range (using 10 tones) leads to a rather smooth increase in transmitted information (or sensitivity as measured by a summed d' between pairs of tones) up to some point where the function either levels off or climbs much more slowly. (In the latter study, the stimuli were 1000-Hz tones, centered at 60 db and presented for $\frac{1}{2}$ sec.

This finding is inexplicable from the standpoint of a Case V Thurstonian analysis (Chapter 7) or by the theory of signal detectability (Chapter 8), since the effect of a stimulus on the psychological scale is supposed to be independent of the effect of others. In other words, as range increases one would expect only that information transmitted would continue to improve in a regular manner until all the available information was transmitted. Some additional factor, not treated by this analysis, must be responsible for the degradation of performance for large stimulus ranges.

Durlach and Braida (1969) have proposed that this "extra" factor might be the range itself. They assume that two types of variance contribute to the total associated with a stimulus. The first is *sensation variance*, which does not depend on the size of the stimulus ensemble. The second is *memory variance*, which does, and is a direct function of the range. When stimuli are packed together, identification performance is most influenced by the sensation variance. As the range increases, however, the memory variance takes over and exerts the most influence. As the argument goes, then, the reason for the relatively poor performance with extended ranges is that subjects are dealing with a more variable stimulus representation. A related explanation was suggested independently by Gravetter and Lockhead (1973).

A quite different view of what's going on in these experiments is offered by Luce, Green, and Weber (1976). They assume the stimulus representation available for judgment is always the same, independent of the number of stimuli or their range. However, the subject's attention is limited, and therefore the degree to which a particular section of the psychological scale is monitored will depend on the range of values possible under a set of experimental conditions. Big ranges are more difficult to monitor than small ones—the attention mechanism has more ground to cover, since it cannot be everywhere at once. In particular, they postulate an "attention band," 10 to 15 db wide, which roves over the relevant range of the continuum. On a specific trial, if the stimulus chances to fall within the band it is adequately received and monitored, and it is subsequently identified with some degree of accuracy. If the stimulus falls outside the band, an inadequate sample is obtained of the internal distribution, and over a series of trials the variance of these samples would be larger than the variance of samples that always fell within the attention band. The idea is that the probability of "hitting" the roving band is reduced with large ranges, and hence the variance associated with a stimulus is increased, leading to a deterioration of identification performance. Unlike the arguments put forth by Durlach and Braida and by Gravetter and Lockhead, range per se is not the important variable in the attention band model. Range indirectly influences performance only insofar as it makes it more difficult for the subject to obtain an adequate sample of the stimulus distribution. (This model is only one part of a more comprehensive theory, which we will return to in the next chapter.)

Whether such an explanation of channel capacity could be generalized to other sensory modalities is unclear at this time. (Thus far, it is mostly limited to audition.) Perhaps a test of the attention band model could be accomplished by using rather long stimulus durations, the argument being that this should allow sufficient time for the attention band to move into the relevant region of the scale, thus always allowing the subject time to secure a good sample of the distribution independent of range. Presumably, performance should improve under such circumstances.

Multidimensional Stimuli

The stricture that only seven stimulus intensities can be perfectly discriminated does not agree very well with our feelings about perception in the everyday environment. The apparent discrepancy between laboratory data and personal experience comes about because the former are based on unidimensional stimuli whereas the latter involve stimuli that usually vary along many dimensions. When more complicated stimuli are employed in the laboratory, the information transmission figures exceed those found in the unidimensional case.

For example, Pollack and Ficks (1954) used auditory stimuli that varied along 8 dimensions, obtained by alternating a tone and noise and changing the parameters of each. Each variable was dichotomous (binary) and included such aspects as the frequency and intensity of the tone, the intensity and range of frequencies of the noise, and the duration of the sound. Subjects made binary judgments for each dimension separately. The sum of the information transmitted was 7 bits, or perfect discrimination among $2^7 = 128$ stimuli. With overlearned stimuli (such as numerals, colors, and position), the total transmission measures can be as high as 15 bits (Anderson and Fitts, 1958; Garner, 1962), but these high measures are based on overly contrived experimental situations and for this reason are deceptive. It would be possible, for example, to use the contents of a set of living rooms as the multidimensional stimuli in an experiment requiring subjects to give the proper labels to a large number of dichotomous variables. For instance, the room has or does not have a rug, the couch is dark or light, the chairs are hard or soft, the person on the couch is male or female. Information transmission would be rather astronomical in this case, but it would be meaningless to say that such an experiment told us much about perception.

Calculation of the information measures for the multidimensional case follows the same rules employed for unidimensional stimuli, although the number of terms involved increases rather dramatically with number of dimensions. Details of these calculations can be found in Garner (1962) and Attneave (1959).

Several empirical generalizations emerge from the research with multidimensional stimuli (reviewed by Garner, 1962).

1.   Although total information transmitted is increased with multidimensional stimuli, the result is less than the amount obtained by summing transmission measures for the unidimensional components judged alone. This suggests that the multidimensional paradigm is not just a way to gather data on a set of independent dimensions. That is, there appears to be some interaction among the dimensions when they are presented simultaneously (or nearly so). This leads to a second generalization.

2.   An increased efficiency of the perceptual system can only be expected for situations where the component dimensions are relatively independent. In the current literature this is known as the problem of perceptual *integrality* (Lockhead, 1966; Garner, 1974). Certain combinations of dimensions are not perceived as a single compound, whereas others are. For example, suppose the dimensions of white-noise (sound) intensity and line length are combined to create a set of multidimensional, noisy lines. It is likely that the auditory and visual components could be processed separately, thus yielding higher total transmission values than when either component was presented alone. On the other hand, some types of dimensions do not remain discriminable from each other when combined. Take, for instance, qualitatively different chemicals that excite the sense of smell (Berglund, Berglund, and Lindvall, 1971). When these chemicals are mixed, the subject is unable to separate the relative contribution of the components to the overall smell experience. In fact, an entirely new quality is induced; it seems more reasonable, therefore, to treat this new compound as a single dimension in its own right. In this case, transmitted information for the compound will approximate that for the individual components.

An intermediate example might be combinations of line length and color. There may be a visual interaction between color and length that would somewhat reduce the amount of transmitted information for a compound, but not to the point where the total was equivalent to the value obtained for one of the components.

At present there is no adequate measure of stimulus compounds that allows us to predict *beforehand* the degree of perceptual integrality. This is an especially difficult research problem, currently under attack from a variety of directions (Anderson, 1970; Feldman and Baird, 1971; Lockhead, 1966; Shepard, 1964; Garner, 1974). It seems clear that the addition of nonintegral dimensions presents a different task for the subject than integral dimensions. However, nobody is exactly sure how best to conceptualize this difference, although Garner's research seems to hold the most promise in this regard.

It is on this note of uncertainty that we close the treatment of information theory and its application to psychophysics. In the final chapter of this work we review the interrelations among different models with an eye toward future developments.

REFERENCES

Anderson, N. H. "Functional measurement and psychophysical judgment." *Psychological Review*, 1970, *77*, 153–170.

Anderson, N. S., and Fitts, P. M. "Amount of information gained during brief exposures of numerals and colors." *Journal of Experimental Psychology*, 1958, *56*, 362–369.

Ash, R. *Information Theory*. New York: Wiley, 1965.

Attneave, F. *Applications of Information Theory to Psychology*. New York: Holt, Rinehart and Winston, 1959.

Baird, J. C. "A cognitive theory of psychophysics: I. Information transmission, partitioning, and Weber's law." *Scandinavian Journal of Psychology*, 1970a, *11*, 35–46.

Baird, J. C. "A cognitive theory of psychophysics: II. Fechner's law and Stevens' law". *Scandinavian Journal of Psychology*, 1970b, *11*, 89–102.

Baird, J. C., Romer, D., and Stein, T. "Test of a cognitive theory of psychophysics." *Perceptual and Motor Skills*, 1970, *30*, 495–501.

Braida, L. D., and Durlach, N. I. "Intensity perception II. Resolution of one-interval paradigms." *Journal of the Acoustical Society of America*, 1972, *51*, 483–502.

Berglund, B., Berglund, U., and Lindvall, T. "On the principle of odor interaction." *Acta Psychologica*, 1971, *35*, 255–268.

Carlson, A. B. *Communication Systems: An Introduction to Signals and Noise in Electrical Communication*. New York: McGraw-Hill, 1968.

Coombs, C. H., Dawes, R. M., and Tversky, A. *Mathematical Psychology: An Elementary Introduction*. Englewood Cliffs, N.J.: Prentice-Hall, 1970.

Durlach, N. I., and Braida, L. D. "Intensity perception I. Preliminary theory of intensity resolution." *Journal of the Acoustical Society of America*, 1969, *46*, 372–383.

Edwards, E. *Information Transmission*. London: Chapman and Hall, 1969.

Feldman, J., and Baird, J. C. "Magnitude estimation of multidimensional stimuli." *Perception & Psychophysics*, 1971, *10*, 418–422.

Garner, W. R. *Uncertainty and Structure as Psychological Concepts*. New York: Wiley, 1962.

Garner, W. R. *The Processing of Information and Structure*. New York: Erlbaum Associates, 1974.

Gravetter, F., and Lockhead, G. R. "Criterial range as a frame of reference for stimulus judgment." *Psychological Review*, 1973, *80*, 203–216.

Hake, H. W., and Garner, W. R. "The effect of presenting various numbers of discrete steps on scale reading accuracy." *Journal of Experimental Psychology*, 1951, *42*, 358–366.

Kemeny, J. G., Snell, J. L., and Thompson, G. L. *Introduction to Finite Mathematics*, 2nd ed. Englewood Cliffs, N.J.: Prentice-Hall, 1966.

Kullback, S. *Information Theory and Statistics*. New York: Dover, 1968.

Landau, S. G., Buchsbaum, N. S., Coppola, R., and Sihvonen, M. "Individual differences and reliability of information transmission in absolute judgments of loudness, brightness and line lengths." *Perceptual and Motor Skills*, 1974, *39*, 239–246.

Lockhead, G. R. "Effects of dimensional redundancy on visual discrimination." *Journal of Experimental Psychology*, 1966, *72*, 95–104.

Luce, R. D. "The theory of selective information and some of its behavioral applications." In R. D. Luce (Ed.), *Developments in Mathematical Psychology*. Glencoe, Ill.: The Free Press, 1960, pp. 5–119.

Luce, R. D., Green, D. M., and Weber, D. L. "Attention bands in absolute identification." *Perception & Psychophysics*, 1976, *20*, 49–54.

Miller, G. A. "The magical number seven, plus or minus two: Some limits on capacity for processing information." *Psychological Review*, 1956, *63*, 81–97.

Pollack, I. "The information of elementary auditory displays." *Journal of the Acoustical Society of America*, 1952, *24*, 745–749.

Pollack, I., and Ficks, L. "Information of elementary multidimensional auditory displays." *Journal of The Acoustical Society of America*, 1954, *26*, 155–158.

Shannon, C. E., and Weaver, W. *The Mathematical Theory of Communication*. Urbana: University of Illinois Press, 1964.

Shepard, R. N. "Attention and the metric structure of the stimulus space." *Journal of Mathematical Psychology*, 1964, *1*, 54–87.

Weber, D. L., Green, D. M., and Luce, R. D. "Effects of practice and distribution of auditory signals on absolute identification." *Perception & Psychophysics*, 1977, *22*, 223–231.

CHAPTER

$$\boxed{13}$$

OVERVIEW:
THEN AND NOW

The effective collaboration of scientists depends largely on their ability to define a common paradigm or standard way of doing things. As viewed by Kuhn (1962), a paradigm is a set of beliefs, attitudes, and assumptions shared by a group of people engaged in the same type of scientific endeavor. Within psychophysics and scaling theory this shared paradigm is that perceptual and cognitive processes are open to quantitative treatment in a framework provided by the experimental method. More specifically, we have the shared notion that human beings can be viewed as measuring instruments that yield scale values in response to environmental stimuli.

This is not to say that there has been a smooth history of progress. Instead, the story of scaling and psychophysics is replete with small revolutions and conceptual reorientations. In the 1920s it was Thurstone's measurement of values without regard to physical correlates. In the 1930s it was the advent of operationism. The new wave in the 1950s was the use of an information-theoretic approach to examine sensory processes. Direct scaling methods together with multidimensional scaling greatly altered the conceptualization of many research problems in the 1960s. In this chapter, we look back as well as forward. Old, but still useful, methods are compared and classified, and a preview is offered of what seems to be in store for the future.

Unfortunately, we cannot measure the effect of a methodology by either the new research opportunities it illuminates or the conceptual reorientation it forces. Probably a better way to proceed is to examine the similarities and differences in data requirements and output representations. That is, we list a possible set of variables by which the methods may be characterized and classified. This helps us see where scaling and psychophysics have been with an eye toward the prediction of future directions.

CLASSIFICATION OF MODELS

There are an infinite number of variables by which the models in the preceding chapters may be classified. We believe, however, that the following eight variables offer a minimal characterization of some utility.

1. *Scalability* The degree to which scale construction (assigning numbers to stimuli) is important.
2. *Scale type for judgments* Whether responses are assumed invariant up to nominal, ordinal, interval, or ratio scales.
3. *Scale type for representation* How the results are organized for presentation independent of the scale type assumed to underlie judgments.
4. *Type of data* Most of psychophysics examines only proximity or dominance judgments.
5. *Unit of measure* A distinction is made between models in which the unit of measure is the difference between means and those in which it is the variance.
6. *Dimensionality* Some models locate stimuli on a unidimensional continuum; others are capable of treating the multidimensional case.
7. *Physical measure of the stimulus* The distinction here is between models that present results in terms of physical units of measure and those that do not.
8. *Sensitivity indices* The primary function of one class of models is to provide sensitivity indices, such as Weber fractions, channel capacities, and exponents. Other models do not lead to such indices.

Each of these eight variables will be expanded upon briefly in the following discussion.

Scalability

Many of the models considered in this book locate stimuli on scales in physical or psychological space. To be more specific, numbers are attached to stimulus objects with the idea that the relations among the objects follow the same rules as the relations among the numbers. By specifying the relations and permissible transformations among the numbers, one defines the scale type.

Scale Type for Judgments

Most of the responses elicited in psychophysical tasks are assumed to be from interval or ratio scales, despite the difficulty of testing the underlying assumptions of such scale types. Models such as information theory, cluster analysis, and the theory of signal detectability require less stringent assumptions about the invariances in a subject's responses. In these cases, ordinal or nominal scale responses are sufficiently invariant to apply the models.

Scale Type for Representation

One worthwhile distinction here is between the type of scale required for a subject to make a judgment and the type of scale assumed by the final representation of results to the outside world—that is, after the model has been applied. The two scale types need not be the same. For example, nonmetric multidimensional scaling requires that similarities among stimuli be ordered in magnitude but not necessarily at the interval or ratio level. On the other hand, a solution in several dimensional spaces is usually considered constrained to an interval scale along each of the dimensions. In fact, with the exception of cluster analysis, all models in this book assume at least an interval scale in the final structure (representation) of the results.

Dimensionality

The majority of psychophysical models deal with unidimensional stimulus and response continua, even if they are theoretically capable of handling more complex situations. Multidimensional scaling and cluster analysis are the only models applied consistently to multidimensional representation of judgments. In the future we expect further generalization of these models and the creation of new ones to process complex responses to multidimensional stimuli.

Type of Data

The comparatively recent models of multidimensional scaling, cluster analysis, and information theory differ from more classical approaches in terms of the type of data generated by subjects. The classical models all require dominance data (stimulus A is larger, brighter, prettier, etc. than stimulus B), whereas more recent models deal with proximity (similarity) data: How close are stimuli A and B? Proximity measures appear to be more generally applicable, since no physical correlate need be specified beforehand. Hence, models that deal with proximity data should become increasingly attractive, especially in fields outside traditional psychophysics.

Unit of Measure

Units of measure in psychophysics are of two varieties: (1) the differences between means of items along a scale and (2) the variance associated with a single mean. Direct scaling methods assume that there is only one response paired with a particular stimulus in a given experimental condition. Any deviation from that "true" value is considered noise and is therefore discarded. Since one does not really know this "true" value, a measure of central tendency is used as a best estimate. The mean is often an appropriate statistic for this purpose. (When fitting Stevens functions, the best-fitting line is itself a measure of central tendency among a set of means.) A similar argument applies to the similarity measures input to a multidimensional scaling or cluster analysis. Again, any deviation from the "true" value is noise (random variation), and the estimate of the central value is used in the similarities matrix.[1]

On the other hand, Fechner functions and Thurstone scaling map response inconsistencies into deviations from the "true" value. The variance, as a measure of the deviations from the best estimate, becomes a unit of measure.

The mean and variance of a distribution are simply units of measure representing empirical findings in alternative ways, so arguments about the relative representativeness of the two measures are not very illuminating. In particular, the practice of referring to those scaling methods leading to Stevens functions as "direct" and those methods involving accumulation of

---

[1]One exception to this is the work of Ramsay (1969), who attempts to extend the Thurstonian analysis to the multidimensional case. The resulting equations are rather unwieldy, but development of such approaches might help to forge a closer connection between classical and modern psychophysics.

jnd's (leading to Fechner functions) as "indirect" should be dropped. Although the relationship between models relying upon the mean and those relying upon the variance has yet to be satisfactorily resolved, this does not imply that they are mutually exclusive ways of dealing with perceptual phenomena.

Physical Measures of the Stimulus

Both Fechner and Stevens functions express sensations or responses in terms of physical measures of the stimulus. The size of the jnd as predicted by a Weber function is also defined in terms of a physical magnitude. In addition, information transmitted is expressed as a function of the amount of uncertainty in the stimulus ensemble. The remaining models do not make explicit use of stimulus measures in the presentation of results, tending instead to emphasize the relations among responses.

Sensitivity Indices

With the exception of the theory of signal detectability, those models not emphasizing stimulus measures do not provide indices of perceptual sensitivity. Weber fractions, exponents, and channel capacities are all indices of the perceptual sensitivity of subjects to diverse stimulus attributes. These indices, along with the d' of the theory of signal detectability, must be somehow connected. A fair amount of theoretical work has gone into schemes to spell out this connection, but at this point nobody seems entirely satisfied with the results.

SUMMARY OF MODELS

In Table 13.1, the models discussed in this book are summarized in terms of the eight variables just noted. In some instances the classification could not be made unambiguously. For these cases we classified according to an interpretation of the broad spirit of the model or in terms of its most usual application. The table is helpful in gaining an overview of the characteristics of a model and its relation to others, but as good psychologists we surely do not want to stop here. What we really want is an opportunity to "see" the structure of the methods space. So let us rearrange things to bring about that opportunity.

Table 13.1 Classification of models

MODELS	Scalability		Scale Type (judgment)				Scale Type (representation)				Type of Data		Unit of Measure		Dimensionality		Physical Measures of the Stimulus		Sensitivity Index	
	High	Low	Nom	Ord	Int	Rat	Nom	Ord	Int	Rat	Prox	Dom	Mean	Var	Multi	Uni	Nec	Unnec	Yes	No
Stevens	*					*				*		*	*			*	*			
IT		*	*				*				*			*		*	*			
Weber	*				*				*			*		*		*	*			
Fechner	*				*				*			*		*		*	*			
TSD	*				*				*			*		*		*		*	*	
GFS	*				*				*			*		*		*		*		*
Thurstone	*			*					*			*		*		*		*		*
MDS	*			*				*			*		*		*			*		*
Cluster	*		*				*				*		*		*			*		*

GFS—Generalized Fechnerian Scaling
MDS—Multidimensional Scaling
TSD—Theory of Signal Detectability
IT—Information Theory

Nom—Nominal
Ord—Ordinal
Int—Interval
Rat—Ratio
Prox—Proximity
Dom—Dominance

Table 13.2   Similarity matrix for models (Entries are the number of agreements in Table 13.1)

	Stevens	IT	Weber	Fechner	TSD	GFS	Thurstone	MDS	Cluster
Stevens	—								
IT	3	—							
Weber	4	6	—						
Fechner	5	5	7	—					
TSD	3	5	7	6	—				
GFS	3	3	5	6	6	—			
Thurstone	3	3	5	6	6	8	—		
MDS	2	2	2	3	3	5	5	—	
Cluster	1	2	2	1	3	3	3	6	—

GFS—Generalized Fechnerian scaling
MDS—Multidimensional scaling
TSD—Theory of signal detectability
IT—Information theory

First, we compute a measure of similarity between pairs of methods. The results are presented in Table 13.2, using a version of the simple matching measure (Chapter 11), where the cell entries are the number of agreements (on the eight variables) counted from the entries in Table 13.1. The higher the number linking two models, the greater the agreement (similarity) in terms of the eight variables.

Finally, to efficiently code this matrix of similarities, we ask the reader to note the order in which the models are listed down the page in both tables. Although we never mentioned it before, lest confusion set in, the order has a rationale behind it. Namely, the list was obtained by running a Shepard-Kruskal multidimensional scaling program (Chapter 10) on the triangular matrix of similarities given in Table 13.2. It turns out that the nine models can be situated quite nicely along one dimension with a stress of 14%. The unidimensional solution is shown in Fig. 13.1. Whether this particular arrangement of models will help stimulate the imagination of theorists remains an open question.

CURRENT DEVELOPMENTS

We have attempted in this book to guide the reader through the fundamental ideas upon which current work in scaling and psychophysics is grounded. In concluding our discussion, it seems appropriate to expand our attention to cover some selected trends in current research. Our hope here is to stimulate others to apply their special skills to the continuing task of unraveling the

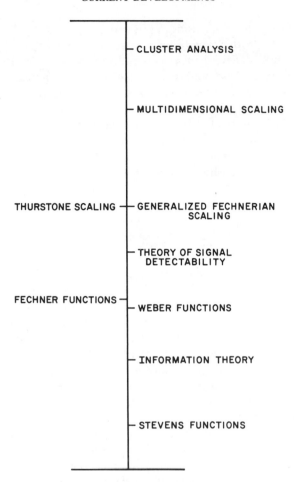

Figure 13.1. Unidimensional scaling of models. The input was the similarity matrix in Table 13.2.

network of variables responsible for the operation of the human perceptual and cognitive systems. In addition, our comments may serve to highlight and review several major issues for those already familiar with the field.

By far the most prevalent entries in today's literature describe rather direct applications of the models outlined in previous chapters. As more perceptual dimensions are investigated, the lists of perceptual indices increase (for example, Weber fractions, exponents, channel capacities); and the scope of multidimensional solutions ranges from social psychology and personality theory to advertising applications (Romney, Shepard, and Nerlove, 1972). Since this type of parametric study yields nothing new *to be understood*, it is best reviewed in a more substantive context. We gratefully leave such reviews to those qualified in specific content areas.

Rather, our discussion will deal only with a few selected aspects of current research that promise some hope for extending, remaking, or displacing previous models. In particular, two regions are singled out for consideration: (1) models of the perceptual and/or cognitive integration of multidimensional stimuli, and (2) general psychophysical theory concerned with understanding the interrelationships among results obtained by different experimental procedures.

Stimulus Integration

One of the continuing problems in perception has been the modeling of how people respond to complex stimuli. The issue of stimulus integration over dimensions or attributes has relevance for such diverse areas as stock market analysis (Clarkson, 1962), person perception (Anderson, 1974), and auditory psychophysics (Levelt, Riemersma, and Bunt, 1972). One of the more sophisticated approaches to this problem is the theoretical work falling under the general title of "simultaneous additive conjoint measurement" (Luce and Tukey, 1964; Krantz et al., 1971). Here, a subject is assumed to rate or judge a set of stimulus compounds made up of the combination of intensities from several attributes or sources (for example, sound and light; sound delivered independently to the two ears; etc.). The question of interest is whether the contributions to the overall rating of the compound can be modeled by an additive combination of the two components.

An empirical example is provided in a study by Levelt et al. (1972), who were interested in testing whether binaural loudness judgments could be modeled in terms of the addition of the two monaural inputs. They employed six different 1000-Hz tones of intensity ranging from 20 to 70 db spaced equally along the continuum. The tones were presented to the two ears simultaneously, thus creating pairs of binaural stimuli. Two subjects rank ordered the loudness of selected pairs of stimuli, and from these ranks it was possible to determine that, indeed, the contribution of the two ears was additive. That is, the judged binaural loudness could be described by a process in which a function of the stimulus intensity entering the right ear (r) was added to a function of the intensity entering the left ear (l). Employing functions ϕ_r and ϕ_l for the right and left ears, this description is equivalent to the following conditions (where β_{rl} represents the binaural function):

1. $\beta_{rl} = \phi_r(r) + \phi_l(l)$
2. $\beta_{r_1 l_1} > \beta_{r_2 l_2}$ implies that the judged loudness of the stimulus pair (r_1, l_1) is greater than the judged loudness of the pair (r_2, l_2).

It is not necessary to actually know the functions ϕ_r and ϕ_l, the analysis seeks only to determine that the contribution of the left ear is independent of the contribution of the right in the binaural judgment of loudness. Only after conditions 1 and 2 are satisfied can we move on to look for the specific functions ϕ_r and ϕ_l. In this way we sidestep the problem of whether the stimulus intensity of a tone should be measured in units of decibels, sound pressure, or some other arbitrary measure. The unit of measure is irrelevant in tests of conditions 1 and 2, since we are asking only whether the right and left stimulus intensities may be rescaled (some way or other) to eliminate interaction effects in their contribution to binaural loudness judgments.

Evaluating this model (conditions 1 and 2) involves a series of tests in the general class called simultaneous additive conjoint measurement structures. The "simultaneous" property means that scale values are obtained for each of the functions β, ϕ_r, and ϕ_l. Conjoint measurement tests often use data that can be represented in a matrix, as in Table 13.3. The judgment entries there are read as follows: $b =$ binaural; r and $l =$ right and left ear inputs; and 1, 2,... = particular stimulus intensities.

A full discussion of all the tests is beyond the scope of this brief summary (the interested reader is referred to Krantz et al., 1971, Chapter 6), but we will mention one test that is always performed when evaluating the additive

Table 13.3   Design matrix of stimulus intensities r_1, r_2, r_3 and l_1, l_2, l_3 presented simultaneously to the right (r) and left (l) ears (after Levelt et al., 1972). $b_{r_i l_j}$ is the binaural loudness judgment of pair $r_i l_j$

		Left Ear			
		l_1	l_2	l_3	$\cdots$
	r_1	$b_{r_1 l_1}$	$b_{r_1 l_2}$	$b_{r_1 l_3}$	$\cdots$
Right Ear	r_2	$b_{r_2 l_1}$	$b_{r_2 l_2}$	$b_{r_2 l_3}$	$\cdots$
	r_3	$b_{r_3 l_1}$	$b_{r_3 l_2}$	$b_{r_3 l_3}$	$\cdots$
	$\vdots$	$\vdots$	$\vdots$		

model. It proceeds in two steps. First all the elements in one column are interchanged with all the elements in another so that the b's in each row increase from left to right. Second, in a similar manner, the rows are interchanged in the resultant matrix so that all b's in each column increase from top to bottom. This is called a test for monotonicity since the elements in each row and column, reading across or down, are monotonically increasing. If the matrix cannot be reordered to satisfy this test, then no functions exist that satisfy conditions 1 and 2. This means that no amount or form of rescaling of the stimulus intensities can ever remove interaction in their joint contribution to the binaural loudness judgment. On the other hand, passing the test only means that functions *may* exist; further tests must be made to verify that functions *actually* exist for the particular matrix of loudness judgments.

Taking into account slight experimental error, Levelt et al. demonstrated that functions ϕ_r and ϕ_l can be found for their loudness matrix. In fact, they subsequently used a scaling technique to fit parameters to a pair of functions that satisfy conditions 1 and 2. Specifically, they showed that judgment of binaural loudness could be described as the addition of two power functions (certainly not a random choice), one for each ear's contribution:

$$b_{rl} = \lambda_r S_r^{n_r} + \lambda_l S_l^{n_l} + k$$

where S_r and S_l are the sound pressure values of the intensities and λ_r, λ_l, n_r, n_l, and k are determined statistically by curve-fitting procedures. The exponents (n_r and n_l) were .44 and .61, respectively, for one subject; .41 and .47 for the other. These values are within the range of loudness exponents generally reported (Marks, 1974).

This method for analyzing conjoint structures is one example among the latest developments in measurement theory. Its goal is to construct a series of tests that determine whether data may be rescaled to satisfy a particular model. Failure to pass these tests completely eliminates the model from further consideration. Passing these tests, on the other hand, justifies application of scaling techniques to determine parameter values. Such techniques have received increasing attention in mathematical psychology (see Falmagne, 1976; and Luce, 1977). These recent developments suggest important applications in many content areas. For instance, one of the more unusual applications concerns research on avoidance learning in rats (Campbell and Masterson, 1969).

Related approaches to the modeling of stimulus combinations are exemplified by the work of Anderson (1974), who relied on the analysis of variance to determine the independence of component dimensions, and the experiments by Feldman and Baird (1971), who relied on substantive psychophysical theory. Neither alternative seems to provide the theoretical possibilities inherent in conjoint measurement techniques, although both are appropriate for special cases.

General Theory

As the reader may have surmised by this point in the book, it is by no means easy to develop theoretical connections among the various psychophysical models. The total understanding of these connections was, of course, Fechner's goal and hence the goal of the field he founded in 1860. It is not surprising that this aspect of psychophysics has received less attention than parametric investigations of special cases. The task of general theory construction has been complicated in recent years by the precipitous growth of the data base that must be explained. Nonetheless, we conclude this chapter by considering several theories in which the general issues of psychophysics are addressed directly.

COGNITIVE THEORY

In a series of theoretical papers, Baird (1970a, b, c) has suggested that the interrelations among psychophysical results can be understood in terms of the alternative cognitive strategies induced by experimental conditions and instructions. Because the theory operates at a rather general level of analysis, exact quantitative predictions cannot always be made, although qualitative predictions are possible. The theory predicts the direction of correlations among quantitative indices such as Weber fractions, channel capacities, and exponents.

First, it is assumed that subjects can perceive a single stimulus in terms of a concatenation of individual elements. The size of each element, say Δx, is constant and proportional to the intensity x of the stimulus, but the ratio $\Delta x / x$ depends on the nature of the continuum and is treated as a perceptual correlate of the Weber fraction.

According to this theory, perceptual channel capacities and Weber fractions should bear a close resemblance (as discussed in Chapter 12). Although one could not expect to find a perfect match between these two indices, as empirically determined, the theory predicts that the size of the Weber fraction for a continuum should be inversely related to its channel capacity. The available data reviewed by Baird (1970a) suggest such a function, but more direct tests are definitely needed on this point.

The differences among Stevens functions, and in particular the logarithmic and power functions, are explained in terms of alternative judgment strategies (Baird, 1970b). For category estimation it is proposed that the subject attempts to distribute perceptual information (a logarithmic measure) equally among the available categories, thus leading to a logarithmic relation between stimulus intensity and judged magnitude, in agreement with Fechner's law.

The argument becomes more involved for the power function where we must consider two continua whose intensities are matched. The essence of the matter can, however, be sketched briefly. The exponent emerges as the ratio of the two channel capacities of the stimulus and response continua. Consequently, the exponent is also related to the two Weber fractions, much in the spirit of the fourfold way (Chapters 4 and 5). Empirical tests of this connection have been encouraging, but they do not offer clear support for the theory (Baird, Romer, and Stein, 1970; Graf, Baird, and Glesman, 1974).

In more recent papers, Baird (1975a, b) has explored a somewhat different theoretical route to the explanation of Stevens functions, based on the model by which one can describe subjects' use of certain numbers in magnitude estimation tasks (Chapter 6). A related two-stage model of the power function has been tested by Curtis and his colleagues (Curtis, Attneave, and Harrington, 1968; Curtis, 1970; Rule, Curtis, and Markley, 1970), while the general view of the connection among alternative indices of perceptual sensitivity is also apparent in some little-known work by the Finnish physiologist Reenpää (1967)[2].

THEORY OF INTENSITY RESOLUTION

In attempting to compare the results obtained from different experimental procedures, one must first ask: "Which aspect of the results are of interest?" Durlach and Braida (1969) have chosen to focus on an aspect of central importance throughout the history of psychophysics: intensity resolution, or more technically stated, response variability conditional on stimulus presentation. Employing loudness perception as their prototype, they propose that response variability, as a measure of perceptual sensitivity, is the same whether a subject is tested with the methods of magnitude estimation, category estimation, or absolute identification.

As noted briefly in Chapter 12, these authors also postulate that the variability associated with a stimulus along the decision axis of TSD is composed of two parts: sensation noise and memory noise. The first depends

---

[2]English-speaking audiences may not have been exposed to his theories, since the major work is written in German.

only on the nature of the stimulus and the relevant sensory system. The second is affected by variables in the experiment that would affect memory for the stimuli, such as the interstimulus time intervals and the range of stimuli. When few stimuli are employed, and they are closely packed, the sensation noise is the factor primarily responsible for the level of intensity resolution attained. When many stimuli are used, and they are spread far apart—for example, in an absolute identification task—the memory noise is the critical determinant of intensity resolution.

In their experiments on auditory perception, Braida and Durlach (1972) used a summed d' measure from TSD as an indication of perceptual resolution for a set of tones judged by alternative psychophysical methods. Although there were clear similarities among results, the sensitivity exhibited in magnitude estimation was consistently less than that found for absolute identification. Nonetheless, the theoretical lines developed by these authors appear quite testable and seem to have stimulated others to search for more adequate explanations of their original data. In the final section of this chapter we examine another class of models that can be applied to the problem of intensity resolution, albeit at a more molecular level.

NEURAL CODING MODELS

Virtually all psychophysical studies report performances that deviate from chance guessing. Without such evidence, in fact, there would be no reason to support the paradigm of the human as measuring instrument. Excluding the influence of extrasensory perception or the possibility that the world does not obey the laws of probability, we must assume that this nonrandomness is due to inputs through our sense organs. The presence of a stimulus excites neurons in a sense organ, producing a series of pulses as the neurons fire repeatedly. The more intense the stimulus, the faster the firing rate. Other neurons are stimulated to fire by the first set, and this process is repeated until the brain receives the message and initiates a response. We are concerned, however, only with the fact that inputs to the brain must originate in the activity at the sense organ level. Information that is not coded at the peripheral level never reaches the brain, so the sensory neurons act as a communications channel carrying only a limited amount of information about the outside world. Now make one additional assumption: All information is contained in the number of neurons activated and in their pattern of firing, since each impulse is considered an all-or-none phenomenon. The generalization of such assumptions to all sensory systems and to alternative experimental procedures (for example, method of constant stimuli, binary choice, magnitude estimation, and absolute identification) constitutes the basis for a powerful theory of psychophysics. Thus far, models of this type have been tested primarily with auditory stimuli, although implications have been drawn for a variety of psychophysical procedures (Green and Luce, 1974). We will concentrate here on the problem of stimulus detection.

The internal interpretation of the neuronal pulse trains is often modeled in one of two ways. The *counting model* (McGill, 1967) assumes that the decision-making homunculus counts the number of pulses within a given time interval. If the number of pulses exceeds a certain level, then a signal or change in signal is reported. Naturally, this report could also be incorrect if there is a spurious burst in neuronal firings in the absence of a signal. The second model is called the *timing model* (Luce and Green, 1972; Uttal and Krissoff, 1968) since the homunculus is assumed to look only at the time interval between pulses. Since a more intense stimulus should stimulate more firings, this would also mean a decrease in the interarrival times of the pulses.

Despite the many similarities of the counting and timing models, they still predict different results in detection tasks. The counting model assumes that one counts the number of neural pulses within a prespecified interval and waits until the end of the interval before responding "signal" or "no signal." Therefore, when asked to respond within a fixed time interval (say, .3 sec), the mean reaction times should be the same for all trials, regardless of the presence or absence of signal. The timing model, on the other hand, states that one monitors the neural pulse train until either a sufficiently short interarrival time is noted or until a response is required by the termination of the trial. This means that all "signal" trials should have shorter mean reaction times than "no signal" trials.

Using these and other predictions it is possible to test these models, but neither is able to handle all the data. This leads to the broader hypothesis that the human observer is able to use either a counting or timing strategy according to the task requirements (Green and Luce, 1973). The "preferred strategy" outside of the laboratory is still a moot question.

This area of study offers many promises and challenges for modeling simple stimulus intensity judgments. One should not believe however, that such research will make obsolete the study of psychological variables emphasized by cognitive theories. In addition, judgments of attributes such as pattern complexity may be more fruitfully studied by other methods (Shepard and Chipman, 1970). To quote an authoritative source: (Fechner, 1966, p. 7).

> Psychophysics should be understood here as an exact theory of the functionally dependent relations of body and soul or, more generally, of the material and the mental, of the physical and psychological worlds.

REFERENCES

Anderson, N. H. "Information integration theory: A brief survey." In D. H. Krantz, R. C. Atkinson, R. D. Luce, and P. Suppes (Eds.), *Contemporary Developments in Mathematical Psychology*, Vol. II. *Measurement, Psychophysics, and Neural Information Processing*. San Francisco: W. H. Freeman, 1974, pp. 236–305.

Baird, J. C. "A cognitive theory of psychophysics. I. Information transmission, partitioning, and Weber's Law." *Scandinavian Journal of Psychology*, 1970a, *11*, 35–46.

Baird, J. C. "A cognitive theory of psychophysics. II. Fechner's law and Stevens' law." *Scandinavian Journal of Psychology*, 1970b, *11*, 89–102.

Baird, J. C. "Information processing in alternative visual spaces." In J. C. Baird (Ed.), *Human Space Perception: Proceedings of the Dartmouth Conference*. Psychonomic Monograph Supplements, 1970c, Vol. 3, No. 13 (Whole No. 45), pp. 183–192.

Baird, J. C. "Psychophysical study of numbers. IV. Generalized preferred state theory." *Psychological Research*, 1975a, *38*, 175–187.

Baird, J. C. "Psychophysical study of numbers. V. Preferred state theory of matching functions." *Psychological Research*, 1975b, *38*, 189–207.

Baird, J. C., Romer, D., and Stein, T. "Test of a cognitive theory of psychophysics." *Perceptual and Motor Skills*, 1970, *30*, 495–501.

Braida, L. D., and Durlach, N. I. "Intensity perception II. Resolution in one-interval paradigms." *Journal of the Acoustical Society of America*, 1972, *51*, 483–502.

Campbell, B. A., and Masterson, F. A. "Psychophysics of punishment." In B. A. Campbell and R. M. Church (Eds.), *Punishment and Aversion Behavior*. New York: Appleton-Century-Crofts, 1969, p. 3–42.

Clarkson, G. P. E. *Portfolio Selection—A Simulation of Trust Investment*. Englewood Cliffs, N.J.: Prentice-Hall, 1962.

Curtis D. W. "Magnitude estimations and category judgments of brightness and brightness intervals: A two-stage interpretation." *Journal of Experimental Psychology*, 1970, *83*, 201–208.

Curtis, D. W., Attneave, F., and Harrington, T. L. "A test of a two-stage model for magnitude estimation." *Perception & Psychophysics*, 1968, *3*, 25–31.

Durlach, N. I., and Braida, L. D. "Intensity perception. I. Preliminary theory of intensity resolution." *Journal of the Acoustical Society of America*, 1969, *46*, 372–383.

Falmagne, J. C. "Random conjoint measurement and loudness summation." *Psychological Review*, 1976, *83*, 65–79.

Fechner, G. *Elements of Psychophysics*. Vol. I Translated by H. E. Adler. New York: Holt, Rinehart and Winston, 1966.

Feldman, J., and Baird, J. C. "Magnitude estimation of multidimensional stimuli." *Perception & Psychophysics*, 1971, *10*, 418–422.

Graf, V., Baird, J. C., and Glesman, G. "An empirical test of two psychophysical models." *Acta Psychologica*, 1974, *38*, 59–72.

Green, D. M., and Luce, R. D. "Speed-accuracy tradeoff in auditory detection." In S. Kornblum (Ed.), *Attention and Performance*, Vol. 4. New York: Academic, 1973, pp. 547–569.

Green, D. M., and Luce, R. D. "Counting and timing mechanisms in auditory discrimination and reaction time." In D. H. Krantz, R. C. Atkinson, R. D. Luce, and P. Suppes (Eds.), *Contemporary Developments in Mathematical Psychology*, Vol. II: *Measurement, Psychophysics, and Neural Information Processing*. San Francisco, W. H. Freeman, 1974, p. 372–415.

Krantz, D. H., Luce, R. D., Suppes, P., and Tversky, A. *Foundations of Measurement*, Vol. I: *Additive and Polynomial Representations*. New York: Academic, 1971.

Kuhn, T. S. *The Structure of Scientific Revolutions*. Chicago: University of Chicago Press, 1962.

Levelt, W. J. M., Riemersma, J. B., and Bunt, A. A. "Binaural additivity of loudness." *British Journal of Mathematical and Statistical Psychology*, 1972, *25*, 51–68.

Luce, R. D. "A note on sums of power functions." *Journal of Mathematical Psychology*, 1977, *16*, 91–93.

Luce, R. D., and Green, D. M. "A neural timing theory for response times and the psychophysics of intensity." *Psychological Review*, 1972, *79*, 14–57.

Luce, R. D., and Tukey, J. "Simultaneous conjoint measurement: A new type of fundamental measurement." *Journal of Mathematical Psychology*, 1964, *1*, 1–27.

Marks, L. *Sensory Processes: The New Psychophysics*. New York: Academic, 1974.

McGill, W. J. "Neural counting mechanisms and energy detection in audition." *Journal of Mathematical Psychology*, 1967, *4*, 351–376.

Ramsay, J. O. "Some statistical considerations in multidimensional scaling." *Psychometrika*, 1969, *34*, 167–182.

Reenpää, Y. *Wahrnehmen Beobachten Konstituieren*. Frankfurt: Vittorio Klostermann, 1967.

Romney, A. K., Shepard, R. N., and Nerlove, S. B. (Eds.), *Multidimensional Scaling: Theory and Applications in the Behavioral Sciences*. Vol. II: *Applications*. New York: Seminar Press, 1972.

Rule, S. J., Curtis, D. W., and Markley, R. P. "Input and output transformations from magnitude estimation." *Journal of Experimental Psychology*, 1970, *86*, 343–349.

Shepard, R. N., and Chipman, S. "Second-order isomorphism of internal representations: shapes of states." *Cognitive Psychology*, 1970, *1*, 1–17.

Uttal, W. R., and Krissoff, M. "Response of the somesthetic system to patterned trains of electrical stimuli: an approach to the problem of sensory coding." In D. R. Kenshalo (Ed.), *The Skin Senses*. Springfield, Ill.: Charles C. Thomas, 1968, pp. 262–302.

AUTHOR INDEX

Pages in *italics* indicate the pages on which the full references appear.

SUBJECT INDEX